BACK FROM EXILE

AMERICAN PHILOLOGICAL ASSOCIATION

CLASSICAL RESOURCES SERIES

John T. Ramsey, Series Editor

NUMBER 4
CICERO
BACK FROM EXILE

translated by
D. R. Shackleton Bailey

CICERO

BACK FROM EXILE:
SIX SPEECHES UPON HIS RETURN

Translated with Introductions and Notes

by

D. R. Shackleton Bailey

Cicero

Back From Exile:
Six speeches upon his return

Translated with Introductions and Notes

by

D. R. Shackleton Bailey

© 1991
The American Philogical Association

Library of Congress Cataloging in Publication Data

Cicero, Marcus Tullius.
    Back from exile : six speeches upon his return / Cicero ; translated, with introductions and notes, by D. R. Shackleton Bailey.
    p. cm. — (Classical resource series / American Philological Association ; no. 4)
    Includes index.
    ISBN: 978-1-55540-627-1
    1. Cicero, Marcus Tullius—Translations into English.
2. Speeches, addresses, etc., Latin—Translations into English.
I. Bailey, D.R. (David Roy Shackleton), 1917- . II. Title.
III. Title: Cicero back from exile. IV. Series: Classical resources series .
PA6307.A4B35 1991
875'.01—dc20   91-31383
                                                            CIP

The cover shows the bust of Cicero in the Vatican, Museo Chiaramonti (XI.15)

CONTENTS

Preface vii

Abbreviations ix

Bibliographical Note xiii

Introduction 1

The Speeches

Speech of Thanks in the Senate 5
    (*Post reditum in senatu*)

Speech of Thanks to the Citizens 25
    (*Post reditum ad quirites*)

On his House 37
    (*De domo sua*)

On the Answers of the Haruspices 103
    (*De haruspicum responsis*)

In Defense of Publius Sestius 137
    (*Pro P. Sestio*)

Examination of the Witness Publius Vatinius 207
    (*In P. Vatinium testem interrogatio*)

Appendix   I Divergences from the Oxford Text 227

              II Roman Names 233

Index   I Persons, Deities, Laws 235

              II Places 253

Glossary of Terms 257

PREFACE

The preface to my edition and translation of Cicero's *Philippics* (University of North Carolina Press, 1986) mentioned two principal objectives: to provide a future commentator (who might be a historian rather than a linguistic expert) with a textual and interpretative foundation on which to build, and to make the speeches more accessible to students and others interested. This book is similarly oriented. It has not been practicable to print a new text, but the form it would take is specified in Appendix I. Places where my translation of a text is semantically different from Peterson's Oxford Classical Text are indicated in the margin. Translators of Cicero's rhetoric in our contemporary climate need all their readers' indulgence; but this version aims at combining fidelity with readability in greater measure than its English precursors. The notes and indexes have been put together with the non-specialist reader in mind.

I am grateful to Professor James M. May for helpful comments contributed as referee and, along with Professors James Clauss and William H. Race, for reading a late version of page proofs and offering suggestions. Professor John T. Ramsey has been lavish of time and trouble, more especially in expanding and improving the notes and indexes. Finally I wish to thank Ms. Laurel Poe Gallagher and Ms. Joellen Loy for typesetting the manuscript.

D.R.S.B

ABBREVIATIONS

(1) All dates are B.C. unless indicated to the contrary.
(2) Crosses (+) in the margin of the translation indicate divergences from Peterson's OCT that affect the sense (see Bibliographic Note).
(3) For the abbreviation SB with superscript, and short title *Onomasticon*, see Bibliographic Note.
(4) For abbreviated forms of praenomens, see Appendix II.

Works by Cicero

Att.	*Epistulae ad Atticum* ("Letters to Atticus")
Brut.	*Brutus* ("On famous orators")
Cael.	*Pro M. Caelio* ("In defense of M. Caelius")
Dom.	*De domo sua* ("On his house")
Fam.	*Epistulae ad familiares* ("Letters to friends")
Flacc.	*Pro L. Flacco* ("In defense of L. Flaccus")
Har. resp.	*De haruspicum responsis* ("On the answers of the haruspices")
Leg. agr.	*De lege agraria* ("On the agrarian law")
Mil.	*Pro T. Annio Milone* ("In defense of T. Annius Milo")
Prov. cons.	*De provinciis consularibus* ("On the consular provinces")
Pis.	*In L. Pisonem* ("Against L. Piso")

Planc.	*Pro Cn. Plancio*
	("In defense of Cn. Plancius")
Q. fr.	*Epistulae ad Quintum fratrem*
	("Letters to his brother Quintus")
Red. quir.	*Post reditum ad quirites*
	("Speech of thanks to the citizens")
Red. sen.	*Post reditum in senatu*
	("Speech of thanks in the Senate")
Scaur.	*Pro M. Scauro*
	("In defense of M. Scaurus")
Sest.	*Pro P. Sestio*
	("In defense of P. Sestius")
Sull.	*Pro P. Sulla*
	("In defense of P. Sulla")
Vat.	*In P. Vatinium testem interrogatio*
	("Examination of the witness P. Vatinius")

Other

AJAH	*American Journal of Ancient History*
AJP	*American Journal of Philology*
BICS	*Bulletin of the Institute of Classical Studies*
	(of the University of London)
Catull.	Catullus
CR	*Classical Review*
HSCP	*Harvard Studies in Classical Philology*
Josephus, *Ant.*	Josephus, *Jewish Antiquities*
Onomasticon	see Bibliographical Note
Ov. *Fast.*	Ovid, *Fasti*
Ov. *Trist.*	Ovid, *Tristia*
Plut. *Cat. min.*	Plutarch, *Lives of Cato the Younger,*
Cic.,	*Cicero,*
Pomp.	*Pompey*
RE	*Realencyclopädie der classischen*
	Altertumswissenschaft (Pauly–Wissowa)
SB[1], etc.	see Bibliographical Note
Serv.	Servius

Suet. *Iul.*	Suetonius, *Life of Julius Caesar*
TAPA	*Transactions of the American Philological Association*
Virg. *Aen.*	Virgil, *Aeneid*

BIBLIOGRAPHICAL NOTE

A stylish English translation of the first four speeches in this volume by N. H. Watts (1935) and a scholarly one of the last two by R. Gardner (1958) are published in the Loeb series. Individual speeches with commentary have been edited by R. G. Nisbet—to be distinguished from R.G.M. Nisbet—(*De Domo* [Oxford] 1939), J. O. Lenaghan (*De Haruspicum Responso*, commentary only: [The Hague] 1969), and L. G. Pocock (*In Vatinium* [Oxford] 1926). H. A. Holden's edition of *Pro Sestio* (London, 1883) is still worth consulting.

References to certain publications of my own are abbreviated as follows. SB^1 = "On Cicero's Speeches," *HSCP* 83 (1979) 237–85 (262–74). SB^2 = "More on Cicero's Speeches (*Post Reditum*)," *HSCP* 89 (1985) 141–51. SB^3 = "On Cicero's Speeches (*Post Reditum*)," *TAPA* 117 (1987) 271–80. SB^4 = "Albanius or Albinius? A Palinode Resung," *HSCP* 92 (1989) 213–14. *Onomasticon* = *Onomasticon to Cicero's Speeches* (Norman, Oklahoma, 1988). "Shackleton Bailey on" such and such a passage in Cicero's letters refers to my Cambridge edition of 1965–80.

I have translated from Sir W. Peterson's Oxford text of 1911, but with many divergent readings as listed in Appendix I. Some of these had already been adopted in the Teubner (Leipzig) editions of the first four speeches (1981) and of the *Pro Sestio* (1986) by T. Maslowski and in J. Cousin's Budé edition of *Pro Sestio* and *In Vatinium* (1965). These divergences are indicated in the translations by a cross in the margin where the translation is affected.

INTRODUCTION

The six speeches in this volume, dating from the period following Cicero's return to Rome in September 57 B.C., are all variously concerned with his exile and restoration. As R. G. M. Nisbet has written, "In spite of all Cicero's rhetoric, his exile was a disaster from which he never recovered, politically or psychologically."[1]

The seeds were sown in the months following the formation of the so-called First Triumvirate at the end of 60. This was a private coalition among three powerful individuals—Pompey, Caesar, and Crassus—and it dominated Roman politics until Crassus' death in 53 and the subsequent rift between the two survivors. Early in 59, against the advice of his bosom friend and correspondent Pomponius Atticus,[2] Cicero rejected recurrent overtures from the Consul Caesar, and in March ventured upon a public attack none the less provocative because no names were mentioned. Retaliation followed in a matter of hours. Caesar and Pompey, in their respective capacities as Chief Pontiff and Augur, put through the adoption of the patrician demagogue P. Clodius Pulcher into a plebian clan, thus clearing the way for him to become a candidate for the tribunate, to which he was duly elected. Clodius was out for Cicero's blood, and the tribunate gave him every opportunity.

Their feud had its origin nearly three years earlier. In December 62 this enterprising young man had been caught in female disguise at the annual rites of the mysterious Good Goddess (Bona Dea; her true name was a secret), at which no male might be present. The rites were celebrated that year in Julius Caesar's house, and Clodius' intrusion was believed to have something to do with Caesar's wife—an affair. Clodius got away, and a bribed jury acquitted him of sacrilege. But Cicero had given evidence

---

1. *Cicero in Pisonem* (Oxford, 1961), p. xvi.
2. See D. R. Shackleton Bailey, *Cicero's Letters to Atticus I* (Cambridge, 1964), pp. 17f.

refuting his alibi, and Clodius vowed vengeance.

Writing to his brother Quintus in the autumn of 59, Cicero was full of misplaced confidence (*Q. fr.* 1.2.16): "I do not think I shall lack general support. It is amazing how people are coming forward with declarations and offers and promises. For my own part, I am in good hope and even better courage—hope because I am confident I shall win, courage because in the present state of the Commonwealth, I am not afraid of anything, even an accident." He went on to say that Pompey and Caesar were lavish with assurances, but that he was not relaxing his preparations on that account. The forthcoming magistrates, including the Consuls-Elect L. Calpurnius Piso (a relative of Cicero's son-in-law) and A. Gabinius, seemed well-disposed.

But in late January or early February of 58, Clodius gave notice of a bill to outlaw any person who had put Roman citizens to death without trial. Cicero was not named, but the reference to Cicero's execution of the Catilinarian conspirators as Consul in 63 was evident. Another bill, in violation of normal constitutional procedure, assigned desirable provinces to the Consuls after their year of office. Their backing was thus secured. Cicero put on mourning, as persons under prosecution customarily did, and the Senate voted to do the same. But the Consuls issued an order forbidding this, and Gabinius high-handedly expelled from Rome a leading Roman Knight and Ciceronian sympathizer, L. Aelius Lamia. Clodius claimed that the "Triumvirs" were behind him, and they did not contradict him. Caesar was about to take up a command in Gaul; an army under his orders was in north Italy, and a small force was outside the city gates. Clodius used it for leverage. Pompey declined to interfere, past promises notwithstanding, and retreated to his country estate in the Alban hills. In the third week of March (probably), Clodius' bills were passed, and Cicero fled from Rome.

He soon regretted it. In contemporary letters he blames himself for losing his nerve and blames his friends, notably the orator Hortensius, for advising him badly (deliberate treachery born of jealousy, as he let himself believe), or, in Atticus' case, for not advising him at all.[3] Naturally, the speeches tell a different story. Again and again his departure is represented as a magnanimous self-sacrifice, accepted to avoid bloodshed. No doubt he half-convinced himself, for his memory was always malleable. Those in his audience who knew the truth must have listened to these self-admiring and self-commiserating disquisitions as impatiently as we (who know the truth even better) read them.

Clodius followed up his success with another piece of legislation exiling Cicero by name and confiscating his property. In a state close to mental breakdown, Cicero made his erratic way down southern Italy to Brundisium, took ship for Greece, and arrived at Thessalonica (Salonika), where a friendly Quaestor, Cn. Plancius, gave him shelter and protection.

In Rome, as the year wore on and passed away, efforts were set on foot for his recall, only to be frustrated by Clodius, supported by another hostile Tribune, by his organized street-warriors, and, tacitly at least, by the Consuls. But these went out of office with the new year and one of their successors, P. Lentulus Spinther, was a firm friend of Cicero, while the other, Q. Metellus Nepos, an enemy of six years standing, proved persuadable. Two of the new Tribunes, T. Annius Milo and P. Sestius, disputed Clodius' control of the streets with rival gangs of their own raising. Most important, Pompey and Clodius had fallen out, and Pompey, with Caesar's grudging assent, came forward in favor of a restoration. The Senate decreed, the Assembly of Centuries passed an appropriate bill, and Cicero landed at Brundisium on 5 August. His progress up Italy was triumphal, culminating in a reentry into Rome on 4 September.

In the eighteenth century the English scholar Jeremiah Markland declared the first four speeches in this volume to be forgeries, and their authenticity was not fully vindicated until Zielinski's researches early in the twentieth showed that they follow the same rhythmical patterns as the rest of Cicero's later oratory.

---

3. See ibid. pp. 19–22.

Bombastic, repetitive, full of self-praise and self-pity, they (and the associated *Pro Sestio*) undeniably deserve some of the harsh things that have been said of them. But they are not all bad. The caricatures of the Consuls of 58 in the *Speech of thanks in the Senate* are among Cicero's best efforts in their kind, and as a lively narrative, what could be better than the account of the Forum riot in the *Pro Sestio* (ss. 75-77)? To students of Roman religion *De domo* and *De haruspicum responsis* offer much of curious interest. And whatever Cicero's exile had done to him, it had not deprived him of his command of Latin words, which even Mommsen had to recognize.

SPEECH OF THANKS IN THE SENATE
(*Post reditum in senatu*)

On 5 September B.C. 57,[1] the day after his return to Rome, Cicero addressed the Senate in an effusion of gratitude: to the House collectively (ss. 1–7), to individual magistrates (ss. 8–28, 30–31), and to Pompey (s. 29). Looking back, he took occasion for a scathing denunciation of the Consuls of 58, Gabinius and Piso (ss. 10–18), and for a relatively brief defense of his flight from Rome. The speech ends with an assertion of his unbroken spirit, supported by comparisons with two distinguished exiles of earlier periods, P. Popillius Laenas and Q. Metellus Numidicus. All of these are motifs with which readers of these speeches will become familiar.

[1] Members of the Senate, if the thanks I am about to render for your unforgettable services to myself and my brother and our children shall be less overflowing than the case demands, I ask and pray you to blame the magnitude of your benefactions, not any natural lack in me. Can any fertility of invention, any wealth of vocabulary, any god-given, transcendent style of eloquence be capable of simply enumerating all you have done for us, let alone of embracing it oratorically? You have restored to me the brother I so sorely missed and me to the most affectionate of brothers.
+ You have restored their parent to my children and my children to me. You have given me back rank, status, fortune, a noble commonwealth, and, source of delight second to none, my country.[2] In a word, you have given me back myself.

[2] I am bound to love my parents, for they transmitted to me life, patrimony, liberty, and citizenship; likewise the Immortal Gods, through whose favor I possessed these things and much else besides; likewise the Roman People, through whose honors[3] I

---

1. For the date, see *Att.* 4.1.5.
2. To a Roman citizen, *patria* ("fatherland") meant Rome first and foremost, though it could also apply to his native town, if that were not Rome—Arpinum in Cicero's case.
3. I.e., elective offices. The quaestorship gave admission to the Senate, but the "loftiest of all ranks" refers to the consulship.

took my place in this august assembly, in the loftiest of all ranks, in this topmost citadel of all the world; likewise this very House, which has often paid me generous tribute in its decrees. But how far beyond term or measure is my debt to yourselves![4] Your signal zeal and unanimity have restored everything to me at one stroke: the benefactions of my parents, the gifts of the Immortal Gods, the honors of the Roman People, and the many testimonials of your esteem. Many are my obligations to you, great are my obligations to the Roman People, to my parents they are beyond count, and to the Immortal Gods I owe everything. In the past I held my several possessions by their grace, but now I have regained all at once by yours.

[3] And so, Members of the Senate, thanks to you I feel I have gained after a fashion something for which no human being should even pray—immortality. Will the day ever come when the recollection and renown of your benefactions to me shall be no more? Even when you were held down by armed violence, terror, and menaces, not long after I left Rome, your entire body recalled me on the motion of my gallant and excellent friend Lucius Ninnius, the loyalest and least timid of my champions in that year of disaster, if I had chosen to fight. But after a certain Tribune,[5] one who took cover under another man's[6] villainy because he lacked the power to tear the Commonwealth to pieces on his own, had denied you the power to make a decree, thenceforward you were never silent on my behalf, never stopped demanding my rights from the Consuls who had bartered them away.

[4] And so by your zeal and authority it came to pass that the very year in which I had chosen calamity for myself rather than for my country produced eight Tribunes who both announced legislation to give me back my rights and more than once brought the matter before you. As for our discrete and law-fearing Consuls,[7]

---

4. Cicero may seem not to notice that he has just mentioned the Senate, but there is no real confusion. The Senate as a continuing institution is distinguished from its present membership to whom Cicero owed his restoration.

5. Aelius Ligus; see Index I and *Sest.* 68.

6. Clodius'.

7. Piso and Gabinius had pretended to be inhibited by Clodius' law against Cicero, which forbade any discussion of his case (cf. s. 8), but what really inhibited

they were held back not by the law passed against me but by one
+ passed about themselves, promulgated by my enemy. But it was
provided in the former law that I might return if and when the
men who almost destroyed Rome[8] came back to life. Thereby he[9]
made two admissions: that he would like those individuals back
alive, and that the Commonwealth would be in great jeopardy if
the enemies and killers of the Commonwealth lived again and I
+ did *not* return. And yet, in that same year, after I had left the
country, when the leading man in our society[10] was guarding his
life with the walls of his house and not with the protection of the
laws, when the Commonwealth was without Consuls, bereft not
only of permanent parents,[11] but of her annual guardians, when
you were forbidden to speak in your House and the clause proscribing[12] me was read aloud—in spite of all, you never hesitated
to link the survival of the community with my restoration.

[5] But then, on the first of January, thanks to the signal and
outstanding merit of Consul Publius Lentulus, you began to decry
a glimmer of light from out the misty gloom of the old year. The
lofty prestige of Quintus Metellus, whose moral excellence
matches the nobility of his birth, and the energy and loyalty of
almost all the new Praetors and Tribunes came to the aid of the
Commonwealth. Gnaeus Pompeius, in valor, glory, and achievement easily the greatest man ever seen in any country, in any age,
in the whole of history, thought it safe to attend the Senate. At
that juncture, your desire for my restitution was so unanimous
that my dignity was already back in Rome, though my person was
elsewhere.

[6] The events of that month afforded you an opportunity to
contrast me with my enemies. I forbore to defend myself, lest on
my account the Commonwealth be stained from Roman wounds:

---

them was that other law which had assigned them their provinces and so bought
their support; cf. *Dom.* 70, *Sest.* 69 (so SB³).

8. The Catilinarian conspirators, executed during Cicero's consulship.
9. Clodius.
10. Pompey. Having fallen out with Clodius, he kept to his house for fear of
violence; cf. *Dom.* 67, *Har. resp.* 49, *Sest.* 69 and elsewhere.
11. The Senate.
12. Cf. s. 8, and Glossary of Terms under "Proscription." Cicero applies the
term metaphorically to Clodius' treatment of him.

they thought proper to block my return, not with the votes of the Roman People but with a river of blood.[13] So, from then on you gave no answers either to Roman citizens, or to our allies,[14] or to foreign kings. The courts rendered no verdicts, the people passed no votes, the Senate no resolutions. You were gazing upon a silent Forum, a voiceless Senate-House, a mute and broken community.[15] [7] The man who by your authority had withstood massacre and arson had left Rome. You saw men roaming the whole city with swords and torches in their hands; you saw the residences of magistrates assaulted, the temples of the Gods set on fire, the *fasces*[16] of a great Roman and an illustrious Consul[17] broken into pieces, the sacrosanct person of a gallant and excellent Tribune [18] not merely touched in violation of his office, but stabbed unconscious. Some of the magistrates, in consternation at the carnage, backed away a little from my cause, part in fear for their lives, part in despair of the Commonwealth. There remained those whom neither terror nor violence, neither hope nor fear, neither promise nor threats, neither weapons nor firebrands, could move from their championship of your authority, and of the dignity of the Roman People, and of my restitution.

[8] Publius Lentulus, parent and guardian spirit of my life, fortune, memory, and fame, took the lead. He judged that his restoration of me to myself and my friends, to you and to the Commonwealth would be a specimen of his worth, an indication of his courage, and a luster to his consulship. From the day he was elected he never hesitated to speak on the subject in the Senate as became himself and the Commonwealth. A Tribune[19] forbade him to do this, reading aloud that remarkable clause which prohibited any reference to you or motion or discussion or speech or

---

13. See *Sest.* 75–77.

14. The term *socii* ("allies") was variously applied. Here it means the native inhabitants of the Roman provinces, whatever their status. The Senate regularly devoted the month of February to hearing delegations from abroad.

15. *Civitas* = "citizenry" or "state."

16. See Glossary of Terms.

17. Presumably Lentulus, but the incident is not otherwise recorded.

18. Sestius. Cf. *Sest.* 79.

19. No doubt Aelius Ligus, if not Clodius himself.

vote or witness.[20] But this entire proscription, as I have termed it,[21] by which a citizen who had done excellent service to the Commonwealth had been snatched away from the Commonwealth without trial, along with the Senate—he regarded it as no law, but as an act of violence.

Once he came into office, what was his first concern, or rather, what other concern did he have except to establish your dignity and authority in the future by preserving me? [9] What a boon the Immortal Gods are seen to have conferred on me in that Publius Lentulus is Consul of the Roman People this year! How much greater the boon if he had been Consul last year! I should never have needed a Consul to heal my hurt, if Consuls had not felled me. I had heard a very wise man and a fine patriot, Quintus Catulus, remark that there had seldom been one bad Consul and never since the foundation of Rome two, except in the Cinnan period; so he used to say that my position would always be very strong, so long as even one good Consul was in office. And right he would have been, if what was true of the past history of the Commonwealth could have held good for all time. If Quintus Metellus, my enemy, had been Consul in that crisis, can you doubt how he would have felt about preserving me when you see how he has supported and subscribed to my restoration? [10] Ah, but the Consuls then in office were petty men, whose base, perverse minds, filled with darkness and greed, could not contemplate or support or understand the very word "consulship"—the splendor of the office, the greatness of the authority it confers. They were no Consuls, but traffickers in provinces, barterers of your dignity. One of them[22] asked me in front of many witnesses what I had done with his lover Catiline; the other[23] asked the same question about his cousin Cethegus. These two—not Consuls but bandits, the most villainous in the memory of man, deserted me, and that in a cause of public and consular concern. Worse, they betrayed me, assailed me, wished me deprived of all

---

20. After the Senate had passed a decree, it was drafted and witnessed as correct by a number of Senators (*scribendo adesse*).
21. See s. 4 and n. 12.
22. Gabinius. Cf. *Dom.* 62.
23. Piso. Cf. *Dom.* 62.

succor, not only from themselves, but from you and the other classes of the community.

[11] What one of them[24] was, however, I and all the world knew. Nobody could augur any good from a fellow whose earliest youth had been openly prostituted to every lust, one who could not fend off men's foul excesses from the holiest part of his body.[25] When he had squandered his own money as energetically as he later squandered the public's, he supported his need and extravagance by turning his house into a brothel. Even so, if he had not fled into the tribunate for sanctuary, he could never have escaped the Praetor's[26] coercion, the multitude of his creditors, and the auction of his possessions. Yet, if in that office he had not carried a bill[27] on the Pirate War, he would have surely been driven by need and rascality to turn pirate himself, thereby causing less public damage than by his conduct as a wicked enemy and corsair inside the city walls. While he sat looking on, a Tribune[28] proposed a law providing that no attention be paid to auspices, no public assembly or elections be blocked by a declaration of adverse signs, that this law not be subject to tribunician veto, and that the Aelian and Fufian laws[29] be invalid—all designed by our forbears as sure public safeguards against revolutionary Tribunes.

[12] Later on, a vast concourse of honest men came from the Capitol, dressed in mourning garb, as suppliants; young men of the highest birth and the whole company of Roman Knights[30] threw themselves at the feet of the shameless pimp. How haughtily the ringleted rake rejected his fellow-countrymen's tears, nay, his country's prayers! Not content with that, he actually mounted a platform and addressed a meeting in terms which his lord and

---

24. Gabinius.
25. His mouth.
26. The City Praetor (*praetor urbanus*), who dealt with litigation between Roman citizens.
27. The Gabinian law of 67, giving Pompey overall command against piracy.
28. Clodius.
29. Passed less than a century before. Their full contents are unknown, but they established the right of magistrates to block legislative or electoral action in assemblies by announcing adverse omens (*obnuntiatio*). See p. 55, n. 52.
30. See Glossary of Terms.

master[31] Catiline would not have ventured to use, had he come back to life—threatening to make the Roman Knights pay for the fifth of December when I was Consul and for Capitol Rise.[32] And not only did he make that threat, he summoned whom he chose, and by a stroke of consular prerogative ordered Lucius Lamia out of the city, a Roman Knight, a person of the highest standing, who favored my restoration as a close friend and loved the Commonwealth as a substantial citizen. And when you voted to put on mourning and actually all did so (all honest men had already done the same), he appeared bathed in perfume and wearing his magistrate's gown,[33] which all Praetors, and Aediles then in office had discarded, to mock your garb of woe and the sorrowing of a grateful community. Further, he did something no tyrant had ever done: he issued an order in which, while having nothing to
+ say against your bemoaning your trouble in private,[34] he forbade you to mourn the nation's misfortunes openly. [13] When he appeared before a meeting in the Circus Flaminius, not as a Consul introduced by a Tribune but as a pirate chief introduced by a brigand, to begin with, what an impressive figure he made! Sleepy, drunken, debauched, his carefully dressed hair reeking with perfume, heavy-eyed, flabby-cheeked, he announced in an alcoholic mutter that he most strongly disapproved of the punishment of citizens without trial. A fine one he to disapprove! Where was such a weight of authority hiding from us all that time? Why were the splendid qualities of this curled dancer wasted so long in brothels and gourmandizings?

As for his colleague Caesoninus Calventius,[35] he had been in public life from youth upwards; nor had he anything to recommend him[36] except a cunning affectation of austerity—neither
+ learning in the law, nor power of eloquence, nor military

---

31. Lit. "husband."
32. Clivus Capitolinus, the slope leading up to the Capitol, where the Knights mustered in arms to support Cicero on 5 December 63.
33. The purple-bordered gown (*toga*) worn by curule magistrates (and boys).
34. Cicero appears to be quoting the words of the edict.
35. Piso's full name was L. Calpurnius Piso Caesoninus. His maternal grandfather Calventius was a Cisalpine Gaul, so that calling him by that name was a facetious insult.
36. I.e., to the public.

expertise, nor eagerness to make people's acquaintance, nor openhandedness. Seeing him in passing, unkempt, ungroomed, sour-visaged, one might have put him down as a graceless oaf, but hardly as a bad lot, a profligate. [14] Talking to this fellow in the Forum, one would have thought, would be just like talking to a log of wood—a mindless, colorless,[37] tongue-tied, dull, churlish specimen, one would have called him, a Cappadocian[38] slave fresh from the auction room. But at home! A foul, lascivious libertine, whose pleasures were not received at the front door but slipped in by a secret entrance. However, this hideous monster began to take an interest in books, and to talk philosophy with Greeklings; then it was that he turned Epicurean, not with any deep commitment to that system, whatever it amounts to, but captivated by the one word "pleasure."[39] His mentors are not those silly folk[40] who spend all day discoursing about Duty and Virtue, and urge us to work hard and well and to face danger when our country calls. *He* prefers the ones who argue that no hour should be void of pleasure and that in every part of our bodies we should always be experiencing some delightful sensation. [15] These gentry he employs as superintendents of his lusts. They track down all manner of pleasures, smell them out, they season and spread the banquet. At the same time they *weigh* pleasures, estimating, pronouncing verdicts, deciding just how much attention each lust deserves.

Instructed in their accomplishments, he held the good sense of our community in contempt. He thought that all his lusts and outrages could be kept secret so long as he brought a grim face down to the Forum. He never fooled *me* for a moment; as a connection of the Pisos by marriage,[41] I knew what a long way his mother's Transalpine blood had taken him from the family. But you and the Roman People *were* taken in, not by brains or eloquence, as happens often enough, but by a beetle brow.

---

37. Lit. "flavorless."
38. I.e., good only for rough, menial work.
39. Epicurus held that pleasure, defined as the absence of pain, is the end of human existence.
40. Such as the Stoics. The description is ironic, of course.
41. Through Cicero's son-in-law, C. Piso Frugi.

[16] Lucius Piso, with a glare (I won't say "mind") like yours, with such a forehead (I won't say "such a life"), with so fine a frown (I can't say "so fine a record"), did you dare to plot my downfall with Aulus Gabinius? You smelt his perfumes and the reek of his wine, you saw the marks of the curling tongs on his forehead; did it not occur to you that, resembling him as you do in fact, you would no longer be able to use your appearance[42] as a cover to hide your vile life? Did you dare to conspire with him to sacrifice the consular dignity, the stability of the Commonwealth, the authority of the Senate, and the fortunes of a well-deserving citizen in a pact for provinces? In your consulship, by your edicts and commands, was the Senate of the Roman People not allowed to come to the aid of the Commonwealth, I do not say by their votes and authority, but even by the wearing of mourning clothes? [17] Did you think you were Consul in Capua (which you actually were at the time),[43] a city once the home of arrogance, or in Rome, a community in which all Consuls before you obeyed the Senate?[44] Did you dare to let yourself be introduced along with your fellow rogue in the Circus Flaminius and to say that you had always been a man of compassion—a phrase by which you tried to present the Senate and all honest men as guilty of cruelty when they saved Rome from destruction?[45] Compassionate! You, who handed me over bound hand and foot to the enemies of the Commonwealth, me, your relation by marriage, whom at your election you appointed first teller[46] for the first Century to vote,[47] whom you called upon third in the Senate on the first of January?[48] My son-in-law, your blood relation, and my daughter, your relation by

---

42. Lit., "brow." There is no reference to patches on the forehead, as has sometimes been supposed.
43. He was Duovir, i.e., co-mayor, corresponding to Consul in Rome.
44. Cicero's rhetoric is apt to outrun the facts. He had to think no further back than the consulship of Julius Caesar in 59 to find this statement refuted.
45. I.e., suppressed the Catilinarian conspiracy in 63.
46. *Custos*, appointed to ensure fair and proper voting. It was a mark of honor to be asked by a candidate to serve in this capacity.
47. *Centuria praerogativa*; see Glossary of Terms under "Centuries."
48. At the first meeting of the year, the presiding Consul determined the order of speaking for the rest of the year within the several categories of ex-magistrates, from Consulars (Ex-Consuls) down.

marriage, were at your knees. You spurned them, in the harshest, most arrogant terms. When together with the Commonwealth I was felled by consular (not tribunician) hands, your criminal impatience was such that in your remarkable gentleness and compassion you did not let a single hour intervene between my destruction and your loot, not even waiting for the general outcry and lamentation to die down. [18] The death of the Commonwealth had not yet been announced when you were receiving your payment for the cost of the funeral.[49] At one and the same time my town house was being ransacked and burned, my goods were
+ in transport to my consular neighbor on the Palatine,[50] and from my Tusculan villa to my other consular neighbor,[51] when these two foul and wicked Consuls were given the Treasury,[52] provinces, legions, commands. How? Why, with the same gangs voting, with the same gladiator proposing, with the Forum void and empty of free men, not to speak of honest men, with the Roman People ignorant of what was afoot, with the Senate beaten down and crushed.

The edifice which these Consuls almost tumbled, you Consuls here present propped up by your courage, aided by the exemplary loyalty and diligence of our Tribunes and Praetors. [19] There was Titus Annius,[53] a gentleman of outstanding quality, of whom I do not know how I should speak, or who will ever speak of such a patriot in the terms he deserves. He saw that a criminal citizen, or rather an enemy within the gates, should be broken in court if legal process was available; but if the courts themselves were hampered or subverted by violence, he realized that audacity had to be overcome by courage, frenzy by resolution, recklessness by policy, a band by rival forces, violence by violence. First he brought a charge of breaking the peace. Finding the courts had

---

49. As undertaker.
50. The house on the Palatine to which Cicero's goods and chattels were removed belonged to Piso's mother-in-law; cf. *Dom.* 62, *Pis.* 26.
51. Gabinius, who owned a villa at Tusculum near to Cicero's, which he later rebuilt on a magnificent scale (*Dom.* 124, *Sest.* 93).
52. Cf. p. 47, n. 20.
53. Milo (see Index I).

been put out of action by the same person,[54] he took measures to prevent that person from carrying all before him by force. He taught the lesson that houses and temples, Forum and Senate-House cannot be defended against brigands in our midst except by high courage and large resources of men and money. He was the first after my departure to take fear from honest men,[55] hope from desperados, terror from this House, and slavery from the community.

[20] Following this principle with equal energy, courage and loyalty, Publius Sestius was ever ready to face any enmities, any violence, any assaults, any danger to his life in the cause of my restoration, your authority, and the maintenance of the community. The cause of the Senate had been assailed by means of public meetings attended by rascals;[56] by continual effort he commended it to the favor of the crowd so effectively that your name became supremely "popular,"[57] your authority at long last an asset universally cherished. He championed me in every way open to him as Tribune and supported me with other good offices like a brother. He sustained me with his clients, freedmen, household, financial resources, and letters, so that it seemed as though he was not only my helper in adversity, but my partner.

[21] As for the other Tribunes, you witnessed their zealous good offices. You saw how eager Gaius Cestilius was to serve me, how keen a supporter of yours, how unwavering in the cause. Then Marcus Cispius: I realize how much I owe him and his father and brother. I had lost their good will in a private lawsuit, but they washed away their private grievance with the memory of my public benefaction. Titus Fadius had been my Quaestor and I was Quaestor to Marcus Curtius' father;[58] their zeal, affection, and courage were in accordance with these ties. Gaius Messius often referred to me in his speeches, for friendship's sake and the Commonwealth's, and independently gave notice of a bill for my restoration at an early stage. [22] If Quintus Fabricius had succeeded

---

54. Clodius.
55. See Glossary of Terms.
56. See Glossary of Terms.
57. See Glossary of Terms under "people's man."
58. Sex. Peducaeus; see Index I under Curtius and Peducaeus.

in carrying through his efforts on my behalf in the face of armed violence, I should have recovered my rights last January. Good will urged him forward, violence checked him, but your authority called him back.

As for the Praetors, you could judge of their sentiments toward me by their behavior. Lucius Caecilius was eager to sustain me privately with all his resources, whereas publicly he announced a law for my restoration in conjunction with almost all his colleagues and did not allow[59] the plunderers of my property to take legal action. Marcus Calidius made clear in the Senate how much my restitution meant to him immediately after his election. [23] Gaius Septimius, Quintus Valerius, Publius Crassus, Sextus Quinctilius, and Gaius Cornutus did everything that lay in their power for me and for the Commonwealth.

I am happy to recall these facts. Nor am I sorry to pass over the acts of wickedness toward me committed by certain folk. I am not in a position to remember injuries; and even if it were in my power to avenge them, I should prefer to forget. My whole life has to turn in a different direction. I have to show gratitude to those who have deserved well of me, treasure friendships tested in the fire, wage war against open enemies, pardon timorous friends, refrain from pointing a finger at the treacherous,[60] and assuage the pain of my leaving with the glory of my return. [24] Even if the only thing left for me to do in all my life were to make men judge me adequately grateful to the leaders only, the prime movers and authors of my restoration, I should hold the life-span remaining to me all too meager for the acknowledgment of my obligations, let alone their repayment.

How long shall I and all mine need to repay this gentleman[61] and his children? How can any memory or force of intellect or amount of observance suffice in face of benefits so many and so great? As I lay in the dust, he was the first to hold out his hand to me, pledging his word as a Consul. He called me back from death to life, from despair to hope, from destruction to salvation. Such

---

59. As City Praetor.
60. Such as (in Cicero's opinion) Hortensius. Cf. *Red. quir.* 21.
61. The Consul Lentulus.

was his affection for me and his zeal for the Commonwealth that he devised a way not only to relieve my misfortune, but to lend it dignity. Could anything happen to me more glorious and splendid than what you decreed on his motion: that all who wished well to the Commonwealth should come from all over Italy to restore and defend me, one man, a man broken almost beyond mending? Only three times in the history of Rome[62] have those words been used by a Consul; used, however, on behalf of the entire Commonwealth and only to those within sound of his voice; but used now by the whole Senate in order to summon Rome's citizens and all Italy from every district and town to uphold the cause of a single individual. [25] What prouder legacy could I leave to my descendants than this, that in the judgment of the Senate no Roman who failed to champion me wished well to the Commonwealth. Accordingly, what with your authority and the Consul's extraordinary prestige, any man who did not come felt himself guilty of a disgraceful, scandalous act.

When that unexampled throng, Italy in person one might almost say, arrived in Rome, this same Consul summoned you in full number to the Capitol.[63] You then had occasion to appreciate the power of native goodness and true nobility. Quintus Metellus was my enemy and the brother of an enemy;[64] but when he fully realized your will, he set aside all private grudges. In a wonderfully impressive speech, with all the weight of his prestige behind it, my excellent and illustrious friend Publius Servilius[65] urged him to be true to the deeds and virtues of his line, their common heritage: let him summon his brother,[66] partner in my achievements, from the grave to advise him, and all those outstanding citizens of the name Metellus, calling them up from Acheron as it were, not excluding the famous Metellus Numidicus, who left his
+ country in former days in a manner deemed honorable by all to be sure, but lamentable nonetheless. [26] And so the miracle

---

62. Cf. *Sest.* 128. The three occasions are not certainly identifiable.
63. At the beginning of July; cf. *Sest.* 130.
64. Clodius. They were half-brothers.
65. P. Servilius Vatia Isauricus (Consul in 79) was a grandson of Q. Metellus Macedonicus.
66. Q. Metellus Celer, Consul in 60. As Praetor he supported Cicero in 63.

+ happened. Metellus, who was my enemy before he did me this great service, stood forward not only to champion my restoration but to approve my dignity.

That day you numbered four hundred and seventeen. All magistrates were present. There was one dissentient,[67] the individual whose law showed him desirous of raising up traitors from their graves. That same day, after you had declared emphatically and at length that the Commonwealth was saved by my devices, this same Consul saw to it that the leaders of the community addressed a public meeting to the same effect on the day following. He himself pleaded my cause most eloquently and it was his doing that with all Italy standing by to listen, no man should hear a word from any hireling or blackguard harsh and hostile to honest men. [27] Having thus aided my restoration and enhanced my prestige, you went further, decreeing that no man should in any way obstruct the matter, and that any person who did so would incur your deep displeasure, and would be acting against the Commonwealth and the welfare of honest men and the general consensus. A person thus acting, so ran your decree, should be brought to your attention immediately. Further, you directed me to come home if they should continue maneuvering for any length of time. Nor was that all. Those who had come in from the country towns were to be officially thanked and requested to be equally zealous in gathering together for the day when public business resumed.[68]

+ Finally, what of the day[69] which Publius Lentulus ordained as my birthday and that of my brother and of our children, one to be remembered by us now living and to all eternity, the day when he summoned me back to my country through the Assembly of Centuries,[70] which our forbears ever wished to be spoken and thought of as the most authoritative form of assembly, whereby the same Centuries which had elected me Consul set the seal of their approval on my consulship? [28] No citizen that day,

---

67. Clodius.
68. When the law would be voted.
69. 4 August.
70. See Glossary of Terms under "Centuries."

whatever his age or state of health, but felt a sacred duty to cast his vote for my restoration. Did you ever see such a throng in the Field,[71] such a distinguished assembly of all Italy and all classes, such personally eminent canvassers,[72] distributers, [73] and tellers?[74] Then it was that thanks to the signal, wonderful benefaction of Publius Lentulus I was not merely brought back to my country, as some illustrious citizens have been in the past, but carried home in a gilded chariot drawn by resplendent horses.

[29] Can I ever seem sufficiently thankful to Gnaeus Pompeius? Both to you, who were all of the like opinion, and to the entire people he declared that the safety of the Roman People had been preserved through me and was bound up with mine. He commended my cause to men of experience, instructed those who lacked it, and at the same time used his personal authority to keep rascals in check and to encourage honest men. For my sake, he urged the Roman People and even implored them as though for a brother or a father. Already, when he was house-bound because of the threat of sanguinary struggle, he had asked last year's Tribunes to announce legislation and make motions in the Senate concerning my restoration. He was himself a magistrate at the time in a recently established colony.[75] There was nobody *there* to cast a bought veto. He attested the violence and the cruelty of a law *ad hominem*[76] by the authority of most respectable persons and by public documents; and he was the first to hold that all of Italy should be entreated to support my cause. He himself had always been my very good friend, and now he worked to make his friends also become friends of mine.

[30] With what services am I to repay my debt to Titus Annius? All his thoughts and actions, his entire career in office, have been nothing but a resolute, constant, courageous, indomitable

---

71. Campus Martius; see Glossary of Terms under "Mars' Field."
72. Before the introduction of the secret ballot, voters were asked which way they voted by *rogatores*. Their subsequent function is uncertain.
73. Of voting tablets.
74. See p. 13, n. 46.
75. Capua; his colleague as Duovir was Piso (see p. 13, n. 43).
76. A law in favor of or against an individual (*privilegium*) was unconstitutional. Cf. *Dom.* 43, *Sest.* 65.

championship of my cause. What am I to say of Publius Sestius, who has manifested his good will and loyalty to me not only in distress of mind but in bodily injuries?

You, Members of the Senate, I have thanked individually and shall continue to thank. I thanked you collectively at the beginning of my address as best I could, though to put my gratitude in adequate words is totally beyond my power. Many have rendered me special services which can in no wise be passed over in silence, and yet it does not suit the present situation and the apprehensions I feel to try to make mention of the kindness I have received from individuals. For it would be difficult not to pass over somebody, and to pass over anybody would be a sin. To you collectively, Members of the Senate, I owe such veneration as I pay to the Gods. But even our worship and prayers to the Immortal Gods are not always addressed to the same deities, but sometimes to one and sometimes to another. So it is with men who have rendered me godlike benefits. I shall have all my life ahead to proclaim and recall what they did for me. [31] Today, however, I thought it fitting to give thanks to our magistrates, and among private citizens to one person,[77] who had approached townships and colonies in my cause, begged the Roman People as a suppliant, and framed the motion which you followed when you gave me back my dignity.

In the days of my prosperity you always did me honor, and when I was in trouble you came to my defense by changing dress, almost by mourning me, as long as you were allowed. We remember the time when it was not customary for Senators to change dress even when they themselves were in danger; but when *I* was in danger, the Senate changed dress until prevented by orders from those who deprived me in my hour of peril not only of *their* protection but of *your* intercession.

[32] Such being the situation I had to face, and seeing that I must as a private citizen clash with the same army[78] which I had defeated as Consul, not by arms but by your authority, I had much to think about. A Consul had said at a public meeting that he

---

77. Pompey.
78. The have-nots and the malcontents that had supported Catiline.

intended to make the Roman Knights pay for Capitol Rise.[79] Some were being summoned by name, others cited to appear in court, others banished. Access to the temples was barred by armed pickets and even by demolition.[80] The other Consul[81] had pledged himself by entering into bargains stipulating personal rewards to desert me and the Commonwealth, more, to betray both to the Commonwealth's foes. There was somebody else:[82] he was at the gates, invested with a military command extending over many years and a large army.[83] I do not say he was my enemy; I know only that when he was said to be my enemy, he held his peace. [33] It was the general opinion that there were two parties in the Commonwealth, one of them demanding my blood because they were at feud with me, the other timid in my defense because they scented a massacre. The party which seemed to be demanding my blood increased the fear of armed conflict by never denying the possibility and so allaying public suspicion and anxiety. I saw the Senate bereft of its leaders, myself assailed or betrayed or left in the lurch by our magistrates. I saw that slaves had been enrolled by name under cover of associations [84] and all Catiline's forces called back to the bright prospect of fire and slaughter almost under the same leaders, that the Roman Knights were in dread of proscription, the country towns of sacking, and everyone of massacre. Now I could, yes, Members of the Senate, I *could* have defended myself by armed force, and many brave men so counselled me. Nor did my own courage falter, courage of which you have had some experience in time gone by.

I saw, however, that if I defeated the adversary in front of me, there were all too many others whom I should have to defeat; whereas if *I* was defeated, many honest men would have to die for
+ me and with me and even after me. Avengers of a Tribune's

---

79. See p. 11, n. 32.
80. Presumably to prevent prayers on Cicero's behalf.
81. Piso.
82. Caesar.
83. The force with Caesar outside Rome was small. His main army was at Aquileia in northeast Italy.
84. *Collegia*—clubs of various kinds. At this period they were often used for political purposes, and the Senate suppressed many of them in 64. Clodius as Tribune passed a law restoring them.

blood[85] were ready at hand; retribution for *my* death would have
to wait for a legal trial or a later generation. [34] As Consul I had defended the public safety without resort to the sword; I did not wish to defend my own by arms as a private citizen. I preferred that honest men should bemoan my lost estate rather than despair for their own. Also, I felt that if I alone were killed, that would be discreditable to me;[86] whereas if many others were killed with me, it would be disastrous to the Commonwealth. Had I indeed thought that unending misery lay ahead for me, I should have chosen death by my own hand rather than an eternity of sorrow.[87] But I saw that I should be out of this city for only so long a time as the Commonwealth herself; so I did not think it right that I should remain after she had been driven out, and as soon as she was recalled she brought me back in her company. The laws, the courts, the prerogatives of the magistrates, the authority of the Senate, liberty, plenty even, all sanctities and holy obligations, divine and human, were in exile as I was. If all this was gone forever, I should have been mourning your ruined fortunes rather than regretting mine; on the other hand, I realized that, should these things eventually be brought back, I must needs return with them. [35] The surest witness to these sentiments of mine is the man who became the guardian of my life, Gnaeus Plancius. Putting aside all the trappings and perquisites of provincial office, he devoted his entire quaestorship to sustaining and preserving me. If he had been Quaestor to me as governor, he would have been to me as a son. As it is, he will be to me as a father, for he was my partaker, not in power, but in suffering.

[36] Therefore, Members of the Senate, since I have been restored to the Commonwealth together with the Commonwealth, I shall abate nothing of my old independence in defending her; in fact, I shall increase it. If I defended her when she owed something to me, what is my duty now that the debt is heavily on my side? Nothing can break or weaken my spirit. You see that my very misfortune stands witness, not of any wrongdoing,

---

85. I.e., Clodius, should he be killed in the struggle.
86. It would show want of support; cf. p. 154, n. 44.
87. Cicero had in fact thought of suicide (*Att.* 3.3).

+ but of two services to the Commonwealth: it was brought upon me because I had defended the community, and voluntarily accepted by me in order that the Commonwealth I had defended might not through me be placed in the gravest jeopardy.

[37] His young sons and a multitude of kinsfolk pleaded to the Roman People on behalf of Publius Popillius, a great aristocrat. A son, a young man who had already proved his worth, supplicated the Roman People on behalf of the eminent and illustrious Quintus Metellus; with him were Lucius and Gaius Metellus, both Consulars, and their children, and Quintus Metellus Nepos, a candidate for the consulship at the time, also Luculli, Servilii, Scipios, sons of female members of the family,[88] all in tears and mourning garb. It was otherwise with me. Only my brother, who proved himself as dutiful as a son, as wise as a father, and as affectionate as the brother that he was, kept my name in ever-recurring wistful public memory and caused my achievements to be held in lively recollection, by dress and tears and daily entreaties. Having made up his mind that if he failed to bring me back through you, he would share my fate and demand the self-same place of dwelling
+ to live and die in, he never feared the magnitude of the undertaking, nor his own isolation,[89] nor the armed violence of our enemies.

[38] My cause had another constant champion and defender, my most worthy and dutiful son-in-law Gaius Piso. My restoration was what mattered to him, not the threats of my enemies or the enmity of a Consul, his relation by blood and mine by marriage, or his assignment as Quaestor to Pontus and Bithynia.

The Senate never passed a decree in the case of Publius Popillius. That of Quintus Metellus was never raised in this House. They were restored by tribunician bills, only after their enemies had been killed. One of them had withdrawn from Rome in obedience to the Senate, the other fled from violence and massacre. As for Gaius Marius, the third Consular before myself in living memory to be driven out in a domestic upheaval, not only was he not restored by the Senate, but he almost wiped the Senate out by

---

88. Cf. *Red. quir.* 6.
89. Not that Quintus stood alone, but he had lost Cicero.

his return.[90] In their cases, there was no consensus among the magistrates, no calling together of the Roman People for the defense of the Commonwealth, no arising of Italy, no decrees of townships and colonies. [39] Whereas I have been summoned by your authority, called by the Roman People, entreated by the Commonwealth, carried back on the shoulders, so to speak, of all Italy. Therefore, Members of the Senate, since things not in my power have been restored to me, I shall take good care not to be lacking in what I can provide for myself. After all, I lost the former and have recovered them, but never lost my courage and my loyalty.

---

90. A number of Senators and many lesser folk were killed in the violence that followed Marius' return to power in 87, some of them certainly by his orders. Cicero, as often, exaggerates.

SPEECH OF THANKS TO THE CITIZENS
(*Post reditum ad quirites*)

> This address to the citizenry, i.e., to a popular assembly specially summoned, will have been delivered shortly after the preceding. With certain differences appropriate to the audience it follows similar lines. Gratitude comes first (ss. 1–5), then the comparison between Cicero's recall and that of earlier victims of injustice to the advantage of the former (ss. 6–11). There follows a selective survey of recent history (ss. 11–17) and, for the future, assurances of patriotic devotion and a spirit undaunted by his ordeal.

[1] Men of Rome, when I offered up myself and my estate on behalf of your safety, tranquillity, and harmony, I made a prayer to Jupiter Best and Greatest and the rest of the Immortal Gods. I prayed that if I had ever placed my personal interests above your welfare, my voluntarily accepted punishment should be permanent; whereas if my past actions had been to save our community, and it was for the sake of your survival that I had undertaken my sad journey hence, to the end that the long pent-up hatred conceived by reckless criminals against the Commonwealth and all honest men be directed upon my single person rather than upon the whole community and its leading members—I prayed that if I had been thus minded towards you and your children, then one day you, and the Senate, and all Italy might come to remember and pity me and to wish me back. Greatly do I rejoice that by the judgment of the Immortal Gods, the testimony of the Senate, the consensus of Italy, the admission of my enemies, and your godlike and immortal benefaction my prayer has been answered.[1]

[2] For indeed, Men of Rome, although a fair and prosperous journey through life without any misfortune to interrupt its even tenor is as much as any man can pray for; yet, if all had been calm and easy for me, I should have missed the enjoyment of an extraordinary, almost superhuman happiness, which, by your

---

1. The Latin expression implies that if the Gods do their part, accepting the sacrifice offered on the terms of the offering, the petitioner must perform what he promised, his vow—though no vow is actually stated here.

kindness, is now mine.

What sweeter gift has nature bestowed upon mankind than children, to each his own? Mine are more precious to me than my life, such is my fondness and such their exceptional qualities. But my pleasure when I first took them in my arms[2] was less than I feel now at their restitution. [3] Nothing ever gave any man more delight than my brother gave me, but I did not feel it so keenly when I had him as when I lost him, and now that you have restored us to each other. All of us take satisfaction in our possessions, but the recovery of what remains of mine now brings me more pleasure than they used to do intact. Friendships, familiar contacts, connections of neighborhood and clientele, even shows and holidays—I have realized the pleasure they yield in the lack better than in the enjoyment. [4] As for honorable standing, station, rank, and the gifts conferred by you,[3] I have always considered them as splendid distinctions, but now that they have been renewed, they seem to shine brighter than if they had never been dimmed. And my country! Words can hardly express the love, the joy of her. The sight of Italy, the populous towns, the landscape, the countryside, the crops, the beauty of our city, the kindness of her people, the dignity of the Commonwealth, the majesty of you, the people! Yes, formerly I used to enjoy all these things as much as any man. But all of them are better relished when missed than when continually sampled, just as a man who has recovered from a serious illness appreciates good health more than one who has never been sick.

[5] Why do I say all this? Why? To let you realize that no speaker was ever so eloquent or possessed of so marvellous and incomparable a style that he could fully enumerate, let alone enhance and embellish in words, the magnitude and multitude of the benefactions you have conferred upon me and my brother and our children. In the necessity of things my parents brought me into the world as a tiny child: to you I owe my birth as a

---

2. *Suscepti*, lit. "taken up," refers to the Roman practice of acknowledging children, i.e., of signifying intent to rear them and not expose them, by the father taking the child in his arms.

3. By election to public office.

Consular. They gave me a brother, but what manner of man he would become none could say: you have restored him to me tried and proven, a paragon of fraternal loyalty. From them in those days I received back a Commonwealth which was almost lost: from you I have received back a Commonwealth which in the judgment of all its citizens was once saved by a single man.[4] The Immortal Gods gave me children; you have given them back. Many other objects of desire I had from the Immortal Gods: but for your will I should be deprived of every gift of heaven. Your honors, to which I had attained gradually, one by one, I now hold from you in their entirety. As much as formerly I owed to my parents, to the Immortal Gods, and to you, so much at this time do I owe in entirety to the whole Roman People.

[6] Your benefaction is greater than I can embrace in words; and by the good will towards me which you have manifested in zealous efforts on my behalf, you are seen not merely to have relieved me of my misfortune[5] but actually to have enhanced my standing. It was not with me as it was with Publius Popillius, a great aristocrat, who had young sons and many other relatives by blood and marriage to plead for his return from exile. It was not as with the illustrious Quintus Metellus,[6] for whom pleaded a son old enough to have proven his worth together with the Consular Lucius Diadematus, a person of the highest consequence, and the Ex-Censor Gaius Metellus with their children, also Quintus Metellus Nepos, who was standing for the consulship at the time, and the sons of sisters,[7] the Luculli, the Servilii, the Scipios. Many indeed were the members of the Metellus family or children of female members who came in supplication to you and your fathers for Quintus Metellus' return. If his own lofty standing and great achievements were not enough, his son's dutiful zeal, the

---

4. After Cicero's restoration the Commonwealth is once again what it was when he saved it in 63.
5. *Calamitas*, a word often used to mean the loss of civil rights.
6. Numidicus.
7. Not Numidicus' sisters. Only one of the ladies referred to was that, the mother of the famous L. Licinius Lucullus and his brother. The other two were sisters of Diadematus and C. Metellus (Caprarius) respectively, and their sons were P. Cornelius Scipio Nasica (Praetor in 93) and C. Servilius Vatia.

entreaties of his kindred, the doleful disarray of the young men, and the tears of their elders could stir the hearts of the Roman People. [7] After those two illustrious Consulars of an earlier day, the third Consular before me in your time and in your fathers' time to undergo this most undeserved affliction to his own eminent glory was Gaius Marius;[8] but his was a different case. He did not return as a result of intercession, but in the course of a civil conflict he recalled himself by arms, with an army. But as for me, I was indigent of kinsfolk, and had no relatives to protect me, nor was there any armed insurrection. Only the wonderful, unparalleled family affection and worth of my son-in-law Gaius Piso, and the daily tears and lugubrious aspect of my unhappiest and best of brothers pleaded with you on my behalf. [8] My brother was the only man whose disarray turned your eyes towards him and whose weeping revived wistful memory of me. He had made up his mind, Men of Rome, in the event of your not restoring me to him, to share my fate. He loved me so well that he called it a sin to have a different dwelling-place from mine, nay, a different sepulcher. When I was present, the Senate and twenty thousand people besides changed dress for me; in my absence you saw one man in the sorry aspect of a mourner. Only he, of those who could appear in public, proved himself a son to me in duty, a parent in beneficence, and in affection the brother he always was. The doleful disarray of my unhappy wife, the incessant grief of my best of daughters, and the childish tears of my little son missing his papa were confined to necessary journeys or, for the most part, to domestic obscurity. So what you have done for me is all the greater in that you have not restored me to a multitude of kinsfolk; you have restored me to myself.

[9] But if I did not have blood-relations, whom I could not produce for myself, to plead for me in my misfortune, I did have many aiders and supporters and advocates of my restoration, for that was something which it lay with my own merit to provide—so

---

8. Note the difference in tone between the references to Marius in this speech (cf. ss. 19–21) and in the speech to the Senate (s. 38). To the mass of people he was a national hero, whereas many Senators remembered his political career with aversion.

many that in this respect I far outdid my predecessors in quantity and quality. The case of the illustrious and gallant Publius Popillius was never officially raised in the Senate, neither was that of Quintus Metellus, that great and dauntless aristocrat, nor that of Gaius Marius, the guardian of your community and empire. [10] The two former were restored by tribunician bills without any senatorial resolution, while Marius was restored not only without the Senate, but after the Senate had been reduced to impotence. In Gaius Marius' restoration it was not the memory of his past achievements that counted but the swords of an army; whereas the Senate constantly demanded that the memory of mine *should* count, and at last made it effective, as soon as that was possible, by a resolution[9] passed in a crowded House. There was no stirring of townships and colonies in their return; whereas all Italy recalled me to my country by her decrees three times over. They were brought back after their enemies had been killed with much shedding of Roman blood; I have been brought back at a time when
+ those who drove me out are governing provinces and on the motion of one of the Consuls,[10] excellent, mild-natured gentleman that he is, who was personally hostile. As for that enemy[11] who to compass my destruction lent his voice to the foes of the community, he was alive in the sense that he was breathing, though in reality he had been consigned to the underworld. [11] That brave Consul Lucius Opimius never urged Senate or people on behalf of Publius Popillius; nor yet on behalf of Metellus (to say nothing of Gaius Marius, who was his enemy) did Marius' suc-
+ cessor, the distinguished orator Marcus Antonius, either alone or together with his colleague Aulus Albinus. On my behalf, on the other hand, the previous Consuls were under constant pressure to refer the matter to the Senate—but they were shy of seeming to act for personal reasons,[12] since one of them was my relative by

---

9. The word *auctoritate* probably refers to the vetoed decree mentioned in *Red. sen.* 3. *Auctoritas* is the regular term for a vetoed decree.

10. In s. 15 and *Dom.* 70, Metellus is said to have put the matter to the Senate jointly with Lentulus.

11. Clodius.

12. Irony.

marriage, and I had taken the other's case on a capital charge.[13]
+ Enmeshed by the pact they had made for provinces, they withstood the protests of the Senate, the mourning of honest men, and the groans of all Italy throughout the year.

On the first of January, however, after the orphan Commonwealth appealed to the Consul as to a legal guardian, Consul Publius Lentulus, parent, guardian angel, and salvation of my life, fortune, memory, and name, once he had made the customary religious motion,[14] judged that his first action respecting secular affairs must be concerning me. [12] The matter would have been settled that day, had not a certain Tribune[15] intervened, a man to whom I had done important favors when he was a Quaestor and I was Consul. The House as a whole and many of its distinguished members begged him to desist. His worthy father-in-law, Gnaeus
+ Oppius, lay at his feet in tears. The Tribune * * * and asked for
+ the night to think things over. He spent it, not in returning his bribe, as some had expected, but in getting more, as became clear from the sequel. Thenceforward no other business was transacted in the Senate. Various obstacles were raised, but the Senate's will was clear, and the case was put before you in January.

[13] At this point the difference between me and my enemies was just this:[16] I saw men being enrolled and formed into companies[17] at Aurelius' Platform.[18] I realized that Catiline's old cohorts had been summoned back to the prospect of massacre. I saw the members of the party, of which I might say I was counted a leader, either betraying my cause or deserting it, partly in jealousy of me, partly in fear for themselves. The two Consuls, bought by a pact for provinces, had surrendered themselves to the enemies of the Commonwealth to be their backers, aware that their own indigence, greed, and lusts could only be sated by handing me over in

---

13. The circumstances are unknown.
14. Concerning the date of the Latin Festival on Mt. Alba. It usually took place in April at a date determined by the Consuls on their entry into office.
15. Sex. Atilius Serranus Gavianus.
16. The difference is actually stated at the end of the section. What intervenes is introductory.
17. Lit. "companies of a hundred." The term *centuriare* is borrowed from military usage.
18. See Index II.

chains to Rome's enemies within the gates. The Senate and the Roman Knights were forbidden in imperious manifestos to shed tears for me or to plead with you in mourning. Pacts for every province, all manner of bargains and reconciliations were being sealed in my blood. All honest men were ready to die for me, or die by my side. In these circumstances I decided not to fight it out in arms, because I believed that either victory or defeat would bring sorrow on the Commonwealth. [14] As for my enemies, when my matter came up in January, they thought proper to bar my return with the bodies of slaughtered citizens and a river of blood.[19]

So in my absence you had a Commonwealth in such a state that the restitution of the Commonwealth and of myself were equally desirable in your eyes. As for me, I did not consider that a Commonwealth existed in a community in which the Senate counted for nothing, any offense could be committed with impunity, the courts of law were non-existent, armed violence was rampant in the Forum, private persons looked for protection to the walls of their houses, not the laws, Tribunes were wounded before your eyes, magistrates' houses attacked with swords and firebrands, a Consul's *fasces*[20] broken, the temples of the Immortal Gods set aflame.

Accordingly, I did not think I had any place in a city from which the Commonwealth had been driven forth; and I doubted not that if ever the Commonwealth were restored, she would herself bring me back in her company. [15] I was quite sure that Publius Lentulus would be Consul for the following year. In those most dangerous days, the crisis of the Commonwealth, when I was Consul, he was Curule Aedile, taking part in all my counsels, sharing all my risks. How could I doubt that he would apply consular medicine to my consular wounds and bring me back to health? He took the lead, while his excellent and mercy-loving colleague at first did not oppose and later actually lent his aid. The other magistrates were almost all champions of my restoration. Among them Titus Annius and Publius Sestius stood out by their

---

19. See *Sest.* 75–77.
20. Cf. *Red. sen.* 7, and see Glossary of Terms.

extraordinary, wonderful good will and zeal on my behalf; they had courage, energy, prestige, auxiliary force in abundance. At the behest of Publius Lentulus, his colleague joining in the motion, with one dissentient[21] but no veto, a crowded Senate enhanced my dignity in terms that could not have been more generous, and commended my cause to you and to all townships and colonies.

[16] Thus it was that my cause, the cause of a man without kin, with no band of kinsfolk to defend him, was continually pleaded before you by Consuls, Praetors, Tribunes, the Senate, and all Italy. All whom you had distinguished with your highest honors and favors were produced before you by the same gentleman; they not only urged you to preserve me, but gave my actions their endorsement, testimony, and praise.

First among them in urging and petitioning you was Gnaeus Pompeius, the first of all mankind, past, present, and to come in worth, wisdom, and glory. He alone has given me, his private friend, all those boons he gave the Commonwealth: welfare, tranquillity, dignity. His speech, as reported to me, fell into three sections. First he showed you that the Commonwealth had been saved by my devices and placed my cause in conjunction with the common welfare, exhorting you to defend the authority of the Senate, the stability of the community, and the fortunes of a
+ deserving citizen. Then in his peroration he said that the Senate, the Roman Knights, and all Italy were petitioning you. Finally, he personally not only petitioned but implored you to restore me. [17] My debt to this man, Men of Rome, goes almost beyond what is right for one man to owe another.

Following his advice, Publius Lentulus' proposal, and the Senate's resolution, by the same centuriate votes with which you had placed me in the position I held through your favors, you replaced me therein. At the same time and from the same platform, you heard men of the highest standing and consequence, leaders of the community, all our Consulars, all our Ex-Praetors, speak with one voice, bearing unanimous witness that I alone had saved the Commonwealth. After Publius Servilius, a gentleman of

---

21. Clodius, presumably.

the highest public distinction, had said that thanks to me the Commonwealth had been handed over unimpaired to succeeding magistrates, the rest spoke to the same effect. And you heard at that time not the opinion merely but the testimony of that illustrious gentleman, Lucius Gellius.[22] He as good as knew that his fleet had been tampered with to his own no small peril, and stated at a public meeting that if I had not been Consul when I was, the Commonwealth would have perished root and branch.[23]

[18] Well, Men of Rome, here I stand, restored to my family and the Commonwealth by so many testimonies, by this resolution of the Senate, by the common voice of Italy and the whole-
+ hearted zeal of honest men, at the instance of Publius Lentulus, and with the agreement of the other magistrates, with Gnaeus Pompeius pleading my cause and all mankind wishing it well, and finally, with the Immortal Gods approving my return by the abundant quantity and low price of grain.[24] So I will make you two promises, Men of Rome, within the limits of my power to perform. First, I shall ever regard the Roman People with the pious reverence which pure-hearted men feel toward the Immortal Gods, and throughout my days your mysterious majesty will be as high and holy to me as theirs. Secondly, I promise that, since the Commonwealth has brought me back into the community, I shall at no point fail in my duty to the same. [19] If anyone supposes that my will has changed or my courage weakened or my spirit broken, he is vastly mistaken. What violence and injustice and the frenzy of criminals could take from me, that was snatched away, robbed, scattered abroad; but what cannot be taken from a brave
+ man remains intact and ever shall.

I saw Gaius Marius, a very brave man and a fellow townsman of mine—for by a strange fatality we both had to wage war with Fortune as well as with Rome's would-be destroyers—well, anyhow, I

---

22. L. Gellius, Consul in 72, had been one of Pompey's Legates in the Pirate War of 67, but the relevance to Cicero's consulship is obscure.

23. The sixteenth-century scholar Paulus Manutius took *classem* (translated "fleet") as a division (class) of the Centuriate Assembly of which Gellius was *custos* (teller or supervisor).

24. The Gods soon changed their minds. On fluctuations in the price of grain at this time, see *Dom.* 14f.

saw him in his extreme old age; not merely was his spirit in no way cowed by the magnitude of his misfortune, it was strengthened and renewed. [20] I heard him deny that he was an unhappy man when he had lost the country which he freed from siege,[25] when he heard of the seizure and plundering of his property by his enemies, and saw his young son sharing the same misfortune; when, sunk in the marshes of Minturnae, his person and his life were saved by a rally of compassionate townspeople, and crossing over to Africa in a little boat, he approached as a needy suppliant those on whom he had bestowed kingdoms.[26] Now that he had recovered his status, said he, and what he had lost had been restored to him, he was not about to lack the courageous spirit which had never failed him.

But between Marius and myself there is this difference: he took vengeance on his enemies by just the means wherein he was strongest, that is by arms; I shall use speech, as I have been wont to do. The former art finds its place in war and civil strife, the latter in peace and tranquillity.

[21] To be sure, Marius in his angry mood cared for nothing but vengeance on his enemies; I shall think even of friends only so far as the Commonwealth will allow me. Actually, Men of Rome, four sorts of people injured me. First, there were some who were my bitter enemies out of hatred of the Commonwealth, because I had saved her in their despite. A second category consisted of persons who wickedly betrayed me under the guise of friendship.[27] A third, of those who were jealous of my glory and prestige, being themselves too lazy to win the same prizes. A fourth, of those whose duty it was to guard the Commonwealth, but who sold my civic rights and the stability of the community and the dignity of that authority with which they stood vested.[28] Well, I shall take vengeance for their several deeds according to the manner of the provocation in each case. I shall punish bad citizens by acting for the good of the Commonwealth, perfidious

---

25. By German invaders menacing Italy at the end of the second century B.C.
26. Cf. *Sest.* 50. "Kingdoms" refers to Marius' settlement of the affairs of Numidia after the Jugurthine War in 105. He made at least one new king.
27. See p. 16, n. 60.
28. The Consuls of 58, Piso and Gabinius.

friends by taking nothing on trust and guarding against all contingencies, the jealous by devotion to virtue and glory, the traffickers in provinces by summoning them home and calling them to account for their provincial administration.

[22] However, Men of Rome, I am more concerned about how to requite you who have deserved so well of me than how to avenge the injuries and cruelty of my enemies. It is easier to avenge an injury than to repay a kindness; to get the better of rascals takes less effort than to square accounts with honest men. Furthermore, it is less necessary to repay our debts to people who have deserved ill of us than to such as have deserved excellently well. [23] Hatred can be softened by pleas; it can be set aside in consideration of the needs of the Commonwealth and the general good; it can be restrained by the difficulty of exacting retribution; it can be appeased by the passage of time. But to be prevailed upon not to pay due regard to benefactors or to sacrifice such a
+ duty for the good of the Commonwealth, unless absolutely necessary, is a sin. Difficulty is no excuse, nor can the memory of a benefaction properly be limited to a period of time. Lastly, laxity
+ in taking vengeance is generally well spoken of, whereas tardiness in requiting benefits such as you have conferred upon me incurs the most severe reprehension and must needs bear the name not only of ingratitude, which is bad enough, but of impiety. Repaying
+ an obligation and repaying a debt are two quite different things. If you keep the money, you don't pay the debt, and if you return it, you don't have it. But he who repays a favor is still grateful; and he who is grateful, repays it.[29]

[24] Therefore I shall keep the memory of your benefaction
+ green in undying good will, nor shall I breathe it out with my last breath, but even when life forsakes me, the records of your benefaction shall yet remain. As for returning it, I make you this promise, to which I shall always be true: I shall never lack diligence in taking thought for the Commonwealth, nor courage in warding

---

29. There is an untranslatable play on words, or perhaps rather some confusion between the normal sense of *gratiam habere*, "feel gratitude," and the literal sense, "have a favor." Perhaps the words translated "Repaying . . . repays it" should be omitted, as in some inferior manuscripts. They seem irrelevant.

dangers from the same, nor honesty in giving as a Senator my views unvarnished, nor independence in crossing the wills of others for the Commonwealth's sake, nor energy in enduring toil, nor the good will of a grateful heart in furthering your interests. [25] In my heart, Men of Rome, shall be rooted this undying concern: that you—who, in my eyes, possess the mysterious power of the Immortal Gods—and your descendants, and all mankind may hold me well worthy of a community which has declared by its unanimous suffrages that only by regaining me could it maintain its own dignity.

ON HIS HOUSE
(*De domo sua*)

Clodius' bill of banishment against Cicero included a clause confiscating his property. His house on the Palatine, acquired from Crassus in 62, was one of the show places of the city. Clodius' house adjoined it, and by indirect means (s. 116) he got possession of Cicero's and demolished it. Part of the site—a very small part, so Cicero says (ibid.)—he combined with the site of a portico (also demolished) erected by the elder Q. Catulus from the spoils of his and Marius' victory over the Cimbri at Vercellae in 102 B.C., and converted the area into a shrine of Liberty, installing what purported to be a statue of the goddess. Thus Clodius made it impossible for the site to be used again for a non-religious purpose, provided the consecration held valid. The dedication was carried out by Clodius and a recently elected member of the College of Pontiffs[1] whose sister he had married.

The law under which Cicero was recalled provided for the restitution of his property. But after his return Clodius raised an objection on religious grounds so far as the house was concerned. The Senate referred the matter to the College of Pontiffs to which Cicero addressed his speech *De domo sua* on 29 September 57 B.C. (*Att.* 4.2.2).

After a brief opening, he turns to justify his proposal on 7 September that extraordinary powers should be conferred on Pompey to regulate Rome's grain supply in response to a shortage which Clodius had used to stir up public unrest (ss. 3–31). Ostensibly this countered an allegation by Clodius, who claimed that Cicero had thereby lost favor with members of the court, the College of Pontiffs, most of whom were conservatives hostile to Pompey. Despite the scorn he pours upon it, Cicero probably felt that the allegation was not unfounded, hence his elaborate defense. There follows an attack upon the validity of Clodius' election to the tribunate and, consequently, on the validity of the bill of banishment (ss. 34–42). But that bill, says Cicero, was invalid on several other grounds and had been so treated by the Senate (ss.

---

1. See Glossary of Terms under "Pontiff."

43–71). He continues with a lengthy repudiation of the term "exile," contumeliously applied to him by Clodius (ss.72–92). A brief digression (ss. 92–94) is followed by another justification of his retirement in March 58 (ss. 95–99). The rest of the speech up to the peroration challenges the legality of the consecration on a variety of grounds, procedural and general.

The Pontiffs decided in Cicero's favor.

In a letter to Atticus (4.2.2) written shortly afterwards, he describes the speech as one of his very best and says that he intends to publish it without delay. Had he taken more time, he might have pruned away some of the redundancies (e.g., in s. 44) and surely would have removed a discrepancy to which L. Schaum drew attention in a dissertation of 1889.[2] In ss. 51 and 106 Cicero clearly states or implies that the consecration was authorized under Clodius' bill of exile. In s. 128 he states the contrary, as also in *Har. resp.* 11 and 13. Schaum's explanation seems the only one possible: Cicero composed the speech in large part before his return, anticipating Clodius' opposition. Back in Rome, he discovered that, contrary to his earlier belief, Clodius (or rather his draftsman Sex. Cloelius) had neglected the lex Papiria, which required that all consecrations be authorized by the people, and added a passage accordingly, but omitted to correct what he had originally written.

[1] Reverend sirs,[3] among the institutions so admirably devised by our ancestors none is more commendable than that system by which the same individuals preside over religious observance and the highest affairs of state.[4] Thus they ensured that our greatest and most illustrious citizens preserve religion by good administration of the Commonwealth and the Commonwealth by wise understanding in matters of religion. Now if ever a cause of the first importance rested with the judgment and prerogative of priests of the Roman People, surely this is such a cause. So great is

---

2. *De consecratione domus Ciceronianae* (Mainz), p. 8.
3. *Pontifices.*
4. In general, members of the College of Pontiffs and other priestly Colleges took part in public life like other people.

its consequence that all the dignity of the Commonwealth, and the welfare of all citizens, their lives, liberty, altars, hearths, and household gods, their goods, fortunes, and dwellings are seen to have been consigned and entrusted to your wisdom, your good faith, and your power. [2] It falls to you to decide this day whether you wish for the future to deprive irresponsible and unscrupulous magistrates of the support of rascals and criminals, or whether you prefer to arm them with the additional weapon of religion. If that curse of the Commonwealth,[5] that destroying flame, shall bring divine religion to defend his ruinous, disastrous tribunate, which he cannot protect by any appeal to human justice, we shall have to look for other rites and priests and religious guides. On the other hand, reverend sirs, you may rescind by your authority and wisdom the work of revolutionary rascals in a Commonwealth which was held down by some, forsaken by others, by others betrayed. If you do so, we shall have good and sufficient grounds to praise our ancestors' prudence in selecting our foremost men for priestly office.

[3] The madman has thought to win some sort of access to your ears by denouncing proposals lately put forward by me in the Senate. Therefore I shall depart from normal sequence in addressing you, and reply to the lunatic's—I will not say speech, for he is incapable of speaking, but clamor. In that he is well practiced, and he has reinforced his skill with aggressiveness beyond bearing, and long-standing impunity.

First I shall put a question to him, crack-brained and crazy as he is: what demon of vengeance for your crimes and villainies torments you into the notion that the reverend gentlemen here present, pillars of the Commonwealth, whose dignity they support not only by their counsels but by their very aspect,[6] are angry because in my speech I linked the welfare of our citizens with an honor to be conferred on Gnaeus Pompeius; or that they will now take a view on a matter of high religious consequence different from the view they took during my absence? [4] He tells me that in those days I stood well with the Pontiffs, but now that I have

---

5. Clodius.
6. The robes and insignia of priestly office.

passed over to the popular side, my stock must needs have fallen.[7] Is that so? Fickleness, or inconsistency, is the worst vice of an untutored populace, which changes its opinions as often as the wind changes quarter. Would you transfer it to these gentlemen? Their sense of responsibility deters them from inconsistency. The fixed, definite character of religious law, the ancient precedents, and the authority of written records restrain them from capricious judgment. He asks me, am I the man whom the Senate could not bear to be without, whom honest men mourned and the Commonwealth missed, by whose restoration we thought the authority of the Senate had been restored—authority which, says he, I betrayed as soon as I arrived in Rome? It is not yet time to speak of my proposal. First I shall answer his impudence. [5] This accursed bane of the Commonwealth admits,[8] does he, that the Senate, all honest men, and the whole of Italy, wanted me, summoned me, called me back for the preservation of the Commonwealth. Such is the citizen whom *he* forced to leave home and fatherland, lest it come to armed conflict between honest men and rascals—forced out at sword point, by the terror of an army, the crime of Consuls, the threats of desperados, the levying of slaves, the blocking of temples, the occupation of the Forum, the seizure of the Senate-House.

"Well, but" says he "you ought not to have gone to the Senate on the Capitol that stormy day."[9] [6] I did not go. I stayed at home while the storm lasted, when it was common knowledge that *you* had gone to the Capitol with your slaves, whom you had long held in readiness for a massacre of honest men, along with your band of armed and desperate criminals. When I heard that report, I kept at home, I do assure you. I did not give you and your gladiators the chance to commence another slaughter. Then it was reported to me that the Roman People had gathered on the Capitol because they were afraid and grain had run short, and that the instruments of your crimes had fled in panic, losing their

---

7. I.e., Cicero's proposal in favor of Pompey had offended the Pontiffs.

8. In Clodius' mouth these questions will have been put sarcastically, but Cicero pretends to take them seriously.

9. The 6th or 7th of September. "Stormy" is metaphorical.

weapons or having them wrenched out of their hands. On that, I went up to the Capitol. I had no force with me, no band; only friends, and not many of them. [7] Could I have done otherwise, when called to the Senate by Consul Publius Lentulus, who had deserved so well of me and of the Commonwealth, and by Quintus Metellus, who, although he was my enemy and your brother, had put my rights and dignity before our quarrel and your solicitations; when so great a multitude of my fellow countrymen summoned me by name to show my gratitude for what they had so recently done for me—particularly as you and your band of runaways were known to have left the area? And you dared call me "our stranger [10] in the Capitol," because I went there when both Consuls were holding a Senate—me, the guardian and defender of the Capitol and all other temples! Are there then occasions when it is discreditable to attend the Senate? Or was the item to be discussed such that I should have rejected it of its very nature and condemned its sponsors? [8] First, I say it is always the duty of a good senator to come to the Senate. I do not agree with those who make it a rule not to attend in difficult times, not realizing that such intransigence on their part played into the hands of those whom it was their purpose to annoy. I may be told that some senators left because they had fears for their personal safety in the Senate. Well, I am not blaming them. I am not inquiring whether there was anything to be afraid of. In my view, every man should judge for himself when and what to fear. Do you ask why *I* was not afraid? Because I knew that *you* had gone away. Do you ask why I did not feel, as some honest men felt, that it was not safe to be in the Senate? I ask in reply why *they* stayed behind when I thought I should not be safe anywhere in Rome. Must I alone be obliged to be afraid both for myself and others, while others are permitted (and rightly so) to fear nothing for themselves in *my* hour of peril?[11]

[9] Or am I at fault because I did not condemn the two Consuls[12] in my speech? Was I, of all men, to condemn those through

---

10. Implying that after his exile, Cicero had ceased to be a Roman citizen.
11. When he was driven into exile. The parallel is rather strained.
12. Lentulus Spinther and Metellus Nepos, who had summoned the Senate to

whose law I myself, a citizen found guilty in no court, who had deserved excellently of the Commonwealth, was not bearing the punishment of convicted offenders? Their signal good will in the matter of my preservation entitled them to indulgence even in wrongdoing, not only from me, but from all honest men. Was I, of all people, to advise the rejection of their excellent initiative, now that I had been restored by them to my former status? What *was* my proposal? To begin with, it was one that common talk had already planted in our minds; also one which had been aired in the Senate in the days preceding; also one which the Senate followed in large numbers, assenting to me. So it was no startling, recent proposition I laid before the House; and if there was anything wrong with it, the proposer is no more to blame than all those who gave it their approval. [10] It may be suggested that the Senate acted under duress, was not free to exercise its judgment. Well, if you tell us that those who left were afraid, you must allow that those who stayed were *not* afraid. On the other hand, if no free decree was possible without the absentees, I may point out that when all were present, there was a move to cancel the decree; and the whole Senate cried out in protest.

Now look at the proposal itself, since I was the first to sponsor it. What, may I ask, is supposed to be amiss with it? Was there no reason to take a new departure? Or did not I, more than most, have a part to play in the matter? Or should we have looked elsewhere for a rescuer?[13]

What could be a more convincing reason than famine, riot, and the schemes of Clodius and his henchmen, who thought that with this opportunity to stir up simple folk he would put new life into
+ his pernicious brigandage, making the price of grain his pretext? [11] The grain-producing provinces either did not have any, or greedy vendors (I suppose) had disposed of it to other lands, or they were keeping it shut up in their custody, so as suddenly to send a new supply and earn more gratitude by coming to Rome's assistance in an actual famine. It was not a doubtful matter of opinion but a danger present before our eyes. We did not forecast

---

consider the grain shortage.
13. Cicero deals with these questions *seriatim* in ss. 10–41.

it by inference, it was already part of our experience; we *saw* it.

The price of grain was rising. There was apprehension, not just of high prices, but of shortage and famine. The people flocked to the temple of Concord, where Consul Metellus had convoked the Senate. Now if this was a genuine movement, springing from public distress and hunger, then surely it was the duty of the Consuls to take the matter up and of the Senate to come to a conclusion. If, on the other hand, the price of grain was a pretext, and Clodius was the agitator, stirring up the riot, were we not all bound to try to take the wind out of the madman's sails? [12] Or perhaps it was both. Perhaps hunger roused the people and he came up like a swelling on an ulcer. All the more reason for medical treatment, to care for the original mischief and the adventitious as well.

So the price of grain was running high and famine loomed. As though this were not enough, stones were thrown. If that was a reaction of popular distress, and no single person was behind it, it was a very serious matter. If instigated by Publius Clodius, nothing unusual; that is how the villain operates. If both—that is to say, if the situation was such as to arouse the populace spontaneously, and ringleaders of riot were ready and armed—was it not a clear case of the Commonwealth herself calling on the Consuls and appealing to the Senate for succor? Actually, it *was* both; that is plain. Nobody denies that the price of grain was acutely high, that the commodity was in extremely short supply, that there was a widespread fear not only of high prices for a long while to come but of downright famine. That this foe of peace and tranquillity would seize upon the situation as a pretext for arson, murder, and plunder, I do not ask you to suspect, reverend sirs, unless you see it for yourselves. [13] Who were the persons named in open Senate by his brother, Consul Quintus Metellus, as having attacked him with stones, even striking him? He named Lucius Sergius and Marcus Lollius. Who is this Lollius? Why, even now he is at Clodius' side, bearing arms; and when Clodius was Tribune, he asked for the job of killing Gnaeus Pompeius, to say nothing of myself. Who is Sergius? Catiline's squire, Clodius' bodyguard, standard-bearer of riot, raiser of shopkeepers, a criminal with a record of assault and battery, a bravo, a stoner, who depopulates the Forum and beleaguers the Senate-House. These and others like them were the ringleaders through whom in time of shortage Clodius planned sudden onslaughts upon Consuls, Senate, and the property and fortunes of the well-to-do, using the ignorant poor as his pretext. He could not survive in settled times, so he had armies of ruffians mustered and enrolled under desperado bosses. Was it not the Senate's business to see that this baleful brand, flung into a heap of inflammable material, ready to burst into civil strife, did not become embedded?

[14] There was reason, therefore, for taking a new departure. Now let us see whether I did not have a part to play, more almost than any other man. Who was it, Clodius, whom your friend Sergius, and Lollius, and the other evil creatures named when the stones were flying? Who did they say was answerable for the price of grain? Was it not I? Did not that nocturnal rally of gangsters, as coached by you personally, demand grain from me—as though I had been in charge of supplies, or was keeping grain tucked away, or had had any say in the matter by virtue of any commission or power? But Clodius was out for bloodshed and had given my name to his gangsters and put it into the minds of simple folk.

When the Senate in unusually large numbers had passed its decree concerning my status in the temple of Jupiter Best and Greatest, with Clodius as the sole dissentient, that very day there was a sudden, unexpected drop in the soaring price of grain. [15] There were those who said the Immortal Gods had expressed their will in approval of my return—which is what I think myself. Others had a different explanation for the phenomenon. They reasoned that hope of peace and concord appeared to center on my return, whereas daily fear of civil strife was the result of my leaving; so when fear of war was almost removed, the price of grain changed. But just as I came back, it climbed again; so I was called to account, since honest men had been saying that grain would be cheap when I came back to Rome. At your instigation, I was named by your gangsters. Not only that, but when your forces had been dislodged and scattered, the whole Roman People gathering on the Capitol summoned me by name to the Senate, though I was indisposed that day. [16] Answering expectation, I came. Many Senators had already spoken when I was called. The speech I made was salutary to the Commonwealth, but I had no choice but to make it. I was being asked to produce abundance of grain at a cheap price—never mind whether I had any control over the matter. Honest men were complaining and demanding; rascals were clamoring, more than I could stand. Well, I delegated the responsibility to a friend who was better able to cope with it. It was not that I was out to lay the burden on one to whom I owed so much; I would rather have sunk beneath it myself. But I saw what everybody else saw: that by his honesty, wisdom, energy, authority, his good fortune even, Gnaeus Pompeius would accomplish what we expected of him with the greatest ease.

[17] It may be that the Immortal Gods are giving the Roman People a benefit consequent upon my return. With my departure came shortage of crops, famine, desolation, bloodshed, fires, lootings, impunity for crime, flight, terror, strife. In the same way, it may seem that fertility, abundant harvests, hope of peace, tranquillity of mood, law courts and laws, public harmony, and the Senate's authority have been brought back with my return. Or perhaps I myself had an obligation to do something for the Roman People on my arrival in return for so great a benefaction, by thinking and advising and taking pains. In any case, I give my solemn word and guarantee that the Commonwealth will not again get into a dangerous crisis over the price of grain such as that into which it was being propelled. I say no more, only what is sufficient for the present emergency.

[18] This duty then was especially mine. Is my proposal censured? Nobody denies the importance of the matter and the very serious danger, not only of famine but of bloodshed, arson, and devastation; for the price inflation was compounded by that spier-out of public woes, who always lights his torch of crime at the fire of the Commonwealth's troubles. He says that nothing extraordinary should have been conferred upon an individual. Well, I shall not answer *you*[14] as I do others, that many great and dangerous wars by land and sea have been entrusted to Gnaeus Pompeius by extraordinary mandate: and anyone who regrets those proceedings regrets the victory of the Roman People. [19] No, that is not

---

14. Turning to Clodius.

the line I take with you; I can use such language to those who maintain that *if* a single individual should be given the responsibility, Gnaeus Pompeius is the right man, but that they are against any extraordinary appointment; adding that after such an appointment has been given to Pompeius, they are in the habit of subventing and maintaining it as befits his dignity. I cannot applaud their view, when I think of Gnaeus Pompeius' triumphs, with which he has aggrandized the name of the Roman People and adorned their empire, summoned by extraordinary mandate to defend our country. But I do approve of their consistency. I, too, had to be consistent, having supported his extraordinary command against Mithridates and Tigranes.[15] [20] With those people, however, I can at least argue. As for *you*, how can you have the effrontery to say that nobody should be given any extraordinary appointment? By a wicked law,[16] without any investigation, you confiscated the property of Ptolemy, King of Cyprus,[17] brother of the King of Egypt, reigning by equal right. You implicated the Roman People in a crime. You launched this empire
+ like an auctioneer's advertisement against the kingdom, property, and estate of an ally and friend of Rome, as his father, grandfather, and ancestors had been before him. And you put Marcus Cato in charge of bringing back this money and taking military action if the king defended his rights. [21] "A fine man," you will say, "upright, wise, brave, and patriotic, wonderfully, almost uniquely commendable for his virtue, good judgment, and style of life." Quite so, but what is all that to you? *You* say that no one
+ should be given any extraordinary public responsibility. Nor is
+ that the only point on which I convict you of inconsistency. In Cato's own case, whom you were not advancing in that affair as befitted his prestige, but getting out of the way as suited your criminal purpose—you had set him up as a target for your henchmen, Sergius, Lollius, Titius, and other ringleaders of massacre and arson; you had called him an executioner of citizens, a

---

15. Conferred by the Manilian law in 66. Cicero supported it in his extant speech *Pro lege Manilia* (*De imperio Cn. Pompei*) ("For the Manilian law" ["On Cn. Pompeius' command"]).
16. Carried by Clodius as Tribune.
17. See Index I.

leading spirit in the putting to death of men without trial, an advocate of cruelty. And this is the man on whom in your bill you conferred an extraordinary command, by name! So little self-control did you have that you could not conceal the reason for that crime of yours. [22] You read out at a public meeting a letter which you alleged had been sent to you by Gaius Caesar. It began "Caesar to Pulcher," and you actually adduced that as a sign of affection, his using surnames only[18] and not adding "Proconsul" or "Tribune." Then, according to you, Caesar congratulated you on getting Marcus Cato out of your year of office and precluding him in the future from talking about extraordinary commissions. Either Caesar never sent you such a letter or, if he did, he did not want it read aloud at a public meeting. But whether he sent it or you forged it, at the least you did give away your purpose in honoring Cato when you read that letter out loud.

[23] However, let us leave Cato out of it. His exceptional qualities and reputation, and his scrupulous integrity in the conduct of that business may be felt to throw a veil over the wickedness of your bill and your political tactics. But who gave rich and fertile Syria, together with the waging of a war against perfectly peaceful natives,[19] and funds (earmarked for buying land) torn from the bowels of the Treasury,[20] and an unlimited command[21] to the foulest, filthiest villain ever born? Previously you had given him Cilicia; then you changed the bargain and transferred Cilicia to a Praetor,[22] likewise irregularly. Syria you gave to Gabinius by name, raising your bribe. And did you not hand over free peoples[23] in chains to Lucius Piso by name—a cruel, treacherous monster,

---

18. So Cicero begins a letter to Volumnius Eutrapelus (*Fam.* 7.32): "As you headed your letter in familiar style (and quite right), without any first names . . ."

19. Cf. p. 65, n. 98.

20. Clodius' bill diverted to the Consuls of 58 funds which Caesar the year before had appropriated for the purchase of land in his agrarian program; cf. *Pis.* 28, 37, 57.

21. I.e., with no fixed time limit.

22. Probably T. Ampius Balbus, governor of Asia at the time; see my note on *Fam.* 3.7.5. In that case "Praetor" is used for Ex-Praetor governing as Proconsul in contrast to the Consul Gabinius.

23. In Macedonia. See R. G. M. Nisbet, *Cicero in Pisonem* (Oxford, 1961), pp. 172f.

stained deep with every crime and vice—although they had been declared free in numerous senatorial decrees and even in a recent bill of Piso's own son-in-law?[24] And despite the fact that the price of your favor, the *quid pro quo* for his province, had been handed over by him to you in my blood, did you not go shares with him in the Treasury? [24] Words fail me. Consular provinces, which that democrat of democrats[25] Gaius Gracchus did not take away from the Senate, but, on the contrary, laid down by law that they must be assigned by the Senate annually—these provinces had been decreed by the Senate under the Sempronian law.[26] You annulled the assignment and gave them irregularly, without drawing of lots, by name to the Consuls[27]—no, to the banes of the Commonwealth. And shall I be taken to task by you for naming a great man, one often chosen to meet our national emergencies, to be in charge of a business of the highest importance, one which had almost been given up as hopeless?

And more: the political scene was dark as night with cloud and storm. You had forced the Senate from the helm, driven the people from the ship, while you, the pirate chief, and your foul crew of marauders made full sail. If you had succeeded in putting through all that you promulgated, determined, promised, and sold, would any place on earth have been exempt from extraordinary commands and the rule[28] of Clodius?

[25] At long last Gnaeus Pompeius was aroused: I shall say what I thought and think within his hearing, no matter how he takes it. Yes, at long last his indignation, too long repressed and buried deep in his heart, suddenly came to the aid of the Commonwealth, raising up a broken community, crippled and enfeebled by its afflictions, cast down by terror, to some prospect of freedom and former dignity. Was not this man a fit person to put in charge

---

24. Caesar. The bill, concerning provincial administration, was part of his legislation as Consul in 59.

25. *Popularis.* See Glossary ot Terms under "people's man."

26. This law of 123 obliged the Senate to name two consular provinces before the Consuls who would govern them were elected.

27. Piso and Gabinius.

28. The term used, *imperium,* may have a special point in that a Tribune did *not* possess the powers which it signified.

of grain supplies by special appointment? *Your* bill,[29] of course, handed over all publicly and privately owned grain, all grain-producing provinces, all contractors, and the keys to every granary, to
+ a dirty glutton, Sextus Cloelius, that beggarly miscreant, the foretaster of your lusts, a partner in your blood,[30] whose tongue even cost you the affections of your own dear sister. From that bill came first high prices, then scarcity, with the threat of famine, arson, massacre, and looting. Your madness menaced every man's fortune and property. [26] And this unconscionable imp actually complains that grain-control was snatched from the filthy mouth
+ of Sextus Cloelius, and that in a most dangerous situation the Commonwealth invoked the aid of the man whom she remembered as the author of her preservation and aggrandizement many times in the past!

Clodius disapproves of all extraordinary legislation. What of the bill which this traitor to his country, this violator of brother and sister,[31] says he carried against me—was not *that* extraordinary legislation? Were you entitled to carry a bill—no, not a bill, but a wicked measure *ad hominem*,[32] for the destruction of a fellow countryman, the savior of the Commonwealth as all Gods and men have now declared, who, as you yourself acknowledge, had not been found guilty nor even charged in any court—and to do so facing the mourning of the Senate, the grief of all honest men, and rejecting the pleadings of all Italy, crushing and imprisoning the Commonwealth? And was *I* not entitled to say my say concerning the welfare of the Roman People, when the Roman People implored, the Senate asked, the situation demanded?

[27] If, in that proposal, the enhancement of Gnaeus Pompei-
+ us' prestige had not been associated with the public interest, it

---

29. Other references to Clodius' grain law mention only its provision for free distributions.

30. Referring primarily to Clodius' sister, whose favors Cloelius is said to share. But there may be an obscene double sense. Cicero may also be playing on the meaning "blood-relative" (cf. Ov. *Trist.* 4.5.29).

31. *Parricida* (translated "traitor") is often used of disloyal citizens, harmful to the *patria* ("fatherland"). The other two terms used, *fratricida* and *sororicida*, involve an obscene sense of *caedo* ("hit"), alluding to Clodius' alleged immoral relations with his brother(s) and sisters.

32. See p. 19, n. 76.

would at least have been to my credit that I was seen as supporting the prestige of one who had lent aid and succor to my existence as a citizen. It is high time people gave up hoping that my position now that I have been restored can be shaken by the same engines with which they overthrew me before, when I stood upright. I suppose our community has never seen a closer friendship between one Consular and another than that which obtained between Gnaeus Pompeius and myself. Has anyone spoken more conspicuously before the Roman People or more often in the Senate on behalf of his dignity? Was any labor, any enmity or conflict too great for me to undertake in that cause? For his part, has he ever passed by an occasion to compliment me, to cry up my achievements, to repay my good will? [28] This combination of ours, our political alliance for the public good, and our very pleasant association in daily life and all manner of mutual attentions, was disrupted by certain individuals using fictitious conversations and slanders. They warned him to fear me, be on his guard against me; whereas to me they portrayed him as my worst enemy. The result was that I could not quite confidently ask him for what I needed from him; whereas he, with his mind poisoned by so many suspicions implanted by certain people in their wickedness, did not quite readily promise me all that the emergency called for. [29] Reverend sirs, I have paid dearly for my mistake. I am sorry for my folly; in fact, I am ashamed of it. The bond between this gallant and illustrious gentleman and myself was not the product of any sudden crisis in my affairs. It arose out of efforts undertaken and foreseen far in the past. And I allowed myself to be detached from such a friendship, not having sense enough to resist the mischief-makers as open enemies or to mistrust them as treacherous friends. So let them finally give up pandering to my vanity with the same old talk: "What is Cicero thinking of? Doesn't he realize how much weight he carries, what he has achieved, how gloriously he has been restored? Why pay compliments to the man who left him in the lurch?" [30] No, no. I do not consider myself as having been left in the lurch at the time, but as virtually handed over to my enemies. Nor do I think I should reveal what was practiced against me in that conflagration of the Commonwealth, nor by what means, nor by whose agency.

If it was in the public interest that I alone should drain that cup of undeserved misfortune on behalf of all, it is also in the public interest that I veil in silence those whose wickedness engineered the mischief.[33] But there is one thing on which only an ingrate would be silent, and so I shall most gladly avow that Gnaeus Pompeius worked for my restoration with zeal and personal authority no less than any one of you gentlemen, and with resources, effort, pleadings, even risk, more than any. When you, Publius Lentulus, were thinking day and night only of my restoration, he was party to all your plans. In setting the campaign in motion, he was your most weighty supporter, in preparing its success he was your most faithful ally; and in bringing it to a conclusion, he was your most valiant auxiliary. He visited the townships and colonies. He implored the aid which Italy was eager to give. He spoke first in the Senate, and, when the House approved his speech, went on to beg my restoration from the Roman People.

[31] So, Clodius, you may as well drop that line of talk in which you intimate that, after my proposal in the Senate about the grain supply, the Pontiffs' attitude changed. Do you really think that their sentiments concerning Gnaeus Pompeius are any different from mine? Or that they are unaware of my obligation, in view of the expectations of the Roman People, of Gnaeus Pompeius' services to me, and of the requirements of my own situation? Or do you imagine that, even if my proposal did offend one or other of these gentlemen—which I am sure it did not—he is going to reach any other decision as a Pontiff on a matter of religion, and as a citizen on a matter of public concern than that imposed by ritual law, and the good of the community?

[32] I realize, reverend sirs, that I have spoken at greater length than I expected or wished to speak on matters extraneous to this case. I was anxious to clear myself in your eyes. Moreover, your kindness in giving me an attentive hearing led me on. I shall make up for it by the brevity of what I have to say about the case itself which you are judging. It has two aspects: that of religious

---

33. Hortensius and other supposedly false friends? But the cryptic phrasing is perhaps to be regarded as a smoke screen put up by the orator to obscure the fact of Pompey's desertion, to which he nevertheless makes sufficiently plain allusion.

law and that of public law. The former, which would require far more words, I shall pass by, and speak only of the latter. [33] It would be presumptuous indeed to try to instruct the College of Pontiffs on religion, divine observances, ceremonies, or rituals. Suppose someone finds this or that in your books—how foolish to tell *you* about it, and how meddlesome to pry into matters on which our ancestors wished you to be the sole consultants and experts!

I maintain that by public law, by the statutes which govern our community, no citizen could be penalized in any such fashion without a trial. I say that even in the regal period it was the rule in this community, a rule handed down to us by our forbears and indeed a distinctive attribute of a free society, that nothing to the detriment of a citizen's rights and property can be ordered without a trial by the Senate[34] or People or an appropriate court. [34] You will note, Clodius, that I am not tearing up all your proceedings by the roots and arguing the manifest truth that your every action was illegal, that you never were a Tribune, that you are a patrician today.[35]

I am speaking before the Pontiffs. Augurs are present. I am dealing with basic public law.[36]

Reverend sirs, how stands the law on adoption? Well, the rule is that the adopting parent must no longer be capable of procreating children and must have tried to do so when he *was* capable. By custom, the College of Pontiffs makes an inquiry into the motive for adoption in each case, the particulars of family and status, and of rites.[37] Were any such inquiries made in Clodius' adoption? The adopting parent was twenty years old, or even less, the adopted son a senator.[38] Was it for children? But he[39] can

---

34. The Senate had no judicial powers, but Cicero is thinking of the Catilinarian conspirators whom he put to death with the Senate's authority.

35. Cicero means that he is *about* to argue that very thing. See SB¹, 264f.

36. "First he marshalls arguments addressed to the Pontiffs, then those addressed to the Augurs (s. 39 *venio ad augures*)" (SB¹, 265).

37. *Sacra gentilicia*, rites proper to each clan (*gens*). An adopted person would normally no longer perform them in his former clan, so the Pontiffs had to see to it that their future maintenance was not compromised by the adoption.

38. And therefore at least thirty. Actually Clodius was some years older.

39. Fonteius, the adopting parent.

procreate, and has a wife by whom he will acknowledge children. So the father will have disinherited his son.[40] And what about the rites of the Clodian[41] clan? Why do they die out, so far as Clodius is concerned? All this should have been the subject of pontifical investigation when he was adopted. [35] Or was he perhaps merely asked whether he wished to throw the Commonwealth into seditious turmoil, and whether he desired adoption, not in order to be that person's son, but to become Tribune and overturn the community from its foundations? Doubtless he answered in the affirmative; the Pontiffs found the motive valid and gave their approval! No inquiry was made as to the age of the adopting parent, as it was in the cases of Gnaeus Aufidius and Marcus Pupius, who, within our memory, adopted Orestes and Piso,[42] being both in extreme old age. These adoptions, like countless others, carried inheritance of name, wealth, and rites; whereas you, Clodius, are no Fonteius, as you ought to have been. You are not your father's[43] heir, and you did not lose your hereditary rites and enter into these adoptive ones.[44] Having thus confused rites, jumbled up families (both the family you deserted and the family you polluted) and turned your back on the legalities of guardianship and inheritance, in defiance of nature, you became the son of a person whose father you are old enough to be.

[36] I am speaking before the Pontiffs. I maintain that this adoption of yours was not in accordance with pontifical law. First, because of your ages: the person who adopted you was of an age to be your own son or—what he actually was.[45] Second, because there is customarily an inquiry into the motive for adoption, to ensure that the adopting parent is seeking under standard pontifical law something he can no longer obtain in the course of nature, and that the adoption is not detrimental to the status of

---

40. I.e., his future son, who would take second place to Clodius.

41. Properly called "Claudian," "Clodius" being a vulgar form affected by the demagogue and used by non-aristocratic members of the clan; cf. s. 116.

42. Cn. Aufidius Orestes, Consul in 71, and M. Pupius Piso, Consul in 61.

43. I.e., adoptive father.

44. In Clodius' case, as in some others known to us, the normal consequences of adoption—change of name and clan rites—did not in practice ensue (presumably by agreement between the parties).

45. An immoral relationship is implied.

the families or to ritual obligations: above all, to ensure that there is no trickery, fraud, or subterfuge in the case. The fictive acquisition of a son must appear to have imitated as closely as possible the acknowledgment of real children. [37] Now what trickery could be more flagrant than this? Here comes a beardless youth, married and in good health, and says he wants to adopt a senator of the Roman People as his son, while all the world knows and perceives that the purpose of the proceeding is not that the latter become the son of the former, but that he cease to be a patrician and become eligible for the tribunate? Nor was there any disguise. No sooner was he adopted than he was emancipated, so as to cease to be the son[46] of his adopter. Why then the adoption?

Approve such an adoption and soon all family rites will die out, rites of which you, gentlemen, should be the guardians. Soon there will be no patrician left. For why should anyone want to be ineligible for the tribunate, restricted in his candidacy for the consulship,[47] unable to get a priesthood, when he might otherwise get one, just because there is no vacancy for a patrician?[48] Whenever for some reason it happens to be more convenient for a man to be a plebeian, he will be adopted in similar fashion. [38] So in a short time the Roman People will have no King of Rites, no Flamens, no Salii,[49] no patricians to fill half of the other priestly Colleges, nor will there be any to sanction assemblies of Centuries and Curies.[50] The auspices of the Roman People would necessarily perish if no patrician magistrates were elected, since there would be no Interrex,[51] because an Interrex must himself be a patrician and be designated by patricians.

Speaking before the Pontiffs, I have stated that your adoption was not approved by any decree of this College, that it took place

---

46. I.e., a son "in his father's power" (*in patris potestate*). Emancipation did not abolish the filial relationship.
47. One of the two Consuls had to be a plebeian.
48. In the three principal priestly Colleges (Pontiffs, Augurs, and Quindecimvirs) patricians were not allowed to outnumber plebeians.
49. See Glossary of Terms.
50. See Glossary of Terms.
51. See Glossary of Terms.

in contravention of all pontifical law, that it is to be regarded as null and void. But the adoption once invalidated, you realize that your entire tribunate has collapsed.

[39] I come to the Augurs. Now I am not scrutinizing any recondite books they may have, nor am I an over-curious researcher into augural law. I know only what I have learned like other laymen, what has often been revealed by answers given at public meetings. They say that proceedings in assembly are against religious law when observation of the heavens has taken place.[52] Dare you deny that such observation did take place the day when the curiate law[53] concerning yourself is said to have been passed? Here we have present Marcus Bibulus, a gentleman of outstanding worth, resolution, and sense of responsibility. I assert that on the very day of the adoption he watched the heavens as Consul. I shall be asked whether I am calling into question the official proceedings of that gallant gentleman Gaius Caesar. Not at all. They are no longer any concern of mine, apart from the weapons that were discharged against my person as a result of his proceedings.[54] [40] But relative to the auspices,[55] certain steps, to which I make only the briefest of references, were taken by yourself. When your tribunate had lost its grip and was plunging to its close, you suddenly emerged as the champion of the auspices. You brought Marcus Bibulus before a public meeting, Augurs likewise. In reply to your question the Augurs stated that when there has been a watching of the heavens, there can be no proceedings in assembly. Marcus Bibulus stated in answer to a

---

52. The right to watch the sky for signs (*servare de caelo*) belonged to curule magistrates (Consuls, Praetors, and Curule Aediles) and (at any rate after 58) Tribunes. An announcement of intention to watch seems to have been regarded as banning a prospective assembly, even though in *Sest.* 78 Cicero implies that, should the convoking magistrate go ahead, an actual announcement of adverse omens by magistrate to magistrate (*obnuntiatio*) was necessary to invalidate it; and this is supported by *Att.* 4.3.3–4. There appears to have been some ambiguity on this point. In 59 the Consul Bibulus shut himself up in his house and declared that he would watch the sky on all assembly days for the rest of the year. Caesar took no notice.

53. See Glossary of Terms.
54. Clodius' adoption, which Caesar promoted as Chief Pontiff.
55. See Glossary of Terms.

question from you that he *did* watch the heavens; he also told a public meeting to which he was introduced by your brother Appius that, inasmuch as your adoption had been carried out against all auspices, you had never been Tribune at all. In fact, your whole political line during the months following was that all Caesar's proceedings should be repealed by the Senate as having been undertaken in violation of auspices.[56] If that happened, you said you would carry me, Rome's guardian, back to Rome on your
+ own shoulders. The folly of the fellow! He wanted Caesar's proceedings repealed, when all the while he was firmly committed to those proceedings through his tribunate.

[41] If the Pontiffs overturn your entire tribunate under pontifical law and the Augurs under auspical observance, what more do you want? Perhaps some still more unambiguous piece of public and statutory law? About noon in court, speaking in defense of my colleague Gaius Antonius, I made some critical observations concerning politics which appeared to me relevant to my unfortunate client's case. Rascals retailed them to certain gallant persons[57] in a form far different from that in which I had spoken them. Your adoption took place three hours later that same day. Well, if the interval of three market days[58] requisite for other legislation can be reduced to three hours for an adoption,[59] I make no objection. If, on the other hand, the same rules hold good, well then, the Senate declared laws of Marcus Drusus, which had been carried in contravention of the Caecilian-Didian[60] law, to be non-binding on the public. [42] You now realize that according to every category of law, ritual, auspical, and statutary, you were never Tribune.

However, I leave all this on one side. I have reason to do so. I notice that certain illustrious personages, leaders of the

---

56. See *Har. resp.* 48f. What occasioned so extraordinary a *volte-face*, as Cicero represents it, is unknown. But his account is likely to be garbled.

57. Meaning Caesar, or Caesar and Pompey.

58. *Trinum nundinum*, twenty-four days, as usually supposed.

59. A reference to the "curiate law," a formality preceding the adoption. See Glossary of Terms.

60. This law, of 98, laid down the minimum interval between the promulgation of a law and its voting, and also forbade the inclusion of measures on different subjects in the same law (cf. s. 53).

community, have declared in various places that you had the right to propose legislation in a popular assembly.[61] Even in my own case, while calling your bill the funeral of the Commonwealth, they said that this funeral, however sad and tragic, had been legally pronounced. They said that, in carrying your bill against a citizen who had deserved well of the Commonwealth, you pronounced her funeral; but that since you did so without violating auspices, your action was legal. I suppose then that I shall be within my rights in not calling into question those proceedings by which your tribunate, which they have approved, was established.

[43] Allow, by all means, that you held office as Tribune as rightfully and legally as that great and illustrious gentleman Publius Servilius, here present:[62] by what right or custom or precedent did you propose a law concerning a citizen who had been found guilty of no offense, by name, depriving him of his civic rights? Inviolable laws[63] prohibit legislation against individuals;[64] so do the Twelve Tables.[65] For that is legislation *ad hominem*. Such legislation has never been proposed; it is in the highest degree cruel, pernicious, and intolerable to this community. When we think of the lamentable word "proscription" and the whole tragedy of the Sullan period, one feature above all others, I imagine, stamps those savageries on our memory: punishment decreed against named Roman citizens without trial. [44] Will you then, reverend sirs, by your judgment and authority give to a Tribune the power to proscribe whom he pleases? For I ask you, what else is the following but proscription: "that ye desire and order that Marcus Tullius do not remain in the community and that his property become mine"—for that is what the bill amounted to, though expressed in other words. Is this an ordinance of the plebs,[66] or a law, or a bill? Can you, gentlemen, or can the

---

61. In *Prov. cons.* 45 this opinion is attributed to an individual distinguished for his prestige and eloquence, perhaps M. Claudius Marcellus, Consul in 51.
62. Present as Pontiff. The comparison is especially appropriate because Servilius came of a plebeian family that had once been patrician.
63. *Leges sacratae*, laws which pronounced a curse against violators.
64. *Privilegium*, legislation *ad hominem*. See p. 19, n. 76.
65. The ancient Roman code of law, drawn up in the mid-fifth century B.C.
66. *Plebei scitum*, a resolution of a plebeian assembly having the force of law.

community endure that a single line of text should suffice to remove a citizen from the community? *I* am now done with all this. I fear no violence, no onslaught. I have glutted the ill will of the jealous, placated the resentments of bad citizens, even sated the heinous perfidy of traitors. In fact, judgment in favor of my cause, a cause which reprobates thought to be a target for popular ill will, has now been pronounced by all cities, all classes, all Gods and men. [45] No, it is to you yourselves, reverend sirs, and your children, and to the rest of the community you should be looking, as behooves your authority and wisdom. Trials before the people[67] were constituted by our ancestors with many safeguards: first, a personal penalty cannot be combined with a pecuniary one; second, no man can be charged without previous notice of the day. The magistrate must present the charge three times, with a day's interval between each presentation, before imposing a fine or other sentence, and then there must be a fourth presentation specifying a trial date at an interval of three market days.[68] Furthermore, accused persons were allowed ample opportunity to soften hostility and arouse pity. The people can be won to forgiveness; canvassing for acquittal is easy. Finally, if that day be canceled for some reason, whether auspices or a legitimate excuse, the whole process and trial are canceled as well. Such are the procedures in law, where there is a charge, a prosecutor, and witnesses. That a person who has not been summoned to attend nor cited nor accused; that hirelings, bravos, and beggarly desperados should cast votes concerning the civic status, the children, and the entire estate of such a person and the result be considered a law—could anything be more outrageous? [46] Now I had official rank[69] to protect me, also my standing, my cause, and the Commonwealth. They were not after my money. Against me was only an unbalanced state of public affairs and a deteriorating political situation. If Clodius could do to *me* what he did, what is going to become of those who lead lives remote from the people's favors

---

67. Such trials were unusual at this period. Most cases were handled by standing or specially constituted courts (*quaestiones*).
68. Translation doubtful. As to "three market days," cf. p. 56, n. 58.
69. Presumably as consular.

and the influence and notoriety they carry, but who on the other hand possess wealth enough to excite the cupidity of all too many beggars and spendthrifts? [47] Once give this license to a Tribune and then take a brief mental look at our younger generation, particularly those who seem already to be casting greedy eyes at tribunician power. Mark my words, whole boards of Tribunes, once this principle has been established, will be found forming combines to deal with the property of the very rich, all the more so as they can offer plunder to the mob and the prospect of largesse.

Now let us see what our skilled and crafty legal draftsman actually proposed: "That ye desire and order that Marcus Tullius be interdicted from fire and water."[70] An intolerably harsh and wicked sentence to be passed without trial even on the worst of criminals. Ah, but he did not make it "be interdicted." What then? "*Is* interdicted." Why, the foul monster, the villain! So this is the bill Cloelius drafted for you, a bill as filthy as his own tongue: a man is interdicted who is not interdicted! My good Sextus, please bear with me: since you are now into logic and relish that taste too, can it be proposed to the people that something is done which has not been done? Can any words so ordain or any votes so establish? [48] Such is the draftsman, the counsellor, the agent through whom you, Clodius, ruined the Commonwealth—the foulest creature on two feet, or four either. You were not so stupid nor so crazy as to be unaware that Cloelius' usual role is to break laws, and other people's to draft them. But none of these people, or any people with any sense of decency, was at your disposal. You could not employ the draftsmen others employ, nor the architects[71] for your buildings, nor call in the Pontiff of your choice.[72] Finally, even when it came to sharing the booty, you could find no buyer or surety outside the ranks of your gladiators, nor any but a thief and a bravo to put this proscription of yours to a vote. [49] So while you were bustling through the Forum in the pink of your potency, the people's fancy-man, these

---

70. I.e., outlawed.
71. On the site of Cicero's house; cf. ss. 100f.
72. To consecrate the shrine of Liberty; cf. ss. 100f.

friends of yours who, secure and happy in that single friendship, had committed themselves to the people's suffrages, were being so roundly rejected that they lost even your very own Palatina.[73] Those who came into court, whether as prosecutors or defenders, met with adverse verdicts in face of your intercessions on their behalf. Finally, that new-fledged[74] Ligus, paid to countersign your bills or indictments, announced his intention of taking action concerning the death of his brother Marcus Papirius—whose unflattering opinion of himself had been signified in his will. He
+ indicted Sextus Propertius, but did not dare to prosecute. Tool of another's domination, partner in his crime, he feared a charge of
+ calumnious accusation. [50] Whoever touched any part of that bill, with finger[75] or voice, plundering or voting, wherever that man went in, he went out rejected and discredited. Are we to speak of such a bill as appearing legally carried?

Another point: this proscription of yours is so phrased as to cancel itself. It runs: "Whereas Marcus Tullius entered a false decree of the Senate..."[76] Very good. If he entered a false decree of the Senate, there is a bill; if not, none. Is not the Senate's judgment sufficiently clear to you: that not only did I not forge a resolution of that body, but I paid it more meticulous obedience than any magistrate since the foundation of Rome?

There are plenty of other ways in which I can show that this law of yours, as you call it, is no law. It covers a number of items, but
+ you carried them at one voting.[77] Do you really suppose that a man such as you, stained with every sort of crime and immorality,
+ supported by the likes of Decius [?][78] and Cloelius, can claim a
+ license which was not permitted to so great a[79] personage as Marcus Drusus, whose counsellors were Marcus Scaurus and Lucius

---

73. One of the four city tribes, mostly made up of humble folk.
74. The epithet is insulting, *novicius* being generally applied to slaves who recently lost their freedom.
75. I.e., raising it to make a bid at the auction of Cicero's property.
76. In respect of the execution of the Catilinarians; cf. *Sull.* 40f.
77. Text doubtful; see Appendix I.
78. The name in the manuscripts, Decumus (= Decimus, a praenomen), can hardly be right. A Decius appears later as a partisan of Mark Antony; see Shackleton Bailey on *Att.* 4.3.2.
79. Text doubtful; see Appendix I.

Crassus, in a number of his laws? [51] You laid it down that I should not be harbored, but not that I should leave Rome; and you yourself could not deny that I had a right to be in Rome. For what could you say? That I had been found guilty? Assuredly not. That I had been driven out? By what right? Anyway, it was not even stated in your text that I should leave Rome. There was a penalty for harboring me, of which nobody took any notice, but not a word about expelling me. However, let that pass. What of the supervision of public works,[80] the inscribing of your name?
+ Don't you think there is a difference between that and the plundering of my property[81] —besides the further fact that under the Licinian law[82] you could not appoint yourself as administrator? Now take your present argument before the Pontiffs. You say you consecrated my house, erected a monument in the precincts, dedicated a statue, all of which you did under one little bill.[83] Does that appear one and the same as what you proposed against me by name? [52] As fully the same, upon my soul, as those two other proposals of yours carried under one law, that the King of Cyprus,[84] whose ancestors were always the allies and friends of this people, should be put under the auctioneer with all his property and that exiles should be brought back to Byzantium![85] He says
+ that he put both operations in the same hands. Well, suppose you put in these same hands the exaction of tribute in Asia, with instructions to proceed thence to Spain; adding that after returning to Rome the person should have the right to stand for the consulship;[86] and, after election, become governor of Syria. Since

---

80. The law will have appointed Clodius to supervise the demolition of Cicero's house and new construction on the site.
81. Cicero here returns to the point that Clodius' bill covered separate items, thus contravening the Caecilian-Didian law.
82. Known only from this passage and *Leg. agr.* 2.21. It barred any person from holding office under a law proposed by himself.
83. See p. 38.
84. Cf. s. 20.
85. Their restoration was assigned to Cato under Clodius' law; cf. Plut. *Cat. min.* 34.
86. Even if he did not present himself as a candidate by the date legally prescribed—such seems to be the implication. This and the other items would appear to relate to a particular individual. Gabinius ("governor of Syria")?

all these items would concern one individual, would they therefore count as one? [53] Just suppose that instead of doing everything through slaves and brigands, you had consulted the Roman People on the matter. Is it not possible that the people would have said "yes" on the King of Cyprus and "no" on the Byzantine exiles? Is not the force and meaning of the Caecilian-Didian law just this, that the people should not have to vote on a combination of items, and thus have to choose between accepting what they do not want or rejecting what they do want?

And again: is it a law if you passed it by violence? Can anything appear done legally if all agree that it was done by force? Granted that in the actual voting, when you held Rome prisoner, there was no stone-throwing or fighting: does that mean that you could manage to ruin the community, wash it down the drain, without extremity of violence? [54] When you were publicly enrolling on Aurelius' Platform[87] not freemen only but slaves drummed up from every street, to be sure, you were not preparing for violence! When you were issuing your orders that the shops be closed,[88] you did not have in view the violence of an ignorant mob, but the moderation and good sense of respectable folk! When you were piling weapons into the temple of Castor, you were merely taking measures to assure that nothing could be done by violence! When you tore up and carted away the temple steps, you barred desperate characters from access and ascent to the temple in order that you might be at liberty to pursue your law-abiding activities! When you summoned to your presence persons who had spoken for my restoration at a gathering of honest men and broke up their supporters with fists and weapons and stones, no doubt of it, you demonstrated your utter aversion to violence!

[55] However, this reckless violence of a crazy Tribune could easily have been overcome and broken by the courage or even the numbers of the honest men. But you were giving Syria to Gabinius and Macedonia to Piso, an unlimited command to both with vast sums of money, asking in return that they allow you a completely

---

87. Cf. *Red. quir.* 13 and see Index II.
88. Shopkeepers in Rome were humble folk, whom Clodius could look to for support; likewise to their slaves.

free hand and lend you their assistance. This they were to do by providing you with an armed band, their own tried and trusty Centurions, money, and troops of slaves;[89] by abetting you with their villainous public speeches; by mocking the authority of the Senate; by threatening the Roman Knights with death and proscription; by terrorizing me with menaces, telling me to expect slaughter and battle; by using their friends to fill my house, crowded as it was with honest men, with the dread of proscription; by depriving me of my concourse of honest men; by robbing me of the Senate's protection; by forbidding that august body not only to fight for me, but even to weep and beg in mourning attire. Was there no violence then?

[56] So why did I withdraw, what was the nature of the fear? I will not say the fear in *my* heart; suppose that I am a born coward. But what of those thousands of brave men, what of my Roman Knights,[90] and the Senate, and all honest men? If there was no violence, why did they escort me on my way with tears instead of holding me back with reproaches or abandoning me in anger? Or was I afraid that, if I were dealt with according to traditional use and practice, I might not be able to hold my own on the spot? [57] What did I have to fear? Indictment and a trial? Or a bill *ad hominem*[91] without any trial? In the first event, was my case an obscure one, or was I incapable of explaining it in words, even if it were generally unknown? Or was it that I could not make it good? Its merits are such that it justified itself of itself, and me, too, in my absence. Would the Senate, and all classes, and those who flocked together from all over Italy to call me back, have been less active to retain and preserve me in person, my case being such that (as the miscreant himself now grumblingly admits) all men have looked forward to my return and recalled me to my former dignity? [58] Well, then, if I had nothing to fear from a trial, was I afraid of a bill *ad hominem*? Would nobody[92] have cast a veto? I was not so poorly off for friends, nor the Commonwealth so

---

89. Or "gladiators."
90. Cicero had been one of them before he became a senator.
91. See p. 19, n. 76.
92. I.e., no Tribune.

denuded of magistrates. If the tribes had been convoked, would they have approved the proscription—I will not say of myself, who had done so much for their welfare, but of any citizen?

If I had been on the spot, is it to be supposed that Catiline's old gang of conspirators, and your troop of desperate beggars, and the new band supplied by these villains of Consuls would have spared my person? Even being absent, after I had yielded to their combined cruelty and wickedness, I could not sate them with my mental suffering. [59] How had my poor wife harmed you people that you harassed her, dragging her off, torturing her with every sort of cruelty?[93] What had my daughter done? Her incessant tears and mournful disarray, which melted all other hearts and eyes, gave you pleasure. What had my little boy done? As long as I was away, nobody saw him but in tears, worn out with grieving. What had he done to deserve your repeated plots against his life?[94] What had my brother done? He arrived in Rome from his province some time after I left. He held his life not worth living unless I were restored. All human beings pitied his grief, the unbelievable, unheard-of misery he displayed. How often he escaped your hands and swords! [60] But why exclaim against your cruelty to me personally and to my family? You and your associates waged war upon my walls, roofs, pillars, and doorposts —all-out, wicked war, inspired by deadly hate. I do not suppose you were blinded by a covetous desire for my plate and furnishings. After I had gone, you devoured every wealthy man's fortune, the revenues of every province, the property of tetrarchs and kings, in greedy anticipation. I do not suppose that Campanian Consul[95] and his dancer colleague[96] were so covetous of my lintels and pillars and folding doors, after you made over to one of them the whole of Achaia,[97] Thessaly, Boeotia, Greece, Macedonia and all the non-Hellenic territories, and the property of Roman citizens; while to the other you had handed over Syria, Babylon,

---

93. Cf. *Sest.* 54, *Cael.* 50. An incident obscurely referred to in a letter from Cicero to his wife (*Fam.* 14.2.2) will have provided the basis for these allegations.
94. This sounds like a mere fairy tale.
95. Piso was Duovir in Capua in 58; cf. *Red. sen.* 17.
96. Gabinius.
97. I.e., the Peloponnese, as in *Pis.* 37 (cf. *Sest.* 94).

Persia—untouched and peaceful nations—for plunder.[98] [61] For that matter, your band and Catiline's cohorts did not expect to satisfy their hunger with the stones and tiles of my buildings. But as with the capital cities of our enemies—not all our enemies, but those against whom we have embarked on a bitter war, a war to the death—we usually raze them, not for plunder but for hate, because, when our minds have been inflamed by a foe's savagery, we always seem to have a residual feud against his buildings and dwelling places * * *[99]

[62] No law was passed concerning me. I had not been ordered to attend, not been absent when summoned. Even on your showing I was a citizen in good standing when my town
+ house on the Palatine was transferred to one so-called Consul, and my country house at Tusculum to the other.[100] Marble pillars from the former were carted to the house of the Consul's mother-in-law in full view of the Roman People. As for the country place, not only the gear and equipment but the very trees were transferred to the property of my consular neighbor and the house itself razed to the ground, not out of greed for booty (there was none), but from hatred and savagery. My house on the Palatine was in flames—no accident, the fire was set—while the Consuls were feasting and receiving the congratulations of the conspirators, one of them boasting himself Catiline's favorite, the other Cethegus' cousin.[101] [63] Such was the violence, reverend sirs, such the crime and fury which I thrust from the necks of all honest men by interposing my own body. I personally took the whole
+ onset, the whole long-accumulated violence of the rascals; it had festered in repressed and silent hate and now, with the advent of audacious leaders, it broke out. Consular firebrands launched by a Tribune's hands, all the nefarious weapons of the conspiracy which I had blunted in years gone by, stuck in my flesh and mine alone. If I had chosen to fight violence with armed violence, as

---

98. Implying that as governor of Syria, Gabinius would be free to attack the non-Roman lands to the east or the south, as Crassus attacked Parthia in 53. Possibly Clodius' bill gave him some encouragement to do so; cf. s.23.
99. The syntax in the Latin is incomplete.
100. The house to Piso, the villa to Gabinius.
101. Cf. *Red. sen.* 10.

many brave gentlemen would have had me do, there were two possible outcomes: I might have won the day, with great slaughter of rascals, who nevertheless were my countrymen; or, after all the honest men had been killed, which was the rascals' dearest desire, I might have fallen along with the Commonwealth. [64] It was evident to me that if the Senate and People of Rome survived I should ere long be returning in triumph; it was inconceivable to my mind that I should, for any length of time, be excluded from the Commonwealth I myself had saved. But supposing I was: I had heard and read that the most illustrious of Romans flung themselves to certain death, into the midst of the enemy, to save their
+ armies;[102] was I to hesitate to devote myself on behalf of the entire
+ Commonwealth? And I had one advantage over the Decii: they could not even hear the tale of their glory, whereas I could witness the spectacle of mine.

So your fury was checked and its onset robbed of impact. All the violence of all the rascals was absorbed in the tragedy of my fall. After so monstrous a wrong, so great a downfall, no scope was left for further savagery. [65] Cato was to have come next,[103] but
+ there was nothing you could do to him except limit your injury to the honor you had paid him.[104] What could you do? Thrust him out, with the job of collecting the Cyprus money? That will mean losing the loot. Never mind, there will be more coming. All that matters is to get him away from Rome. Thus it was that Marcus Cato, whom you loathe, was banished to Cyprus under the pretense of doing him a favor. The two individuals whom the rascals could not face were expelled; in the one case by means of a highly discreditable preferment, in the other of a highly honorable calamity.

[66] And, to show you that Clodius has ever been the enemy of virtues rather than of persons, after I had been expelled and Cato dispatched elsewhere, he turned upon the very man whom in his public statements he used to claim as his adviser and abettor in all

---

102. The famous "devotion" of P. Decius Mus at the battle of Veseris in 340 and of his son at Sentinum in 295.
103. Not "Cato had been my closest adherent."
104. See ss. 20–22.

his actions both past and present—Gnaeus Pompeius. He saw that Pompeius was universally accounted as far and away the leading man in Rome, and he judged that Pompeius would not indulge his madness much longer. He stole out of Pompeius' custody the son of a friendly monarch,[105] a stranger, a captive, hoping that, having provoked so brave a spirit by such an affront, he could use the same forces in the clash as those against which I had declined to fight and risk the lives of honest men. At first he had the Consuls to abet him, but later Gabinius broke the compact; Piso, however, remained faithful. [67] You saw Clodius' work—the carnage, the stone-throwings, the routs. You saw with what ease, even after he had been deserted by the stoutest and boldest of his followers, he deprived Pompeius of the Forum and the Senate-House with weapons and daily attempts against his life and kept him shut up in his home. You may judge from that how formidable was this violence in its oncoming stages and in its aggregate: torn apart, extinguished, it still terrorized Gnaeus Pompeius.

[68] All this was apparent to a very wise man, a friend devoted to the Commonwealth, to me, and to the truth: Lucius Cotta. When he addressed the Senate on the first of January, he gave it as his view that no legislation should be passed for my return. I had been careful for the Commonwealth, he said, had bowed to the storm, had proved a better friend to you and the rest of the community than to myself. I had been driven out by armed violence, men organized for massacre, and a revolutionary despotism. No legislation affecting my rights as a citizen could have been passed, nothing had been put legally into writing, nothing had any claim to validity; all had been accomplished in defiance of law and tradition, recklessly, tumultuously, by force and fury. If that document were a law, the Consuls were not entitled to put the matter before the Senate, nor he himself to address the House.[106] But they had so done and he was so doing. Therefore the House should not decree that legislation on my case be

---

105. Tigranes, king of Armenia, whose son of the same name had been brought to Rome by Pompey.
106. Cf. *Red. sen.* 8.

proposed; that would mean accepting as a law what was not a law at all. No speech could have been truer, graver, better, or more in the public interest. In branding Clodius' criminal madness it essayed to banish the prospect of any similar disaster in times to come. [69] Gnaeus Pompeius, who delivered a most eloquent speech on the same theme, and you, reverend sirs, who defended me in your speeches and recommendations, were no less aware that the "law" is no law, but rather an ebullition of the moment, an interdict born of crime, the voice of fury. But you were concerned lest a wave of popular resentment might break upon me at some later date if it should appear that my restoration had taken place without the people's sanction. With the same consideration in mind, the Senate accepted a motion by the gallant Marcus Bibulus directing your College to make a ruling with regard to my house; not that they doubted the utter absence of legality, religious propriety, and equity in Clodius' proceedings, but they had apprehensions lest some day somebody in such a plenitude of rascals might arise to allege that some element of religious sanction[107] persisted in my residence. That Clodius' "law" is no law was declared by the Senate every time it expressed itself on my case. For, according to Clodius' text, it was forbidden do so, [70] as did not escape the notice of that pair of legal purists,[108] Piso and Gabinius. When a crowded Senate daily and insistently called upon them to lay my case before the House, they replied that they had no objection in principle, but were debarred by Clodius' law. True enough, they were; but the law which debarred them was the one the same Clodius had passed with respect to Macedonia and Syria.[109] *This* one, Publius Lentulus, *you* never held to be law, either as private citizen or Consul. As Consul-Elect you often spoke of my case in the Senate on the motion of Tribunes, and from the first of January onward, until all was concluded, you put my case to the Senate, you promulgated a bill, carried it; none of which would have been open to you if that document had been a

---

107. *Religio*, "a supernatural feeling of constraint, usually having the force of a prohibition or impediment," *Oxford Latin Dictionary*. Cf. "taboo."
108. Lit. "fearful of laws and law courts."
109. Cf. p. 6, n. 7.

law. Your colleague Quintus Metellus, Publius Clodius' brother, likewise, when he joined you in putting my case to the Senate, declared it null and void, contrary to the opinion of Piso and Gabinius, who had no connection with Publius Clodius whatsoever. [71] They were afraid of Clodius' law, those two; how carefully did they observe other laws? As for the Senate, whose judgment weighs heaviest when it comes to the validity of laws, it declared that law null and void every time my case was submitted to it. And in the bill you carried concerning me, Publius Lentulus, you had the same point in mind. It provided, not that I should be free to return to Rome, but simply that I should return. You did not wish to propose that I should be free to do what I *was* free to do, but that I should resume my place in public life as one
+ summoned by command of the Roman People rather than as one restored.

[72] Did you dare, you monster of mischief, to call such a person an exile—you, who were branded with such heinous crimes and infamies that you turned every place you visited into the close resemblance of a place of exile? What, after all, is an exile? Simply in itself the word denotes misfortune, not dishonor. When is it dishonorable? In reality, when it is the punishment of wrongdoing, but also, in general estimation, if it is a punishment imposed
+ on a person found guilty of a crime. Well, do I incur that name through my own wrongdoing or by judicial verdict? The former neither you, whom your satellites call "lucky Catiline," dare any longer say nor any of those who used to say it. Nobody at this time of day is so ignorant as to call my actions as Consul wrongdoings; in fact, nobody is so bad a patriot as not to admit that our country was saved by my devices.

[73] Is there anywhere on earth a communal council, great or small, which has not declared itself on my actions in the most flattering and glowing terms? The Senate is the supreme council of the Roman People, of all peoples and nations and monarchs: it passed a decree calling on all who wished well to the Commonwealth to come to Rome solely to defend one man, myself, declaring that the Commonwealth could not have survived without me and would cease to exist unless I returned. [74] Next in prestige

comes the order of Knights: all the companies of tax-farmers[110] passed most generous and eloquent resolutions concerning my Consulship and public actions. Then we have the Clerks,[111] who handle public accounts and records along with us senators; they did not wish their declared judgment on my services to the Commonwealth to be left in obscurity. There is no association[112] in this city, not "villagers" nor "hillmen"[113] (since our ancestors wished the city populace also to have its committees and councils, so to speak) that did not pass resolutions in the most generous terms supporting not only my restoration, but my dignity. [75] As for those wonderful, never-to-be-forgotten resolutions of municipalities and colonies and all Italy, I feel that they not merely recalled me to my country, but gave me a ladder to heaven.

Ah, to think of the day when you, Publius Lentulus, submitted the law for my reinstatement! That day, the Roman People saw itself, realized its own multitude and majesty. As all agree, Mars' Field[114] never knew so numerous and splendid an assembly; every variety of men, age, class, contributed to the spectacle. And I say nothing of the unanimous judgment and consensus of communities, tribes, provinces, monarchs—the world, in fact—concerning my service to all mankind.

I come to my arrival, my entry into Rome. Did my country give me the welcome due to a beacon of salvation returned and restored to her, or receive me as a cruel tyrant, which is what you comrades of Catiline used to say of me? [76] That one day, on which the Roman People honored me with its thronging, jubilant escort from the city gate to the Capitol and thence to my home,[115] gave me such happiness that I no longer regard your felonious violence as an evil to be fended off, but rather as a boon worth the purchasing.

---

110. The *publicani,* most if not all of them Roman Knights, were sometimes regarded as representing the order. See Glossary of Terms.
111. See Glossary of Terms.
112. Cf. p. 21 n. 84.
113. *Pagani* and *montani,* together practically equivalent to "city populace."
114. See Glossary of Terms.
115. Obviously not the house on the Palatine which Clodius had destroyed, but a temporary residence, possibly a family house in Carinae which Cicero earlier had made over to his brother.

+   That misfortune, if that is the right word, has swept away the whole trail of slander, and nobody any longer dares find fault with my Consulship, now that it has been approved by so many weighty and eloquent judgments, testimonials, and resolutions. In fact, when you utter this slander, so far from taunting me with anything discreditable, you are adding luster to my glory; which makes you the most foolish of all possible or imaginable fools. By a single insult you admit that I have saved my country twice over: once, by an action which *you* thought deserving of condign pun-
+ ishment and which everybody else considers as something to be handed down to immortality, if that be possible; and a second time, when with my own person I took the brunt of the fiery onset aimed at all honest men by you and many more besides, rather than endanger in arms the community which I had saved without resort to them.

[77] We may agree, then, that in my case there was no punishment of wrongdoing. Was there punishment consequent upon judicial verdict? What verdict? Who ever called me to account under any law? Who brought a charge or named a day? Can one unconvicted of any offense undergo the penalty of one convicted? Is this a doctrine for a Tribune, a people's man?[116] But in what can you call yourself a people's man—except when you officiated "on behalf of the people?"[117] It is a legal principle handed down
+ from our ancestors that no Roman citizen can lose either his personal independence or his citizenship except by his own authority. You might have learned that from your own experience. Although nothing in that adoption of yours was done legally, still I suppose you were asked whether you gave authority that Publius Fonteius should have power of life and death over you, as father over son. Now I put it to you: suppose you had said no or nothing, and suppose the thirty curies[118] had nonetheless made the order, would such an order have been valid? Certainly not. And why not? Because our ancestors, who were not democrats in sham pretense

---

116. *Popularis.* See Glossary of Terms under "people's man."
117. Allusion to the Bona Dea scandal. At her festival "sacrifice was offered on behalf of the people" (traditional formula).
118. See Glossary of Terms.

but truly and wisely such, established the legal principle that no Roman citizen can lose his freedom without his consent. [78] They even ordained that if the Board of Ten[119] gave an adverse decision on a claim to free status, in such a case, and in such a case only, the matter thus determined might be brought back to the courts as often as the party wished.

As for citizenship, no man shall ever lose it by any order of the people without his consent. Roman citizens migrating to Latin colonies could not become Latins[120] unless they had so authorized and entered their names. Persons condemned on capital charges did not lose Roman citizenship until they had been received into the community into which they had moved for the purpose of "turning" (that is, changing) "soil." They were impelled to do that, not by taking away their citizenship, but by interdiction of roof, water, and fire.[121] [79] On the proposal of Dictator Lucius Sulla, the Roman People in the Assembly of Cen-
+ turies took away citizenship from a number of municipalities. They also took away their lands. As regards the lands, the measure held good; that was the people's prerogative. As regards citizenship, its effectiveness did not even last as long as the military power of the Sullan regime. When men of Volaterrae were still in arms, Lucius Sulla, victor and restorer of the Commonwealth, was unable to deprive them of citizenship through the Assembly of Centuries; and today they enjoy Roman citizenship along with us, and excellent citizens they are. And was Publius Clodius, the subverter of the Commonwealth, able to take citizenship away from a man of consular rank by summoning a meeting, through the
+ hired agency of beggars—nay, of slaves—led by Fidulus,[122] who asserts that he was out of town that day? [80] If he is telling the truth, how unscrupulous of you to engrave his name,[123] and how

---

119. See Glossary of Terms.
120. See Glossary of Terms.
121. Equivalent to outlawry.
122. On the name see D. R. Shackleton Bailey, *Two Studies in Roman Nomenclature* (1976), p. 39.
123. On the bronze tablet recording the text of the law passed, prefaced by a statement that Fidulus cast the first vote in the tribe that was called upon first in the order of voting.

desperate to boot! Even with a liar's latitude, could you not fake a better backer? On the other hand, if he was indeed the first to cast a vote (which he easily might be, after passing the night in the Forum for lack of a roof to shelter under), why should he not swear he was in Gades, seeing that you got a jury to believe *you* were in Interamna?[124] Is this the sort of legal safeguard for citizen rights and freedom of which you, as a democrat, approve—that any one of us be liable to lose our citizenship if a Tribune propose
+ "that ye desire and order" and a hundred Fiduli say "yes, we do"? Our ancestors then were undemocratic when they laid down legal principles concerning freedom and citizenship which neither
+ times of violence nor magisterial authority nor a prior judgment nor the otherwise so far-reaching power of the entire Roman People can shake. [81] And you, snatcher of civic rights, carried a bill in redress of public wrongs,[125] which mightily pleased a certain Menulla of Anagnia; so much so that he put up a statue to you in my house, where the very site, recalling so egregious a wrong of your committing, made nonsense of the bill and of the inscription
+ on the statue. His respectable fellow townsmen were far more indignant at this happening than at the crimes which that same gladiator had perpetrated in Anagnia.

[82] However, if there is nothing in the text of that very bill of
+ yours for which Fidulus denies having voted, whereas you cling to your backer in order to gild your distinguished tribunate with his prestige—to resume, if nothing in your bill prevented my remaining on the roll of citizens and even in that rank in which the honors bestowed by the Roman People have placed me, will you still loose your tongue at me? And that, though you see how many declarations of the Senate, the Roman People, and all Italy, following upon the heinous crime of the previous Consuls, have done me honor, though even during my absence you could not deny that by the terms of your own bill I was a senator? Where had you proposed that I be interdicted from water and fire? Grac-
+ chus so proposed concerning Publius Popillius, and Saturninus

---

124. Allusion to Clodius' alibi in the Bona Dea affair, contradicted by Cicero's evidence. See p. 1f.
125. Nothing more is known of this.

concerning Metellus—rank agitators assailing excellent and courageous citizens. But their proposals were that those persons *be* interdicted, not that they *were* interdicted—an impossible proposal. Where did you provide that the Censor[126] should not enroll me as a senator in my grade? That provision is written into all such laws, even when the interdiction applies to persons judicially
+ convicted. [83] Question your legal draftsman Cloelius about these points, tell him to appear. To be sure, he is in hiding, but if you give orders for a search, they'll find the fellow lurking at your sister's with his head bowed low.[127] Nobody in his right mind ever called your father[128] an exile. He was a fine citizen; yes indeed, quite unlike his children. When a Tribune promulgated a bill against him, he preferred not to appear because a fair hearing could not be expected under Cinna's regime; and he was deprived of his command. The penalty was legal, but carried no discredit in his case because those were times of violence. How, then, could the penalty of a convicted person apply to me, for whom no trial date was ever set, who answered no charge in court, who was never cited by a Tribune—particularly as no such penalty was ever prescribed, even in the bill itself? [84] And let me call your attention to the difference between what happened to your father, gross injustice as that was, and the circumstances of my own case. That excellent citizen, your father, himself the son of an illustrious personage[129] (a stern character he was; if he had lived, I'll be bound that *you* would not be alive[130]), was passed over by his nephew Lucius Philippus when he read the roll of the Senate. Philippus could not dispute the validity of proceedings taken under a regime under which he had been willing to hold the censorship, which he did at that very period. On the other hand, Lucius Cotta, an Ex-Censor, stated in the Senate on his oath that, if he had been Censor during my absence, he would have read

---

126. See Glossary of Terms.
127. With obscene implication, as in s. 25 and elsewhere.
128. Appius Claudius Pulcher, Praetor in 89, Consul in 79.
129. Appius Claudius Pulcher, Consul in 143.
130. A Roman paterfamilias had power of life and death over his family and occasionally exercised it.

out my name as senator in my grade.[131] [85] No one nominated a juror in my place. None of my friends made a will when I left Rome but made me the same bequest as if I had been in residence. No citizen, no non-citizen even, hesitated to harbor and help me, contrary to your bill. Finally, not long before the bill for my recall was passed, the whole Senate voted thanks to those communities "which had harbored Marcus Tullius." Just "Marcus Tullius"? No, there was more: "a citizen who has rendered the Commonwealth a great service." And do you, a single pernicious citizen, deny the restitution of one whom, after his expulsion, the whole Senate always regarded as a citizen, and a citizen beyond the ordinary?

[86] Well, but the annals of the Roman People, the records of antiquity, tell us that Kaeso Quinctius and Marcus Furius Camillus and Gaius Servilius Ahala, all of whom had rendered great service to the Commonwealth, none the less incurred the violence and wrath of a people stirred up against them. Found guilty in the Assembly of Centuries, they fled into banishment, only to be reinstated to their former high position by the same people when its anger was appeased.[132] Here, then, we have convicted persons whose mishap did not detract from the glory of their illustrious fame, but actually enhanced it. For, while to complete life's journey without pain or injury is the most desirable lot, to be wanted back by his countrymen does more to immortalize a man's glory than never to have suffered at their hands. Now *I* left Rome without any trial before the people, and I have been reinstated with the most generous declarations on all hands. Shall *my* mishap be ground for insult or reproach? [87] Publius Popillius was a brave citizen, always a steadfast optimate. But in his whole career nothing shed more luster on his name than that very exile. Who would remember his services to the Commonwealth had he not been expelled by the rascals and restored by the honest men? Quintus Metellus had a brilliant record of generalship, he was a distinguished Censor, his whole life was redolent of lofty principle; but it was his exile that carried this great man's fame into the memory

---

131. I.e., as Consular (an "Ex-Consul").
132. According to other accounts, Kaeso Quinctius (see Index I) died in exile.

of all posterity. These persons were expelled unjustly, but legally. They were brought home, after their enemies had been killed, by tribunician legislation, not by the authority of the Senate, not by the Assembly of Centuries, not by the resolutions of Italy, not by the yearnings of the community. But the wrong done them by their enemies did not blemish their reputations. I, on the other hand, left Rome with status intact, I and the Commonwealth were absent together, I returned gloriously, while *you* lived and your
+ brother was Praetor, on the motion of one Consul and with the acquiescence of the other. Do you think your crime ought to be a reproach to *me?*

[88] Suppose the Roman People, stirred up by anger or resentment, *had* thrown me out of the community, and then later, remembering my services to the Commonwealth, pulled themselves together and rebuked their own rashness and injustice by restoring me. Even then, surely nobody would be so unreasonable as not to think that such a judgment of the people should be counted to my honor rather than to my discredit. But now! Nobody on earth summoned me to trial by the people. I could not have been found guilty since I was never prosecuted, and though I was driven out, I could have had the upper hand if I had fought; on the contrary, I have always been championed, advanced, decorated by the Roman People. How, then, can any man set himself ahead of me, even when it comes to democratic politics? [89] Perhaps you think the Roman People is that people, made up of hirelings and persons who are instigated to do vio-
+ lence to magistrates and beleaguer the Senate, which prays every day for massacre, arson, and looting—the "people" which, nonetheless, you could not bring out in numbers without closing the shops, the "people" over which you had set the likes of Lentidius, Lollius, Plaguleius, and Sergius as leaders. A majestic presentation of the Roman People, one to strike awe into the hearts of monarchs and foreign nations and races most remote—a multitude assembled from slaves, hirelings, criminals, and beggars! [90] No, the true beauty, the true shape of the Roman People was the shape you saw in the Field on that occasion when even you were at liberty to speak in opposition to the authority and zeal of the

Senate and all Italy.¹³³ *That* is the people, the lord of kings, victor and ruler over all nations, which you saw, you villain, on that glorious day when all the leaders of our community, and all men of all classes and ages, were casting their votes, not (so they believed) for the welfare of a citizen, but of the whole citizen body. The shops had not been closed to bring *them* to the Field—the country towns were closed!¹³⁴ [91] With this people I would have had no trouble resisting your headlong fury, your impious villainy, had there been Consuls in the Commonwealth at the time—or if there had absolutely *not* been Consuls. But I did not choose to take up the public cause against armed violence without public protec-
+ tion. Not that I disapproved of the gallant Publius Scipio's cour-
+ age, private individual though he was, in the case of the Tribune Tiberius Gracchus; but Consul Publius Mucius, who was thought
+ rather sluggish in his conduct of public affairs, once they had been conducted for him, promptly defended and even commended Scipio's action in many senatorial decrees. I, on the other hand, would have had to fight in arms with the Consuls after you had been killed, or else with both you and them if you were alive. [92] There was much else besides to apprehend at that
+ time. It would have come down to the slaves,¹³⁵ take my word. Such was the hatred for honest men which possessed the wicked survivors from that old conspiracy, searing their nefarious hearts.

At this point, you actually tell me not to boast. You say my habit of vaunting myself is intolerable. You are a wag: you make out that I am in the habit of calling myself Jove and saying that Minerva is my sister—so witty, so amusing! Well, my presumption in calling myself Jove is less remarkable than my ignorance in supposing Minerva to be Jove's sister. But at all events, *I* take a virgin for my sister; *you* did not let yours be a virgin. Now isn't it perhaps you who are by way of calling yourself Jove, since you would have every reason to call the same lady your sister and your wife?

[93] Now, since you reprove my habit, as you allege, of

---

133. Cf. *Sest.* 108.
134. Because their inhabitants had gone to Rome to vote on Cicero's restoration. On the shops, cf. p. 62, n. 88.
135. I.e., "the slaves would have taken over"; cf. s. 110 fin. So in *Sest.* 47 and see SB³, 273f. But the expression is not very precise.

boasting about myself, let me ask:[136] has anyone ever heard me talk about myself except when driven by necessity to do so? Consider this: if it is my habit to reply to charges of theft or bribery or immorality that my devices, dangers, and ordeals saved my country, then I am to be regarded not so much as boasting of my achievements as acknowledging the truth of the accusations. But in fact, until these late times of tribulation in the Commonwealth, the only charge ever leveled at me was that of cruelty, relating to that one crisis when I saved my country from ruin. Well, was it fitting for me to leave that slander unanswered or to answer it humbly? Not so. [94] I always held it in the public interest to maintain in words the splendor and dignity of that glorious act, which I had accomplished for the survival of my country on the authority of the Senate and with the approval of all honest men; all the more so as I, alone in this Commonwealth, had gained the right to declare under oath before the Roman People that this city and this Commonwealth had survived through my exertions.[137] This slander of cruelty is now extinct; they see that it was not as a ruthless tyrant, but as the gentlest of parents that I was missed, recalled, summoned by the eager wish of every citizen. [95] Another slander has sprung up. My leaving Rome is brought against me. To this reproach I cannot reply without the highest self-praise. After all, reverend sirs, what ought I to say? That I fled because of a guilty conscience? But the act with which I was reproached involved no guilt; on the contrary, it was the finest in human history. That I was afraid of a trial before the Roman People? Nothing of the kind was proposed; but if it had been, I would have emerged with glory doubled. That the honest men failed to come to my defense? That is false. That I feared to die? That is dishonoring. [96] So I have to say something I should not be saying unless forced; for I have never said anything about myself that might be thought vainglorious in order to claim credit, but only

---

136. On this passage see SB[1], 266.

137. Retiring magistrates took an oath that they had done nothing in office contrary to law. At the end of his year as Consul, a hostile Tribune (Metellus Nepos) forbade Cicero to address an assembly following the taking of the oath. Cicero then substituted a different oath: that he alone had saved the Commonwealth. And the people repeated it after him (*Fam.* 5.2.7).

to ward off calumny. So I say it and say it as loudly as I can: when violence instigated by all the desperados and conspirators was making its onslaught, not so much upon me as upon all honest men through me, under the leadership of a Tribune, and with the backing of the Consuls, with the Senate cast down, the Roman Knights terrorized, and the whole community tense with anxiety, I saw that little of the Commonwealth would be left if I won the day, and nothing if I lost it. Thus judging, I bewailed the parting from my poor wife, the orphan plight of my beloved children, the predicament of my absent brother, best and most affectionate of brothers, the sudden ruin of so well-established a family. But before all these considerations I placed the lives of my countrymen, preferring that the Commonwealth should tumble with the departure of one, rather than perish with the destruction of all. I hoped that if honest men lived, I could be raised from the dust—as actually happened—whereas if I perished along with the honest men, there would be no bringing the Commonwealth back to life. [97] I suffered much, reverend sirs, no one can believe how much. I do not deny it, nor do I claim for myself the philosophy which some thought I should have shown, when they talked of my being unduly cowed and downcast. Torn from such a variety of many blessings, blessings which I leave unspoken because even now I cannot name them without tears, could I deny my humanity and disown the common sentiments of nature? If I could, I should not call my action praiseworthy or claim to have conferred any benefit on the Commonwealth, since I should only have abandoned for its sake commodities which I could forego with equanimity; and I should reckon that there was more of insensibility than courage in such hardness of mind, like a calloused body which feels nothing when it is burned. [98] No, no; to undergo such mental anguish voluntarily; to suffer alone, while your city survives, the fate that befalls a conquered people whose city has been taken; to see yourself torn from the embrace of your family, your house demolished, your property dissipated; to lose country itself for country's sake; to be robbed of the most splendid honors the Roman People can bestow, hurled from the topmost rung of reputation's ladder; to see enemies in purple-bordered gowns claiming the funeral expenses before the death has

been bewailed;[138] to undergo all this in order to preserve your
+ countrymen, and to do so feeling the pain of it, not so philosophic as those whom nothing concerns, but loving your family and yourself as common humanity demands: there is the glory, the shining, transcendent glory. For a man to give up with equanimity, for the sake of the Commonwealth, benefits which he has never prized or enjoyed argues no very remarkable degree of patriotism; but whoever, for the same sake, lets go things from which he is parted only with the deepest pain, he is a true patriot, placing his country's welfare before the love of his own family.[139]
+ [99] So this demon, this bane of his country, shall hear me say it, since he has challenged me, though he burst in the hearing: I saved the Commonwealth twice: once when, as a Consul in civilian dress, I defeated armed insurrection; and again when, as a private citizen, I yielded to armed Consuls. From both crises I reaped a rich reward: from the earlier in that I saw the Senate and all honest men wearing mourning for my sake by the Senate's authority; and from the latter in that the Senate and Roman People and all mankind both privately and publicly declared that the Commonwealth could be saved only by my return.

[100] But this return of mine, reverend sirs, depends on your verdict. If you place me in my residence—as you always did throughout the struggle—by your good will, counsel, resolutions, and declarations, I will see and feel myself truly restored. On the other hand, if my house is *not* returned to me—and even supplies my enemy with a memorial of my suffering, his crime, and the public calamity—who would regard this as a return, and not rather as an everlasting punishment? Reverend sirs, my house is in
+ view of almost the entire city. If that monument, or rather tomb, inscribed with my enemy's name remains on its site, I must go elsewhere rather than live in a city where I should be seeing trophies of victory set up over myself and the Commonwealth. [101] Could I possess a mind so callous or eyes so unabashed as to live

---

138. "Gabinius and Piso claimed their provinces and other perquisites as though they were undertakers rendering an account" (R. G. Nisbet). Cf. *Red. sen.* 18.

139. This sentence merely repeats less eloquently what has just been said; see p. 38.

in the city of which the Senate, with the assent of all, has so often declared me savior and to look upon my house,[140] which my enemy, or rather the common foe, demolished, and upon the shrine which he erected and set before the eyes of the community, so that the tears of honest men might never dry?

Spurius Maelius aspired to despotism. His house was leveled and the justice of the retribution approved by the very name "Aequimaelium," because it was "fair to Maelius" in the judgment of the Roman People. For the same reason, Spurius Cassius' house was demolished and the temple of Tellus[141] put in its place. In Vaccus' Meadows stood the house of Marcus Vaccus, which was confiscated and destroyed in order that his misdeed[142] would be marked and commemorated by the name of the place. Marcus Manlius drove the attacking Gauls back from the slope of the Capitol, but he was not content with the glory of that patriotic deed. He was convicted of aspiring to depotism. So his house was demolished and is covered by the two woods which you see. Such, in the view of our forbears, was the greatest punishment that could be devised for wicked, criminal citizens. Am I to undergo and bear the same punishment, for our posterity to think of me as the author and leader of a criminal conspiracy instead of its suppressor? [102] What of the dignity of the Roman People, reverend sirs? Can it bear such a stigma of dishonor and inconsistency while the Senate lives, and while you are our leaders in public counsel? Can it bear that the house of Marcus Tullius Cicero seem to have been joined with the house of Marcus Fulvius Flaccus in commemoration of punishment publicly ordained? Marcus Flaccus was put to death by decision of the Senate because he had acted with Gaius Gracchus contrary to the welfare of the Commonwealth. His house was demolished and confiscated. Some time later, Quintus Catulus set up a portico on its site out of the spoils taken from the Cimbri. When that firebrand and demon of his country[143] captured, occupied, and held Rome with forces

---

140. I.e., the site.
141. The Earth Goddess.
142. See Index I.
143. Clodius.

captained by Piso and Gabinius, at a single stroke he proceeded to destroy the monument of the illustrious dead,[144] and to join my house with Flaccus' house, thus causing one who had been declared by the Senate our country's guardian to suffer—now that the Senate had been crushed—the same punishment that the Senate had once meted out to a subverter of society. [103] Will you allow *this*[145] portico to stand on the Palatine, the fairest site in Rome, planted there for all mankind to remember forever as evidence of tribunician recklessness, consular crime, the cruelty of conspirators, the calamity of the Commonwealth, and my suffering? For the love you bear and have always borne to the Commonwealth you would be eager to tear down that portico, not merely with your votes but, if need were, with your hands—unless perchance any of you are deterred by a superstitious regard for that holy priest's dedication! [104] Here we come to a source of unfailing merriment to the ribald, whereas the more serious among us cannot hear of it without profound indignation. Did Publius Clodius, who robbed the house of the Chief Pontiff[146] of religious sanctity, import it into mine? Do you gentlemen, the overseers of our rites and observances, take *him* for your authority and instructor in state religion? Ye Gods Immortal (I desire you to hear what I say), does Publius Clodius care for your rites, does he tremble before your divinity, does he suppose that all human affairs are bound up with your worship? Does he not make mock of the authority of all these eminent persons here present? Does he not abuse your solemn dignity, reverend sirs? Can a religious word fall, or slip, from those lips? With that same mouth of his, he launched a foul, blasphemous attack upon religion when he railed at the Senate for passing a rigorous decree upon a religious matter.[147] [105] Look at this devout individual, reverend sirs, and, if it please you, tell him, as good priests will, that religious scruple has its limits; it should not degenerate into superstition. Anile superstition: under what fanatic compulsion did you step in upon

---

144. I.e., the portico of Catulus (d. 61 or 60 B.C.).
145. Built by Clodius; cf. s. 116.
146. Caesar, in whose house the rites of the Bona Dea were being celebrated in 62 when Clodius intruded.
147. The Bona Dea affair; see p. 1.

a sacrifice in another's man home? Was your intellect so enfeebled that you thought the gods would be insufficiently placated unless you involved yourself in women's rituals as well as men's? Your ancestors went about their private observances and presided over state priesthoods; did you ever hear of one of them attending at a sacrifice to the Good Goddess? No, not even that one who went blind.[148] From this we see how often in life popular opinion errs. Appius, who had never knowingly looked at what it was unlawful for him to see, lost his sight. Clodius, who defiled rituals not merely by looking at them, but by outrageous impurity and immoral act,[149] is not punished in his eyesight; his mind is blinded instead. When so pure, so devout, so stainless, so god-fearing an authority tells you that with his own hands he tore down the house of an excellent citizen, and with the same hands consecrated it, how can you fail, reverend sirs, to be profoundly impressed?

[106] Now, Clodius, let us examine your consecration. You say you had carried a bill giving you permission. Did that bill not contain a proviso invalidating any item contrary to law?[150] Will you, then, gentlemen, determine it lawful that the dwelling, altar, hearth, and household Gods of each one of you be subject to the caprice of Tribunes? That, whoever is the object of somebody's onslaught by means of an incited crowd, the victim of a sudden assault, it be lawful not only to dash his house to the ground in a sudden storm of temporary insanity, but to bind it with a religious sanction for all time to come? [107] For my part, reverend sirs, I have always been told that in undertaking religious obligations, the chief point is to arrive by interpretation at what appears to be the will of the Immortal Gods. Nor is there any piety toward the Gods without a worthy conception of their divinity and disposition; it must be held a sin to seek of them anything wrong or improper. That filthy creature, all-powerful as he then was, could find no human being to whom he could assign my house or hand

---

148. Appius Claudius Caecus, the famous Censor (312 B.C.), who went blind in his old age.
149. The rendezvous with Caesar's wife; see p. 1.
150. Such a proviso was customary.

it over or grant it as a gift. He himself was aflame with desire for the site and the building; and, for that sole reason, had constituted his worthy self owner of my property in that baleful bill of his. And yet, even in the midst of his madness, he did not venture to occupy my house, though he burned with desire for it. Do you suppose that the Immortal Gods wished to move into the house of one through whose efforts and policy they themselves hold possession of their temples, after the wicked banditry of a criminal had torn it to the ground? [108] No citizen in all our great people—except for those of Publius Clodius' contaminated, bloodstained gang—touched a single item of my property, none but defended me in that time of trouble to the extent of his capability. As for those who did contaminate themselves by some contact with the
+ loot as partners or purchasers, in no judgment, public or private, could they escape penalty. Well then, out of this property, of which no man touched a single item but was universally accounted a thoroughpaced villain, did the Immortal Gods covet
+ my house? On the contrary, your beauteous Liberty expelled *my* household Gods and the spirits of my hearth, to establish herself as in a captured dwelling. [109] What is more sacred, more closely guarded by religious safeguards than the home of each and every citizen? Here are the altars, the hearths, the household Gods; here are focused the family rites, observances, and ceremonies. The home is an asylum held sacred by all; to tear any man away from his home is a sacrilege. All the more firmly, gentlemen, should your ears reject Clodius' fury. That which our forbears ordained by religious sanctions as safe and holy, he has not only sacrilegiously jarred, but torn down in the name of religion itself.

[110] But let us examine this goddess. Good [151] she must be, because she has been dedicated by *you.* "She is Liberty," says he. So you installed Liberty in my house, after removing her from the length and breadth of Rome! You treated your colleagues like slaves,[152] vested though they were with exalted power; access to the temple of Castor was closed to us all; in the hearing of the Roman People you ordered your lackeys to trample upon this

---

151. Alluding to Bona Dea.
152. Lit. "denied that they were free men," i.e., treated them like dirt.

illustrious personage here present,[153] a gentleman of the highest birth, elected by the people to the highest offices, a Pontiff, a Consular, and a man of singular good nature and modesty—I cannot sufficiently wonder how you dare look him in the face; you thrust me forth without a trial, bringing in tyrannical laws *ad hominem*; you kept the world's greatest man[154] a prisoner in his house; you occupied the Forum with armed bands of desperados. And after all this, did you undertake to install the image of Liberty in a house that was itself evidence of your cruel despotism and the Roman People's pitiable bondage? Was it right for Liberty to drive from his house the one man but for whom the whole community would have fallen under the yoke of slaves?

[111] Now, whence came this Liberty of yours? I have made careful inquiry. It is said there lived in Tanagra a woman of the town. Her marble image was placed in a tomb not far from Tanagra. A certain nobleman,[155] not unconnected to our devout priest of Liberty, brought the statue to Rome to adorn his aedileship, for he had in mind to outdo all his predecessors in the splendor of his show. So with wise economy he brought back to his house all *objets d'art* surviving in temples and places of public resort throughout Greece and all the islands—for the sake of the Roman People. [112] Then, realizing that he could cheat the aedileship and be returned as Praetor[156] by Consul Lucius Piso if only he had a competitor whose name began with the same letter as his own,[157] he put his aedileship[158] in two places: his strongbox and his property in the suburbs. This statue taken from a harlot's tomb he gave to Clodius, to be a symbol of *their* license rather than Rome's liberty. Indeed, a goddess not to be trifled with! The likeness of a harlot, the ornament of a tomb, abstracted by a thievish hand, installed by a sacrilegious one. Shall *she* drive me from

---

153. Identity uncertain. M. Terentius Varro Lucullus, Consul in 73, would fit.
154. Pompey.
155. Clodius' brother Appius, a notorious plunderer of Greek art treasures.
156. The Roman *cursus honorum* ("sequence of offices") ran: Quaestor, Aedile or Tribune, Praetor, Consul; but the second stage was sometimes passed over.
157. Implying that voting tablets on which the candidates' names were abbreviated could be misattributed.
158. I.e., the money he would have had to spend and the art treasures he had assembled.

my house? Victorious over our humbled community, shall she be decked with the spoils of the Commonwealth? Shall she be in that monument which was placed as evidence of the Senate's subjugation to perpetuate a disgraceful memory?

[113] Ah, Quintus Catulus—shall I call on the father first or the son? The son's memory is fresher and more closely associated with my own achievements—how greatly were you mistaken when you used to think that I should be most richly rewarded in public life, more richly day by day! You used to say that it was against nature that there be two Consuls in the community both hostile to the Commonwealth.[159] Well, two Consuls were found to hand over the Senate in bondage to a crack-brained Tribune, to prohibit its members by manifestos and magisterial authority from pleading for me and supplicating the people, to look on while my house was demolished and sacked, and, finally, to give orders that the charred remnants of my possessions be transported to their own residences. [114] Now I come to Catulus the elder. You, Quintus Catulus, desired that Marcus Fulvius' house should be a memorial of your spoils, though his daughter had married your brother. You wished all memory of one who had conceived designs destructive to the Commonwealth to perish utterly from men's eyes and minds. What would you have said if you had been told when you were building that portico that a time would come when a Tribune, who had disregarded the Senate's authority and the judgment of all honest men, would demolish your monument, overturn it, while the Consuls looked on and even lent their assistance, and would join it with the house of a citizen who, as Consul, had defended the Commonwealth under the Senate's authority? Would you not have replied that such a thing could happen only if the Commonwealth were overturned?

[115] But mark the fellow's insufferable insolence, combined with a precipitate, unbridled greed. Did *he* ever devise a monument or any act of religion? What he wanted was a spacious, magnificent residence, combining two very large, well-known mansions. At the very moment when my departure robbed him of a pretext for a massacre, he pressed Quintus Seius to sell him his

---

159. Cf. *Red. sen.* 9.

house. When Seius refused, he first threatened to obstruct his lights. But Postumus[160] swore that while he lived, Clodius should not get that house. Our bright young man saw what had to be done from Seius' own words. Without the slightest concealment, he murdered him by poison, then bought the house at almost half as much again as its value, after wearing out the other bidders. Where's all this tending? [116] Well, almost all that house of mine is unconsecrated; hardly a tenth part of it was added to Catulus' portico. The promenade, the monument, and that Liberty from Tanagra to signify the crushing of freedom—these were pretexts. Clodius had set his heart on a portico three hundred feet long on the Palatine with a splendid view, paved, with rooms adjoining, a magnificent peristyle, and all else such as to outdo all other houses in spaciousness and dignity. And when this man of religion was simultaneously buying and selling my house,[161] even in that murky time he did not venture to set his own name to the purchase. Instead, he put up that fellow Scato, whose energy had made a beggar of him. Scato no longer had a roof to shelter him from the rain in his Marsian homeland, but Clodius had him claim to have bought a famous house on the Palatine. The lower part of the premises Clodius assigned not to his own Fonteian clan but to the Clodian, which he had abandoned. Out of its many members none gave in his name except desperate beggars and criminals. Will you, reverend sirs, give your approval to such a strange mixture of heterogeneous intents, such impudence, insolence, and rapacity? [117] He reminds us that a Pontiff was present. Are you not ashamed to say in a hearing before the Pontiffs that *a* Pontiff was present, and not the College of Pontiffs, especially since as Tribune you could require or even compel attendance? Never mind: you did not bring in the College. Well, *which* member was present? There was need of authority, which all these gentlemen here possess, but still, prestige increases with age and official rank. There was also need of science. If all the College has attained it, the fact remains that length of tenure adds

---

160. I.e., Q. Seius Postumus.
161. As administrator Clodius sold the house to Scato (see below), but in reality he bought it himself.

expertise. [118] Well then, who *was* present? "My wife's brother,"[162] says Clodius. If we ask for authority, he is not yet old enough to have acquired it; and anyhow, such authority as the young man may possess must be considered as diminished by so close a connection. As for science, if that was desired, who was less expert than a Pontiff who had entered the College only a few days previously? And he was yet more bound to you by a recent favor, in that he found himself, your brother-in-law, put before your brother by birth.[163] To be sure, you took care that your brother cannot hold it against you.

Do you call this a dedication? You could not bring the College in nor yet a Pontiff honored by the Roman People with political office nor even * * *,[164] though you had some close friends in the College. The person who attended—if he *did* attend—was there at your instigation, his sister's request, and his mother's compulsion.[165] [119] Have a care then, reverend sirs, how your ruling in my case affects property in general. Would you suppose that the house of any one of us can be consecrated on the word of a Pontiff, if he puts his hand on the doorpost and says this or that? Were not such dedications, such hallowings of temples and shrines, established by our ancestors to the glory of the Immortal Gods without any evil consequences to citizens? A Tribune has been found, equipped with Consular forces, to rush in a paroxysm of frenzied aggression upon a citizen whom the Commonwealth herself has raised up with her own hands from the dust as he lay stricken. [120] Now supposing a man like Clodius (for would-be imitators will not be wanting) makes a violent assault on someone *not* like myself, someone to whom the Commonwealth owes no such debt, and consecrates his house through the agency of a Pontiff: will you by the authority vested in you decide that

---

162. L. Pinarius Natta.

163. C. Claudius Pulcher, who had been a candidate to fill the vacancy into which Pinarius was elected; cf. *Scaur.* 34. The point of the following sentence is obscure.

164. Text doubtful. The manuscripts have "nor even a young man." "A man of mature age" would make sense. Cf. SB[1], 266.

165. Implying immoral relations between Clodius and his mother-in-law; cf. ss. 134, 139. Pinarius' sister (i.e., half-sister) was probably Fulvia, later married to Curio and Mark Antony; see Index I, under "Pinaria."

such an act should be valid? Perhaps you will ask: "Whom will he find in the College?" Cannot the same person be both Pontiff and Tribune? The illustrious Marcus Drusus, the Tribune, was a Pontiff. If he had laid hold of the doorpost of the house of his enemy Quintus Caepio and uttered a few words, would Caepio's house have been dedicated? [121] I say nothing of pontifical law or the words of the actual dedication or religious sanction or ritual. I do not disguise my ignorance of such matters; even if I had knowledge of them, I should conceal it, not wishing to seem tiresome to others and meddlesome to yourselves—not but what particulars of your discipline often leak out and percolate even to laymen. I think I have heard that in a dedication, a doorpost has to be grasped; for the doorpost is where, in a temple, we have the entrance and folding doors. Nobody ever grasped the doorpost of a promenade in dedication. If Clodius dedicated a statue or an altar, that can be moved without any scruple of religion. But it will no longer be open to him to say that, since he has said that the Pontiff grasped the doorpost.[166]

[122] Here I am, talking about a dedication, arguing about pontifical law and religion, contrary to my declared intention. But even if I were to concede that everything had proceeded with the customary words according to ancient traditional practice, I should still defend myself with Commonwealth law. By the departure of the citizen through whose sole agency the Senate and all honest men had so often declared the community to be intact, you and two very villainous Consuls held the Commonwealth in the grip of a detestable brigandage. Grant that you had used some Pontiff to dedicate the house of one who had refused to let the country he had saved perish on his account: could the revived Commonwealth endure it? [123] Reverend sirs, if you admit this sort of religious sanction, you will soon be saying good-bye to the common rights of property. Allow that if a Pontiff lay hold of a

---

166. The doorpost ritual, Cicero argues, could not apply to a portico open on all sides. Yet Clodius evidently intended to dedicate the portico. Should he claim that he was dedicating a particular object in the portico, such as a statue, that object could be moved without any violation of religion. However, since he had already brought in the doorpost, he could not so claim. Such seems the best that can be made out of this obscure passage.

doorpost and transfer words composed for the worship of the Immortal Gods to the ruin of citizens, the holy name of religion shall validate the injustice: then, if a Tribune in words no less
+ ancient and hallowed by custom, consecrates somebody's possessions, will not the same apply? Within our fathers' memory, the possessions of Quintus Metellus[167] —your grandfather, Quintus Metellus,[168] and yours, Publius Servilius, and your great-grandfather, Publius Scipio—were consecrated by a Tribune, Gaius Atinius, whom as Censor Quintus Metellus had expelled from the Senate. A brazier[169] was placed on the Rostra and a flute player was in attendance.[170] What was the result? Did the Tribune's antic, derived from some very ancient historical precedents, injure the great and illustrious Metellus? Assuredly not. [124] We saw a Tribune do the same to Censor Gnaeus Lentulus.[171] Did he thereby put Lentulus' possessions under any sort of religious embargo? But never mind others: you, yes you, covered your head, called a meeting, set up your brazier, and consecrated the possessions of your friend Gabinius, the man on whom you had bestowed all the realms of Syria, Arabia, and Persia.[172]

If that action was void of effect, what could be the effect when *my* property was consecrated? But if it is valid, how did that greedy monster, who in your company had devoured the blood of the Commonwealth, raise a villa at Tusculum to the clouds out of the bowels of the Treasury,[173] while *I* was not allowed even the sight of my ruins—I, who prevented all Rome from suffering a similar fate? [125] Well, forget Gabinius. Did not a very gallant and

---

167. Macedonicus.
168. Creticus.
169. For libations or incense.
170. As generally supposed, music and the veiling of the head (cf. s. 124) served to avoid observation of bad omens.
171. Cn. Cornelius Lentulus Clodianus, Censor in 70. Nothing more is known of this incident.
172. When, after Cicero's banishment, Clodius turned his gangs against Pompey (see p. 7, n. 10), Gabinius remained loyal to Pompey, with whom he had close ties, and thereby exposed himself to attack by Clodius, including the attempt by Clodius to consecrate Gabinius' property. Clodius' colleague, the tribune L. Ninnius, who was friendly to Cicero, tried to adopt Clodius' tactic against him by consecrating *his* property (s. 125).
173. Cf. p. 47, n. 20.

excellent gentleman, Lucius Ninnius, follow in your footsteps and consecrate *your* possessions? Do you say that his act should not be valid because it concerns yourself? Then the rules you laid down in that splendid tribunate of yours were for you to use for the ruin of others, and to reject when turned against you. If, on the other hand, that consecration is legitimate, what item of your possessions can stand clear? Or does consecration have no binding force, while dedication carries religious sanction?[174] Then what was the sense of your solemn appeal to the flute player, or of the brazier, or of the prayers, or of the archaic language? Why did you want to lie and cheat, and abuse the power of the Immortal Gods to make men afraid? For if what you did in my case—to say nothing of Gabinius'—is valid, your house and anything else you own is certainly consecrated to Ceres. But if that was a farce, are you not the most unclean thing in creation? You have defiled all that is sacred either with lies or with debauchery. [126] "I now admit," says he, "that it was a wicked thing I did to Gabinius." Yes, for you see that the penalty which you set up against another has been turned against yourself. Very well, you specimen of all crimes and infamies, in Gabinius' case you make that admission. His career we have seen: an immoral boy, a licentious young man, a disreputable beggar later in life, a brigand as Consul. Even that calamity which you tried to bring upon him could not have gone beyond his deserts. But in my case, you hedge on your admission, and claim that what you did before one young man has greater weight than what you did in front of an entire public meeting.

[127] "A dedication," says he, "has great religious force." Does it not seem to you, gentlemen, that you are listening to Numa Pompilius? Learn, Pontiffs, and you, Flamens. You, too, King,[175] learn from your fellow clansman, though he has left your clan—learn, all the same, from this votary the comprehensive principles governing all religious observances. Well then, in a dedication do we not ask who dedicates, and what and how? Or are you so

---

174. The distinction between the two terms is a difficult problem; see R. G. Nisbet's edition, Appendix VI.
175. King of Rites (see Glossary of Terms). A man by the name of L. Claudius (*Har. resp.* 12).

mingling and confounding these matters that anyone who likes can dedicate anything he likes any way he likes? Who were you, the dedicator? By what principle, what law, what precedent, what power? When had the Roman People put this matter in your charge? I observe that there is an ancient tribunician law which forbids the consecration of a building, or a piece of ground, or an altar except by order of the Plebs. Its proposer, one Quintus Papirius, did not then envisage *this*, or suspect that there would be some danger of the dwellings or possessions of citizens unconvicted of offense being consecrated. Such a thing was not to be thought of, nobody had done it, nor had Papirius any reason to forbid it and so appear to be not so much deterring it as calling attention to the possibility. [128] But temples were consecrated, not the dwellings of private citizens, but what are called sacred edifices; lands were consecrated, not like my estates were, at will, but when an army commander consecrated lands taken from the enemies of Rome. Altars were set up to invest the site of their consecration with a sacred character. Such consecrations he forbade except by order of the Plebs. Well, if you interpret these provisions as applying to my house and lands, I make no objection. But I ask what law was passed enabling you to consecrate my house, when this power was conferred upon you, by what right you acted. Nor am I now arguing about religion, but about the property of us all; nor yet about pontifical law, but about public law. The Papirian law forbids the consecration of buildings except by order of the Plebs. Let us grant, if you will, that this relates to our homes and not to public temples: show me one word about consecration in that same bill of yours,[176] if it is a bill and not the voice of your crime and cruelty. [129] If you had been able to think of everything in that shipwreck of the Commonwealth, or if, in that conflagration of the community, your draftsman had been giving his whole mind to framing those bills of yours—those monstrosities, I should rather say—instead of drawing out notes of hand with Byzantine exiles and Brogitarus' representatives, you would have had everything in legal form, in words, if not in substance. But so much was going on all at once:

---

176. See p. 38.

bonds being signed,[177] bargains for provinces being struck, royal titles being sold, all manner of slaves being enrolled street by street throughout Rome, enemies being reconciled, new posts of authority being assigned to the younger generation,[178] poison being prepared for the unfortunate Quintus Seius, plots being hatched for the assassination of Gnaeus Pompeius, the empire's
+ champion and guardian, so that the Senate would have none to protect it, and honest men would mourn eternally, and the Commonwealth, captured by the treachery of Consuls, would be at the mercy of tribunician violence. With all these important activities in progress, small wonder that much escaped his attention and yours, especially in a state of mental excitement and occlusion.

[130] I ask you, gentlemen, to observe the power of this Papi-
+ rian law in a business of this nature, though that business be respectable, unlike Clodius' contribution, which was full of crime and madness. Quintus Marcius as Censor had commissioned a statue of Concord and set it in a public place. Gaius Cassius as Censor transferred this statue to the Senate-House and then consulted your College as to whether there appeared to be any objection to his dedicating the statue and the Senate-House to Concord. Let me invite you, reverend sirs, to compare the two men, the two situations, and the two projects. Cassius was a very discreet and highly respected Censor; Clodius an exceptionally villainous and unscrupulous Tribune. The political situation on the earlier occasion was tranquil, based upon the freedom of the people and the guidance of the Senate. Under Clodius that freedom had been crushed and the Senate's authority destroyed. [131] The former project was entirely just, wise, and reputable; a Censor, to whose judgment the dignity of the Senate was committed by the ordinance of our ancestors, which Clodius has abolished, wished to dedicate a statue of Concord in the Senate-House and to dedicate the Senate-House to that Goddess. His intention was excellent, entirely praiseworthy. In linking the actual location and consecrated area of the public council with the worship of

---

177. Probably for bribe money, payable to Clodius, in the first case. As for Brogitarus, see Index I and p. 118, n. 43.

178. The reference is unknown.

Concord, he considered himself to be giving senators a direction to speak without partisan dissensions. Whereas *you* held the community enslaved by weapons, fear, manifestos, laws *ad hominem*, by a force of desperados on the spot, and by the terror and threat of an absent army, by a partnership, a nefarious bargain with the Consuls; and you set up the image of Liberty as an impudent mockery rather than for any pretense of religion. Cassius placed a
+ statue of Concord, which could be dedicated with no injury to anybody, in the Senate-House; *you* placed a representation, not of
+ public liberty, but of your own license, on the blood and bones, so to speak, of a citizen who had rendered the Commonwealth great service. [132] And yet Cassius referred the matter to the College;
+ to whom did *you* refer? If you had had some private project under consideration, some religious expiation or institution of a domestic character, you would still have brought the matter before a Pontiff, following the ancient practice observed by others. When setting up a new shrine in the most celebrated part of Rome, an impious, unprecedented type of foundation, did you not think it proper to consult to the public priests? If you did not see fit to call in the College of Pontiffs, did none of these gentlemen now present, eminent by virtue of years, rank, and authority, appear a suitable person to consult about a dedication? You did not despise their exalted standing; you feared it. Would you have dared to ask Publius Servilius or Marcus Lucullus—by whose advice and authority I, as Consul, snatched the Commonwealth from the hands and jaws of you and your like—about the proper form of words and ritual for consecrating a citizen's house? A citizen, yes; but let me add, one whom first the leader of the Senate,[179] then all classes, next the whole of Italy, and finally all nations had testified as being the savior of this city and empire. [133] What would he have said, this wicked, pernicious disgrace to the community? "Please, Lucullus, please Servilius, be present while I dedicate Cicero's house, and say the words for me to repeat, and hold the doorpost." Your audacity and impudence are quite exceptional,

---

179. I.e., the younger Catulus, who seems to have been the first to hail Cicero as *parens patriae* ("father of the fatherland"; cf. *Sest.* 121, *Pis.* 6) after the Catiline affair. As a title, *princeps senatus* was almost certainly abolished by Sulla.

but even you would have dropped your eyes, lost countenance and voice, when those personages who, in their dignity, uphold the image of the Roman People and the authority of the empire, scared you from their presence with a crushing rebuke, told you that it would be an act of impiety for them to take part in your
+ madness and lend assistance to crime, to the murder of the fatherland. [134] Aware of this, you betook yourself to your brother-in-law; he was not chosen by you, but left alone by his colleagues. And yet, if he is descended from ancestors who, as tradition relates, learned their rites[180] from Hercules himself when he had finished his labors, I do not believe he was so heartless in the troubles of a brave man[181] as to place a tombstone over his head as he lived and breathed. Maybe he said nothing, did not act at
+ all, only lending his image and name in another's wrongdoing by way of retribution for his mother's indiscretion.[182] Or, if he did stumble through some words and touch a doorpost with a trembling hand, assuredly he did not accomplish anything in proper, unexceptionable fashion, according to established usage. He had seen his stepfather Murena as Consul-Elect bring to me as Consul, along with the Allobroges,[183] the proof of a conspiracy for general destruction; he had heard from Murena that I saved him twice, once individually[184] and a second time along with the whole nation. [135] When this newly appointed Pontiff, undertaking his first religious function since entering into his priestly office, started to speak, can anyone doubt that his tongue went mute, that his hand went numb, that his fear-stricken mind gave way— especially since, out of so large a College, he saw neither King nor Flamen nor Pontiff and was forced against his will to become a participant in another man's crime, and pay the heavy penalty of a vile connection?

---

180. According to legend, the cult of Hercules at the Ara Maxima in Rome was originally taught to the Pinarian clan (and another, the Potitian, which died out) by Hercules himself; cf. Virg. *Aen.* 8.269.

181. Cicero himself. "Brave" (*fortis*) is in keeping with the earlier reference to the heroic Hercules.

182. Cf. p. 88, n. 165.

183. Envoys from this Gaulish tribe who happened to be in Rome gave Cicero evidence implicating the Catilinarian conspirators.

184. By his defense (the extant speech *Pro Murena*).

[136] But to return to the public law governing dedications—which the Pontiffs themselves have always accommodated, not only to their own rituals, but also to the orders of the people: you can find in your registers that Censor Gaius Cassius consulted the College of Pontiffs concerning the dedication of the statue of Concord, and that Chief Pontiff Marcus Aemilius answered him on behalf of the College: that, in the opinion of the College, unless the Roman People commissioned him by name and unless he was acting by its order, the statue could not properly be dedicated. Another instance: in the consulship of Titus Flamininus and Quintus Metellus,[185] Licinia, a Vestal Virgin of the highest birth, invested with a most sacred priestly office, dedicated an altar, chapel, and sacred couch under the Rock.[186] Did not Praetor Sextus Julius by authority of the Senate refer her action to this College? Then Chief Pontiff Publius Scaevola answered on behalf of the College: "That which Licinia, daughter of Gaius, has dedicated in a public place without order of the people appears to have no sacred character." How strictly and conscientiously the Senate handled this matter you will readily perceive from the text of its decree. Please read out the Senate's decree.

[The decree is read.]

[137] Do you observe that the City Praetor was directed to make sure that no sacred character should attach and that any engraving or inscription should be removed? What have we come to? In those days, the Pontiffs forbade a Censor of stainless character to dedicate an image of Concord in a consecrated precinct; later the Senate, by authority of the Pontiffs, ruled that an altar already consecrated on hallowed ground be removed and did not allow any written memorial of that dedication to remain. Whereas you—our country's stormcloud, a tornado whirling away peace and quiet—after violating all religion, you mingled with the name of religion what you demolished and built amid the shipwreck of the Commonwealth, when darkness reigned, and the Roman People had sunk beneath the waves, and the Senate had been thrown

---

185. 123 B.C.

186. On the southeast slope of the Aventine. The temple of Bona Dea was located there (cf. Ov. *Fast.* 5.148 ff).

overboard and ejected. You set it, as a memorial of the Commonwealth you had destroyed, upon the vitals of one who by his own exertions and perils had saved Rome. You removed the name of Quintus Catulus and engraved it with a mark that signified the distress of all honest men.[187] Did you expect the Commonwealth to tolerate that structure any longer than she, along with myself, was banished from Rome's walls?

[138] Now, reverend sirs, if the person dedicating did not have the right, and the thing dedicated was wrong, it can hardly be necessary for me to prove my third point: that he did not carry out the dedication by the usages and formulae which ritual requires. I have said from the outset that I shall say nothing about your science, or about sacred observances, or arcane pontifical law. What I have hitherto argued concerning the rules of dedication was not researched from some secret sort of writings; it was common knowledge, taken from the public acts of magistrates, laid before your College. But there are more recondite matters which fall within your province: what it was legitimate to say, dictate, touch, hold. [139] But suppose it were clear that all had proceeded with the science of a Tiberius Coruncanius, who is said to have been the most expert of Pontiffs; or suppose Marcus Horatius Pulvillus, he who resolutely dedicated the Capitol, refusing to give way when many jealous folk tried to stop him with trumped-up religious objections—suppose Horatius had presided over a dedication of this nature: even so, there could be no power of religion in a crime; certainly none in the alleged act of an inexperienced youth, a newly appointed priest, brought to the scene by the entreaties of his sister and the threats of his mother.[188] Ignorant, reluctant, without colleagues or books or adviser or acolyte, furtive, with mind and tongue a-tremble—ay, and with that foul, sacrilegious foe of all religion, who had so often made unholy appearance as a woman among men and a man among women, he conducted the business in such disorderly haste that neither mind nor voice nor tongue held steady. [140] It was reported to you, reverend sirs, at the time, and later became the talk of the

---

187. Text doubtful.
188. Cf. p. 88, n. 165.

town, how Clodius uttered and behaved throughout otherwise than as your records prescribe: words out of order, omens adverse, continually correcting himself, hesitating, nervous, wavering. Nor is it in the least surprising that in so criminal and crazy an enterprise, even audacity was powerless to suppress fear. Imagine a pirate, a robber of temples, who consecrates an altar on a desolate shore, prompted by dreams or some religious scruple: however barbarous and savage, would his soul not shudder when he is driven to placate by prayers the divine power which he violated by his crimes? What do you suppose was the spiritual turmoil of this marauder of all temples and dwellings, of all Rome, when he nefariously consecrated a single altar in deprecation of so many crimes? [141] Puffed up though he was by the insolence of arbitrary power, armed though he was with audacity beyond belief, it was impossible that he should not tumble headlong in the doing of it, often make mistakes, especially with a Pontiff and instructor who was obliged to teach before he had learned. Great power lies in the divinity of the Immortal Gods, great power also in the Commonwealth. Seeing the guardian and protector of their temples feloniously driven forth, the Immortal Gods refused to move out of their temples into his dwelling. So they dismayed Clodius' moonstruck brain with anxiety and alarm. As for the Commonwealth, though expelled along with me, she appeared before the eyes of her suppressor, already demanding her restitution and mine from his flaming, uncontrollable fury. What wonder then if, harried by terror, goaded by madness, driven headlong by crime, he could neither follow established rituals nor enunciate a single hallowed formula?

[142] So matters stand. Now, reverend sirs, I beg you to turn your thoughts away from this detailed argument of mine back to the Commonwealth as a whole, which in the past, you have sustained in the company of many brave men, but which in this cause, you support alone. Think of the perpetual authority of the entire Senate, always in my cause magnificently led by yourselves. Think of the splendid insurgency of Italy, the rally of the country towns. Think of the hustings, the united voice of all the Centuries, with you as their leaders and instigators. Think of all the financial companies, all the classes, all those who flourish in the present

and expect to flourish in the future. All of them will regard their good will and judgment with respect to my standing as committed, indeed commended, to your hands. [143] Finally, the Immortal Gods themselves, who protect this city and this empire, appear to me to have made the actual enjoyment of my return to Rome, with its attendant congratulation, subject to the judicial power of their priests for a reason: they desired it to be plain to all peoples and posterity that divine will has brought me back to the Commonwealth. For this, reverend sirs, is what return and restitution mean: recovery of house, dwelling, altars, hearths, and household Gods. Clodius tore away their roof and dwelling place with his own ruffianly hands. And when, under the captaincy of the Consuls, he took the city—as it were—he felt he must destroy this one house as belonging to the stoutest of her defenders. Now through you, these household, family Gods of mine will be restored to my house along with myself.

[144] I call upon thee, God of the Capitol, whom the Roman People have named "Best" because of thy benefactions, and "Greatest" because of thy power; and thee, Queen Juno, and thee, Minerva, Guardian of the City, who hast ever stood my aid in counsel and my witness in trial: hear my prayer and petition.[189] Ye also, ancestral and family deities of my household, who above all others sought and brought me back, whose dwelling is the subject of this my suit, and ye who preside over this city and Commonwealth,[190] I call upon ye, from whose temples and shrines I warded off that evil, devouring flame; and thee, Mother Vesta, whose pure priestesses I protected from the fury and crime of madmen and whose everlasting fire I did not suffer to be extinguished by Roman blood or mingled in a conflagration of all Rome. [145] If, in the Commonwealth's hour of impending doom, I exposed my life to the fury and swords of desperate men on behalf of your rites and temples; and if, a second time, when they sought to use the struggle in which I was engaged for the destruction of all honest men, I called upon ye to witness and commended myself and my family to your care; and if I then

---

189. Actually, no prayer is offered, though it is implied in what follows.
190. The penates (household Gods) of Rome.

devoted myself and my life on certain terms—namely, that if, on the one hand, both at that time and during my consulship, I had disregarded all personal interests, profits, or rewards and given my every care and thought and vigil to working for my country's welfare, then it should be granted me to enjoy a restored Commonwealth; whereas if, on the other hand, my devices had been of no benefit to my country, I should suffer in perpetuity, torn from my dear ones: if all this be true, then I shall consider this devotion of myself as cancelled and forfeited[191] when, and only when, I have been restored to my dwelling.

[146] At present, reverend sirs, I am banished not only from my house, of which you have taken cognizance, but from all Rome, despite the appearance of restoration. For the most important and populous quarters of the city look toward that monument—no, that national wound. Don't you see that I must needs shun and flee that spectacle more than death?[192] Do not then, I beg, let one, by whose return you thought the Commonwealth would be restored, be deprived not only of the appurtenances of
+ his rank, but even of the sight of the city to which he belongs. The plundering of my property, the razing of my house, the laying waste of my estates, the Consuls' ruthless seizure of booty from my possessions—these do not disturb me. Such things I have always accounted ephemeral and unstable; gifts, not of character and intellect, but of Fortune and circumstance. I never thought their acquisition and abundance so desirable as wisdom in their enjoyment and patience in their loss. [147] My wordly wealth has now been trimmed and limited more or less to my personal needs. To my children I shall leave a sufficiently ample patrimony in their father's name and memory. But I cannot be deprived of my house without signal humiliation to the Commonwealth, and pain and disgrace to myself—the house which was snatched away by a
+ crime, occupied in an act of brigandage, and rebuilt in a show of religion yet more felonious than its demolition.

If you recognize that my return is welcome and pleasing to the Immortal Gods, to the Senate, to the Roman People, to all Italy,

---

191. Cf. *Red. quir.* 1 fin., where the word *convictos* is used somewhat differently.
192. Cf. s. 101.

to the provinces, to foreign nations, and to you yourselves, who have ever held a prime place and authority in the matter of my restoration: I beg and adjure you, reverend sirs, now that by your authority and support and votes you have brought me back, to place me also in my dwelling, since the Senate so wills, with your own hands.

ON THE ANSWERS OF THE HARUSPICES
(*De haruspicum responsis*)

The haruspices (inspectors of entrails) practiced a system of divination evolved in Etruria (*Etrusca disciplina*), with predictions drawn from prodigies (abnormal phenomena such as we read of in Livy), lightning, and the entrails of sacrificial victims. They gradually received recognition in Rome, and in Cicero's time were a group of sixty under a Chief Haruspex, consulted on occasion by order of the Senate. Such an occasion gave rise to this speech, which, in the customary sequence, follows *De domo* but is probably to be assigned to early May of 56.[1]

The day prior to its delivery Cicero and Clodius had clashed in the Senate as described in the first two sections. Cicero goes on to disclaim any intention of prosecuting Clodius unless provoked—he will leave that to Milo. In s. 9 we reach the main topic, an interpretation given by the haruspices to a portentous noise, as of clashing arms, observed in a district near Rome. Clodius had seized on a reference in their response to "profanation of sacred and hallowed places" as indicating the rebuilding of Cicero's house on the area consecrated to Liberty. This Cicero rebuts (ss. 9–17 and again 30–33). The remainder deals with other points in the response. The speech ends with a plea for an end to the "discords and dissensions among the optimates" to which the haruspices had adverted, i.e. to the bad blood between Pompey and the senatorial leaders such as Bibulus and the Luculli.

Cicero takes the attitude of an unquestioning believer in the efficacy of the "Etruscan Discipline," which he certainly was not, though he respected it as a part of the state institutions handed down from earlier times. No doubt many of his fellow senators were in the same position. As a practiced advocate he had no trouble putting himself in the appropriate psychological posture, quite oblivious of private reservations.

---

1. See Lenaghan's discussion in the introduction to his edition.

[1] Yesterday, Members of the Senate, I felt it incumbent upon me to repress Publius Clodius' shameless effrontery. Your dignity and the presence in large numbers of Roman Knights, to whom the Senate was giving audience, moved me strongly, as Clodius with his absurd questions held up the cause of the tax-farmers in the interests of Publius Tullio of Syria,[2] to whom he had sold himself lock, stock, and barrel; and whose favor he was currying before your very faces. As soon as I advanced the threat of prosecution, I checked his crazy swagger. It took only a couple of words to stop the bold, bounding gladiator in his tracks. [2] Even so, he reacted: quite forgetting who our Consuls are, pale with agitation, he suddenly flung out of the Senate-House, uttering certain threats which time has rendered empty and harmless, the bogies of the Piso-Gabinius regime. I started to follow him as he left, and then it was that I reaped a rich reward: you all stood up and the tax-farmers bore me company. Suddenly the madman halted, lost countenance, color, and voice. He looked back; and as soon as he caught sight of Consul Gnaeus Lentulus, he almost collapsed on the threshold of the Senate-House—recollecting his dear friend[3] Gabinius, no doubt, and missing Piso.

What shall I say of this exhibition of unbridled, headlong hysteria? I can find no words more severe to wound him than those with which our venerable fellow member Publius Servilius struck him lifeless on the spot. Even if I were able to match Servilius' extraordinary, almost superhuman force and gravity, I am sure that weapons cast by an enemy would appear less sharp and heavy than those discharged by his father's colleague.[4] [3] All the same, I should like to explain my action to those who thought I was carried away by indignation yesterday and that anger made me go almost further than the considered counsels of wisdom would have required. I did nothing in anger or uncontrolled impulse, nothing that I had not well weighed and pondered beforehand.

---

2. The matter at issue will have had to do with Gabinius' government of Syria, where he had fallen foul of the tax-farmers. P. Tullio is an odd name for a Syrian, perhaps corrupt. "Syrian" can hardly be taken as contemptuous ("Syrian-fancier"—he was presumably standing up for the provincials).

3. Irony, since Clodius had broken with Gabinius; cf. p. 90, n. 172, *Pis.* 27.

4. P. Servilius Vatia Isauricus and Appius Claudius Pulcher were Consuls in 79.

Members of the Senate, I have never made any secret of my enmity to the pair.[5] It was their obligation to defend me and the Commonwealth, it was in their power to save both. Summoned to consular duty by their very insignia of office, summoned to my cause not only by your authority, but by your entreaties, what did they do? First they deserted me, then they betrayed me, finally they attacked me. For the profits of a wicked bargain they wished me totally overwhelmed and extinguished along with the Commonwealth.

The calamities which, as generals in their bloody, baneful spells of command, they could not avert from the walls of Rome's allies nor inflict upon the cities of Rome's enemies—razing, burning, demolition, depopulation, devastation—these they brought upon all buildings and lands belonging to me, and took their plunder. [4] On these demons, these firebrands, yes, on these destructive monsters who well-nigh ruined this empire, I have declared war to the death, I say it. And yet I have gone only so far as your suffering and that of all honest men—not mine and my family's—called for. As for Clodius, I hate him no more today than on the day I learned that he had been shot out of the Chief Pontiff's residence, and out of a sacrilegious intrigue, in women's clothes,
+ scorched by sacred fires.[6] I saw then, yes then, far ahead I saw what a storm was brewing, what a tempest hung over the Commonwealth. I could see that so unconscionable a crime, such monstrous audacity existing in a young man of reckless spirit, noble birth, with a hurt to avenge, could not be held within bounds of public peace; that the evil, if left unpunished, would one day burst out and destroy the community. What happened later added but little to my hatred. [5] For nothing that he did against me was done from hate of myself, but from hate of morality, of dignity, of the Commonwealth. He injured me no more than he injured the Senate, the Roman Knights, all honest men, all Italy. And he committed no worse a crime against me than

---

5. Piso and Gabinius, but their entry is abrupt and something may have fallen out of the text.
6. Allusion to the Vestal Virgins, keepers of the sacred flame, who carried out the rites which Clodius violated.

against the Immortal Gods themselves. This crime with which he outraged them had never been committed before; but his attitude toward me was only what that of his bosom friend Catiline would have been if he had won the day. That is why I never thought it proper to bring charges against him, any more than against that block of wood who calls himself Ligus—we should not know where he came from otherwise.[7] Why should I pursue such a brainless brute, corrupted by my enemies' fodder and acorns?[8] If he has come to a sense of what a crime he has upon his conscience, I don't doubt that he is very unhappy;[9] but if he does not see it, there's the risk that he might plead stupidity!

[6] A further point: universal expectation sees Clodius as a victim assigned and devoted to our gallant and illustrious Titus Annius. It would be grossly unfair if I were to get in first and rob him of his promised, appointed credit when I myself have regained my civic status and dignity thanks to his efforts. I think of him as another Publius Scipio, born to bring death and destruction upon Carthage, which city he alone overthrew at last—he, the emissary of destiny, after many commanders had beleaguered and assailed and shaken and *almost* taken her. Just so Titus Annius seems to have come into the world to repress, extinguish, and utterly destroy that pest: the Gods' gift to the Commonwealth. It took *him* to find the right method of not only beating but binding an armed fellow citizen, who was putting some people to flight with stones and steel, keeping others[10] shut up in their homes, terrorizing the entire city, the Senate-House, the Forum, and all the temples with fire and slaughter.

[7] No, I shall never by my own volition rob such a man and such a benefactor of mine and Rome's of his legal prey, especially as he not only took the quarrel upon himself on my account but actually sought it. If, however, even now that Clodius is tied up in

---

7. See p. 169, n. 83. Ligus ("Ligurian") was a cognomen in a consular branch of the gens Aelia. In *Sest.* 69 Cicero implies that Clodius' ally Aelius Ligus had acquired it by adoption or otherwise. He had already used the motif in his speech *Pro Cluentio* (72) in 66 B.C.

8. Indicating a pig, a proverbially stupid animal.

9. No need, therefore, to pursue him.

10. Pompey in particular.

all manner of judicial threats, enmeshed by the hatred of all honest men, hampered by the apprehension of chastisement not long to be deferred—if even now he comes at me with faltering steps and tries to attack me despite impediments, I shall fight back and put down the attempt, with Milo's permission or perhaps even
+ with his assistance. Yesterday, for instance, when both of us were
+ on our feet, he threatened me: I merely hinted a menace of legal proceedings. Down he sat: I said no more. If he had given notice of prosecution, as he threw out he would, I should have seen that he received a two-day summons from the Praetor.[11] Let him think and regulate his conduct on this basis. If he is content with the crimes he has already committed, he is now earmarked for Milo. If he brandishes a club at me, I shall immediately pick up the weapons of legal process.

[8] Not long ago, Members of the Senate, he addressed a public meeting. The speech was reported to me in full. Let me tell you first the general argument and gist, and when you have had your laugh at this fellow's impudence, I shall tell you about the
+ whole harangue. Clodius discoursed on cults, rites, and ceremonies, Members of the Senate; yes, Publius Clodius! He complained of neglect, violation, contamination of rites and cults. No wonder you find it ludicrous. Even his own meeting laughed at him. Here was a fellow with a hundred senatorial decrees in his hide, as he himself likes to boast, all passed against him in defense of religious observances;[12] a fellow who carried immoral conduct into the sacred couches of the Good Goddess, violating rites which it is a sacrilege for a man's eyes to look upon, even accidentally, not only by masculine eyes but by a gross act of immorality.[13] And he protests at a public meeting about neglect of religious observances! [9] So we are now waiting for his next speech—on chastity! For what is the difference? Chased from a holy altar, he wails about religious rites and observances; why should he not quit his sisters' bedrooms to champion modesty and chastity? He read out at the meeting this recent response of the haruspices about the

---

11. "The shortest notice allowed by the law." See Lenaghan's note.
12. In connection with the Bona Dea affair.
13. See p. 83, n. 149.

noise; now along with much else the response refers, as you have heard, to "profanation of sacred and hallowed places." He claimed that this applied to my house as having been consecrated by that most scrupulous of priests, Publius Clodius.

[10] I am glad to have been presented with a fair, indeed an obligatory reason for saying my say about this whole phenomenon, perhaps the most important of its kind to be reported in this House for these many years past. You will find that the portent and the response are solely to warn us, as though by the voice of Jupiter Best and Greatest, of Clodius' criminal madness and of the grave dangers that impend. [11] First, however, I shall clear my house of religious sanction, if I can do so truthfully and to everyone's satisfaction; but if the slightest scruple appear to remain in any mind, I shall obey the signs and religious mandate of the Immortal Gods patiently, indeed cheerfully.

But where is there in all this great city a house so clear and free of this suspicion of religious sanction? To be sure, your houses, Members of the Senate, and those of the rest of the community are, for much the most part, clear of any such; but mine is the one and only house in Rome which has been cleared by every kind of pronouncement. I appeal to you, Lentulus, and to you, Philippus: the Senate decreed, in view of this response of the haruspices, that you should consult the House concerning sacred and hallowed places. Can you consult it about my residence, the only one in Rome, as I have said, which was cleared of all religious sanction by all kinds of pronouncements? First, my enemy himself in that stormy night of the Commonwealth did not touch it[14] by a single letter relating to religion, though he wrote up the rest of his enormities with a pen wet from the filthy mouth of Sextus
+ Cloelius. Then, the Roman People, to whom belongs supreme power in all things, in an assembly of the Centuries, by the votes of all ages and classes ordered that the status of this same house remain as it was. Later still, you, Members of the Senate, decreed that the College of Pontiffs be consulted about the religious status of my residence—not that the matter was in any doubt, but to muzzle this demon, should he remain any longer in the city he

---

14. I.e., in his law against Cicero; cf. *Dom.* 128.

wanted to destroy.

[12] Is any scruple of religion so grave that a reply, a word, from Publius Servilius or Marcus Lucullus singly would not free us from our doubts and utmost misgivings? The Roman People, the Senate, the Immortal Gods themselves have ever held a decision of three Pontiffs sufficiently sacred, august, and religiously valid, whether concerning public ritual or the principal games or the ceremonies of the household Gods and Mother Vesta—or that very sacrifice which is offered for the welfare of the Roman People[15] and which has never, since the founding of Rome, been violated except by this holy champion of religion. But my house was cleared of all religious sanction by the unanimous ruling of Publius Lentulus (Consul and Pontifex), Publius Servilius, Marcus Lucullus, Quintus Metellus, Manius Glabrio, Marcus Messalla, Lucius Lentulus (Flamen of Mars), Publius Galba, Quintus Metellus Scipio, Gaius Fannius, Marcus Lepidus, L. Claudius (King of Rites), Marcus Scaurus, Marcus Crassus,[16] Gaius Curio, Sextus Caesar (Flamen of Quirinus), and the Minor Pontiffs Quintus Cornelius, Publius Albinovanus, Quintus Terentius: that they did after hearing the case, in two different places[17] with a large concourse of the greatest and wisest in our community standing by. [13] I declare that never since rituals were instituted, and they are coeval with Rome herself—on no subject, not even on capital charges against Vestal Virgins, has the College made a ruling in such numbers.[18] In an inquiry into delinquency, the larger the attendance the better, for the Pontiffs' interpretative function is

---

15. At the rites of Bona Dea.

16. Whether this Marcus Crassus is the father (the "Triumvir") or the son is uncertain, but his position is low on the list, which (after the Consul) is arranged in order of seniority. So eminent a person as Crassus Senior should have got his priesthood earlier. He may have been an Augur, and as such ineligible for the pontificate. The Chief Pontiff Caesar, now in Gaul, and L. Pinarius Natta, who had consecrated Cicero's house and was not a senator (therefore not one of the Pontiffs who adjudicated), are omitted.

17. One of these occasions was, of course, 29 September, when Cicero made his speech *De domo*. The other may be the discussion in the Senate on the following day, as Lenaghan suggests.

18. Even if this were true, it has to be remembered that Sulla raised the number of Pontiffs from nine to fifteen.

of such a nature that they have the power of judges; whereas in a matter of religious observance an elucidation can properly be given by a single experienced member of the College—which would be harsh and inequitable in a capital trial. And yet you will find that the Pontiffs ruled on my house in larger numbers than have ever ruled on the rites of the Virgins.

Next day a very full meeting of the Senate took place. As Consul-Elect, you, Lentulus,[19] initiated the motion, after Consuls Publius Lentulus and Quintus Metellus put the question. All Pontiffs of senatorial status were present. Many other senators standing high in honors conferred by the Roman People spoke on the College's ruling, and all of the same attended as witnesses to drafting.[20] It was determined that in the Senate's judgment my house had been cleared of religious sanction by the ruling of the Pontiffs.

[14] Well then, is it likely that the haruspices are referring to this particular "sacred place," which among all places in private possession has the peculiar status of having been pronounced not sacred by the very authorities who have charge of sacred matters? But let the Consuls put the matter to the House, as is their duty under the Senate's decree. Either the inquiry will be assigned to them (and they were the first to give an opinion concerning this house and clear it from all religious sanction); or the Senate will make a ruling itself (and it has made one earlier on in very large numbers, with none dissenting except our overseer of sacred matters); or (as will doubtless happen) the matter will be referred to the Pontiffs, to whose authority, integrity, and experienced judgment our ancestors have commended rites and cults both public and private. What other reply can they give than the one they have already given? There are many houses in Rome, Members of the Senate, and I dare say almost all of them are held on very good title—but a private title, one of inheritance or authority[21] or conveyance in either form.[22] I assert that no other house is

---

19. Marcellinus.
20. See p. 9, n. 20. So large a number of witnesses was probably very unusual.
21. I take this as a title resting on an affidavit by a person of credit.
22. *Mancipium* and *nexum*. The exact nature of these two modes of acquiring ownership (the latter obsolete in Cicero's time) has been much discussed. See

protected both by an unimpeachably private title and by every special public title imaginable, both human and divine. [15] Firstly, it is in the process of being rebuilt at public expense by authority of the Senate; secondly, it is protected by the safeguard of so many senatorial decrees against the nefarious violence of this gladiator. To begin with, last year you gave the responsibility of ensuring that I be free to build without violent disturbance to the same magistrates to whom the Commonwealth is customarily commended in moments of extreme peril.[23] Then, after he had brought devastation on my residence with stones, fire, and steel, the Senate further decreed that the perpetrators came within the provisions of the law of violence, which is directed at persons assailing the entire Commonwealth. And on your initiative, Consuls (the bravest and best Consuls in human memory), the same Senate decreed in large numbers that whosoever harmed my house would be acting against the public interest. [16] I assert that there are more senatorial decrees on record concerning my house than concerning any public work or monument or temple; that mine is the only house since this city came into existence which the Senate thought fit to have rebuilt at the expense of the Treasury, cleared by the Pontiffs, defended by the magistrates, and avenged by the courts.

Publius Valerius[24] was publicly granted a house on Velia Hill in recognition of his signal services to the Commonwealth; my house on the Palatine has been publicly restored. He was given a site; I have been granted walls and roof. He had to maintain his title himself under private law, mine is under public protection by all magistrates. If I had gained these privileges for myself or received them at hands other than yours, I should not be parading them in
+ front of you, for fear of appearing vainglorious. But the house you have given me is under attack by the tongue of the person whose hand earlier demolished it, only to be restored by *your* hands to me and my children. I am speaking of your actions, not mine, and have no fear that this my public acknowledgment of

---

Shackleton Bailey on *Fam.* 7.30.2.
23. The Consuls.
24. Poplicola, Consul in 509 and later.

your benefaction will be taken for arrogance rather than for gratitude.

[17] And yet who would not pardon me if, after the ordeals I have passed through for the common good, I were occasionally betrayed into boasting by a feeling of indignation when I rebut the calumnies of rascals? I observed a certain person murmuring yesterday. They told me that he was saying that I had become unbearable, because of a reply that I gave to this same foul traitor when he asked me what community I belonged to:[25] "one," I said, "which could not do without me." You and the Roman Knights approved my answer. He, I imagine, groaned. Well, what was I to say? I am putting the question to *him*, the gentleman who finds me unbearable. That I am a citizen of Rome? That would not have been a very sophisticated[26] retort. Or should I have said nothing? That would have let the matter go by default. Is it possible for anyone who has engaged in great affairs and attracted unpopularity to make a sufficiently impressive answer to an enemy's insults without self-praise? As for Clodius, not only does he make any reply he can when challenged, he is glad to be told what to say by his friends.[27]

[18] My case is made out. Now let us see what the haruspices are saying. I admit that I was gravely disturbed by the alarming nature of the phenomenon, the gravity of the response, and the unanimous and consistent voice of the haruspices. Perhaps I may seem to some a closer student of books than other people who have as much to do as I have; but that is not to say that I am apt to take pleasure in writings that deter and detach our minds from religion, or even to read them at all. Our forebears tell me to practice our religion and teach me how. I have so high an opinion of their wisdom that I consider any who, I won't say attain to it, but who appreciate it at its proper worth to be wise enough, and more than enough. Fixed and established ceremonies, so they held, are the province of the Pontiffs. For the proper

---

25. Implying that he was still an exile.
26. *Litterate*, taken as virtually equivalent to *docte*, "cleverly"; so SB[1], 268.
27. Apparently implying that Clodius could think of nothing good to say about himself.

conduct of business we have the Augurs, for ancient oracular prophecies the books of Apollo's seers,[28] for the expiation of portents the system of the Etruscans. This last has proved its validity in our own lifetime. They foretold the disastrous beginnings of the Italic War and later the well-nigh fatal crisis of the Sulla-Cinna epoch; later still they warned us, not long ago and in no obscure terms, of the recent plot[29] to burn Rome and destroy the empire.

[19] And then, if I had time to spare, I also got to know that wise and learned men had spoken much and left much in writing concerning the mysterious power of the Immortal Gods. These writings, I recognize, are most admirable productions; but they make us think that our forebears taught their authors rather than learned from them. After all, who is so mindless as not to feel that there are Gods when he looks up into the sky? Who could take for the work of chance all those phenomena which proceed by so mighty a power of intellect that scarcely anyone by exercise of any skill can keep track of their sequence and necessary course? Or who, realizing that the Gods exist, could fail to realize that this great empire of ours was created and augmented and retained by their power? However highly we might like to think of ourselves, Members of the Senate, we are not more numerous than the Spaniards nor physically stronger than the Gauls nor more cunning than the Carthaginians; we do not excel the Greeks in the arts nor the Italians themselves and the Latins in that home-grown, native good sense proper to this people and this land. It is in piety and religion and this one form of wisdom which consists of perceiving that all things are ruled and guided by divine power that we Romans have surpassed all other peoples and nations.[30]

[20] Not to dwell further, then, on a matter so plain, let me ask you to pay close attention and direct your minds as well as your ears to the words of the haruspices. "Whereas in the Ager

---

28. The Sibylline books of prophecies, kept by a priesthood of fifteen members, Clodius being one; cf. s. 26. The original books had been destroyed by fire in 83, but others were assembled to replace them.

29. Catiline's in 63.

30. Similarly Horace (*Odes* 3.6.9): *dis te minorem quod geris, imperas* ("because you walk humbly with the Gods, you rule").

Latiniensis a loud noise and a clashing has been heard,"—let us forget the haruspices, forget that ancient system delivered to Etruria by the Immortal Gods themselves, as men say. Can we not be our own haruspices? In an area quite close to Rome a hidden noise and a dreadful clashing of arms was heard. Poets tell us that the giants made war upon the Gods. Which of those giants would be so irreligious as not to acknowledge that so strange and mighty a disturbance is a sign from heaven, portending and fortelling some great event to the Roman People? On that, the text runs: "Expiations are due to Jupiter, Saturn, Neptune, Tellus, and the heavenly Gods."[31] [21] That tells me which deities have been offended, to whom expiation is due, but not the human transgressions on account of which it is due. "Games carelessly celebrated and profaned." Which games? I appeal to you, Lentulus—your priestly office[32] is concerned with the sacred cars, the races, the preliminary chant, the games, the libations and the banquets of the games—and to you, Pontiffs, to whom the Banqueters of Jupiter Best and Greatest report any impropriety, whether of omission or of commission, so that by your ordinance those same proceedings may be enacted anew—what games were carelessly celebrated, when were they profaned and by what offense? You will reply on behalf of yourself and your colleagues, also on behalf of the College of Pontiffs, that nothing took place in the way of negligent disregard or criminal profanation and that all the hallowed ritual of the games was observed with the utmost ceremony in every detail.

[22] Which then were the games that, according to the haruspices, were carelessly celebrated and profaned? Those at which the Immortal Gods themselves and the Mother from Mount Ida ordained that you, Gnaeus Lentulus, whose ancestor's[33] hands

---

31. After Jupiter come three non-heavenly deities: Saturn, (identified with Kronos, ruler of the Titans), Neptune (sea), and Tellus (earth).

32. That of the *septemviri epulones* (seven banqueters). They were particularly responsible for the *epulum Iovis* (banquet of Jupiter) at the Roman and Plebeian Games, held in September and November, and apparently for the ritual correctness of the celebrations as a whole.

33. P. Cornelius Scipio Nasica, commissioned to bring the image of Cybele (the Great Mother) from Pessinus to Rome in 204.

welcomed her to Rome, should be a spectator. If you had not chosen to attend the Megalesian games that day, I doubt whether we should be alive now to deplore what occurred. A countless host of incited slaves, got together by our devout Aedile[34] from every street in Rome, was at a signal suddenly let loose from every archway and doorway and burst onto the stage. Then it was that you showed your courage, Gnaeus Lentulus, the same courage that your great-grandfather[35] once showed as a private citizen. The Senate, the Roman Knights, and all honest men rose and followed you—followed your name, your authority, your voice, your aspect, and your dash—after *he* had handed over the Senate and People of Rome, penned up as they were on the packed benches, hampered by the crowd and the narrow quarters, to a mob of jeering slaves.

[23] Now if a dancer[36] stops dancing, or a flutist suddenly stops playing, if the boy whose father and mother are alive loses control of the chariot or lets the reins slip, if the Aedile makes a mistake in his words or in handling the chalice, the games are improperly celebrated, the errors are expiated, and the Immortal Gods are appeased by a reenactment of the games. But suppose fear is set in the place of enjoyment, suppose the games are not interrupted but totally cancelled, suppose those festal days almost become funeral days for the entire community by the criminal action of one who chose to put sport into mourning—shall we have any doubt which games that noise declares to have been profaned?

[24] If we care to remember what tradition tells us about various deities, this Great Mother, whose games were violated and profaned and almost converted into a massacre and ruin of our community—this Goddess, we are told, traverses the fields and woodlands with a rattling and a rumbling.[37] She, therefore, and none other, let you and the Roman People know that a crime had been committed and showed us a danger signal.

---

34. As Curule Aedile, Clodius had charge of the Megalesia, held in April.
35. P. Cornelius Scipio Nasica Serapio, who led the murderous attack on Ti. Gracchus in 133.
36. *Ludius*, who danced to the flute in the preliminary procession.
37. Or, as Lenaghan suggests, the Latin terms may refer to the roaring of Cybele's lions and the wild music of her followers.

\+ Concerning those games, need I recall that our forebears ordained they should take place and be celebrated on the Palatine opposite the temple of the Great Mother, in her sight, at her festival? The usages and institutions attached to them make them especially holy, solemn, and sacred. It was at these games that Publius Africanus the Elder, as Consul for the second time, first gave the Senate seats in front of the body of the spectators[38] —only for this filthy pest to profane them! Free men who came to watch, or even for religious reasons, could expect to be manhandled. No married woman attended because of the slaves who crowded the benches. So those games, a ceremony so sacred that it was fetched from the ends of the earth to be located in this city, the only games even the name of which is not Latin, announcing in the very word a cult we sought from abroad and adopted in the name of the Great Mother—these games were celebrated by slaves, watched by slaves; in short, with *him* as Aedile, the whole Megalesia belonged to slaves.

[25] Immortal Gods! How could you speak to us better if you were with us, walking in our midst? You have told us that games were profaned, you say so plainly. Could there be any worse defilement, disfigurement, perversion, confusion than this—the entire slave population freed by a magistrate's permission, let loose onto one stage and put in control of the other,[39] so that one body of spectators was at the slaves' mercy, the other entirely made up of them? If a swarm of bees had invaded the stage or the auditorium at the games, we should feel obliged to call in haruspices from Etruria. Now we all see vast swarms of slaves let loose on a fenced-in, cooped-up Roman People, and we think it of no consequence? If there *had* been a swarm of bees, it may be that the haruspices would have warned us out of their Etruscan books against a slave rising. [26] We should have guarded against the danger if it had been foreshadowed by a separate, different portent, but now that it portends itself, now that the danger lies in

---

38. A fragment quoted by Asconius (69 Clark) from the lost speech *Pro Cornelio* says that Scipio as Consul in 194 merely allowed this to be done.

39. "What is meant by the two *caveae* or the two *scaenae* [auditoria and stages] is an utter mystery" (Lenaghan).

the very manifestation which heralds the danger, have we no fear? Did your father celebrate the Megalesia in such a fashion? Did your uncle?[40] Does he actually talk to me of his family, after preferring to celebrate his games in the manner of Athenio or Spartacus, rather than of Gaius or Appius Claudius? When *they* celebrated games, they ordered slaves to leave the auditorium: *you* sent slaves into one auditorium and ejected free men from the other. Thus at your games, the slaves, who once used to be moved away from the free men by the voice of a crier, segregated the free men from themselves, not by voice but by main force.

Did it not enter your mind, as a priest of the Sibyl,[41] that our forebears were prompted to seek those rites by the books of your College—if I can so call the books which you research with your blasphemous heart, read with your profaned eyes, touch with your contaminated hands? [27] Once upon a time, when Italy was exhausted by the Punic War and harried by Hannibal, at the behest of this seeress[42] our forebears adopted these rites from Phrygia and established them in Rome. They were received by a man who was judged to be the best of the Romans, Publius Scipio, and by a woman who was accounted the most chaste of matrons,
+ Quinta Claudia—your sister has the reputation of imitating her old-time austerity to an astonishing degree. Neither the connection of your ancestors with these observances nor the priestly function itself, through which this whole cult was constituted, nor the office of Curule Aedile, which normally has this cult under its special care, prevented you from profaning those most holy games with all manner of outrage, defiling them with turpitude, involving them in crime. [28] But that should not surprise me. For a bribe you sacked the very domicile of the Mother of the Gods, Pessinus itself, and sold the whole area and shrine to an infamous scoundrel, Brogitarus the Gallogreek, whose envoys used to distribute cash among your gang in the temple of Castor when you were Tribune. You sold the whole place and shrine, you dragged the priest from the very altar and sacred couch, and

---

40. C. Claudius Pulcher, Aedile in 99, gave a memorable show.
41. See p. 113, n. 28.
42. The Sibyl.

upset all those institutions to which ancient tradition, Persians, Syrians, and all monarchs ruling over Europe and Asia have ever paid the most scrupulous respect; which our own ancestors held in such reverence that in a Rome and Italy studded with shrines our generals made vows to this Goddess in the greatest and most dangerous wars and discharged them in Pessinus itself at the high altar in that very place and shrine. [29] Deiotarus, the most faithful ally our empire has in the world and the most attached to the name of Rome, was its devout worshipper and protector; but you handed it over to Brogitarus, sold it for money, as I have said. And yet you actually order that this same Deiotarus, whom the Senate has often deemed worthy of the royal title, who has been complimented by the tributes of our most illustrious commanders, be addressed as "king" along with Brogitarus. We have so addressed the former, following the decision of the Senate: *you* have so addressed the latter, following—money. * * * I shall consider the other a king the day he has the wherewithal to repay what you lent him on note of hand.[43] Deiotarus has shown himself a true king in many ways, but never more clearly than in this affair. He did not give you a penny. While not repudiating that part of your bill which accorded with the Senate's decision in pro-
+ viding that he be king, he regained control of Pessinus, which you had criminally violated and stripped of priest and holy things, to keep it in its former sanctity. He does not permit Brogitarus to profane the immemorial rituals and had rather that his son-in-law[44] lose your present than this shrine lose its time-honored religious character. However, to go back to these responses of the haruspices, in which the first item concerns games, I trust everyone will acknowledge the prophecy[45] and the response to be entirely directed at *Clodius'* games.

[30] Next we come to sacred, religious places. Astounding impudence! You dare to speak of my house? Ask the Consuls or the Senate or the College of Pontiffs to rule on yours. Mine has

---

43. In addition to money advanced by Clodius, the bond presumably covered a bribe to be paid out of Brogitarus' plunder; cf. *Dom.* 129.

44. Brogitarus.

45. I.e., the portent. Or should we read *praedicatum* (Courtney, *CR* 10 [1960], 97), "the declaration," for *praedictum?*

been cleared by rulings from all three, as I have already said. But in the house you occupy, after getting Quintus Seius, a Roman Knight of unblemished character, quite openly murdered, I assert
+ there was a chapel. I shall offer clear proof of it from censorial records and the memory of many individuals. Once this matter is
+ taken up (and under the Senate's recently passed decree, it must
+ necessarily be referred to us),[46] I have some things to say about religious places. [31] When I have dealt with your house, in which a chapel has been walled up (someone else[47] did that, true, you have only to demolish the masonry), I shall consider whether I must say a word about others. Some think it falls to me to open up the depository[48] of Tellus. They say it used to be out in the open until not long ago, and that is my own recollection. Now, they say, the holiest part of the temple, the most sacred place, is incorporated into a private vestibule. I have several reasons for concern here. The temple of Tellus is in my curatorship. The person[49] who did away with that depository used to declare, after my house had been cleared by the Pontiffs' ruling, that the ruling went in favor of his brother. Also, with the present high price of grain, bad harvests, crop shortages, I am concerned about the worship of Tellus, and all the more so because by the same portent an expiation is said to be due to that Goddess.

[32] Perhaps I am speaking of ancient history. To be sure, it is laid down by the law of nature and the common law of nations, even if not written into any civil statute, that mortals cannot acquire by prescription anything belonging to the Immortal Gods.
+ However, let us leave things of long ago aside. Shall we also leave aside what is going on at this very moment, before our very eyes? Everybody knows that only the other day Lucius Piso did away with a large and highly sacred chapel of Diana in the Caeliculus. Persons living in the neighborhood are present, and there are many in this House who have been in the habit of performing annual clan sacrifices at a prescribed spot in that very chapel.

---

46. Editors read *vos* ("you" pl.), but the manuscripts have *nos* ("us"), and Cicero speaks as a senator to senators. Cf. s. 11.
47. Seius or an earlier owner.
48. *Magmentarium*, a storeroom for meat left over from sacrifices.
49. Clodius' brother Appius; see E. Courtney, *CR* 10 (1960), 98–99.

And do we ask what places the Immortal Gods are claiming back, what they mean, what they are talking about? Are we unaware that very sacred chapels have been undermined, walled up, covered over, and worse, disgustingly befouled by Sextus Serranus?

[33] Could *you* make my house a religious place—with the mind you had lost, the hand with which you had torn it down, the voice with which you had ordered it set on fire, the law which you had not written even in your heyday of impunity,[50] the sacred couch which you had defiled,[51] and the statue taken from a harlot's tomb which you had placed in a general's monument?[52] What is there in the way of religious sanction about my house except that it abuts the wall of a foul doer of sacrilege? And so for fear that any of my people might accidentally look into *your* house
+ and see you at those rites[53] of yours, I shall raise my roof even higher than yours, not in order to look down on you, but to block your view of the city you wished to destroy.[54]

[34] However, let us look now at the remaining responses of the haruspices. "Envoys slain in violation of earthly and heavenly law." What does this mean? I hear talk of Alexandrians,[55] nor have I anything to say to the contrary. I recognize that the rights of ambassadors are not only fenced around by human protection, but also palisaded by divine ordinance. But I have a question to put to that personage who as Tribune discharged all the

---

50. Meaning that Clodius' law against Cicero contained no such provision. See p. 108, n. 14.

51. Apparently a reference to the Bona Dea affair (cf. ss. 8, 28).

52. Placed in the shrine of Liberty adjoining the rebuilt portico of Catulus, which that general had erected using the spoils of the Cimbric War (last decade of the second century). See *Dom.* 111-14.

53. Improper goings-on.

54. "It appears that from Cicero's house it was possible to see something of what went on in his neighbor's . . . and he announces his intention of putting a stop to this by raising the height of his own roof. It seems to follow that Clodius' house was the higher of the two, so that a person standing on Cicero's roof might find himself looking through Clodius' top-story windows. To obviate this Cicero would only need to raise his roof to nearly the same height as Clodius'. But he is going to raise it even higher in order to achieve the further object of blocking Clodius' view of Rome. This seems to call for *tollam <etiam> altius* (sc. *tuo tecto*)." (SB[1], 268).

55. The chief of a mission from Alexandria had recently been poisoned in Rome at the instigation of the exiled King Ptolemy XII.

informers from prison into the Forum, at whose discretion all operations of dagger and poison now take place, who made out notes of hand with Hermarchus of Chios: does he know that Hermarchus' bitterest opponent, Theodosius, an ambassador to the Senate sent by a free community, has been knifed?[56] I am sure the Immortal Gods were no less indignant on his account than on that of the Alexandrians. [35] Nor do I now lay everything at your door. The outlook would be rosier for us if you were the only infamous character around. There are others, a fact which adds to your self-confidence and brings us close to a justified pessimism. Everyone knows that Plator of Orestis, which is a free district of Macedonia, a distinguished nobleman in those parts, came to Thessalonica as envoy to our Imperator,[57] as he called himself. That worthy, having failed to extort money from Plator, flung him into prison and then sent his own physician to sever the veins of an ambassador, an ally, a friend, and a free man—a foul, cruel murder.[58] He did not want blood on his own axes,[59] but defiled the name of Rome with a crime that can be expiated only by his own punishment. What must his executioners be like, when he uses even his doctors not for saving life, but for taking it?

+ [36] But let us read out what follows: "Good faith and oath neglected." In itself I do not find this easy to interpret, but from what ensues I suspect it refers to the flagrant perjury of your jurors on that occasion when the cash would have been snatched out of their pockets if they had not asked the Senate for a body-
+ guard.[60] Another reason why I suspect this reference is to them is that, as I consider, it is the most notorious and conspicuous act of perjury in this community; also that you yourself are, after all, not

---

56. Nothing further is known about this.

57. L. Piso; cf. *Pis.* 83. He had been saluted *imperator* by his soldiers after an important victory won by his lieutenants; see R. G. M. Nisbet, *Cicero in Pisonem* (Oxford, 1961), p. 179.

58. According to *Pis.* 83 (delivered over a year later), Plator, in whose house Piso had been a guest, came to Thessalonica on Piso's orders with a safe conduct. Piso had him killed as described here in return for a bribe from the people of Dyrrachium. Of his mission mentioned here, nothing is known.

59. See Glossary of Terms under *fasces*.

60. Cicero adapts a witticism of Q. Catulus about the corrupt jury in Clodius' trial for sacrilege; see *Att.* 1.16.10.

being called to answer a charge of perjury by those with whom you swore a conspiratorial oath.[61]

[37] And I observe that the following is subjoined in the response of the haruspices: "Ancient and secret sacrifices carelessly performed and profaned." Are these the words of haruspices or of the ancestral household Gods of Rome? There are many, no doubt, who might be suspected of such a misdeed? Who but this one individual? The language identifying the violated rites is obscure? How could anything be put more plainly, more scrupulously, more emphatically? "Ancient and secret." I declare that your prosecutor Lentulus,[62] an impressive and eloquent speaker, used no words more often than these, which are now uttered out of the books of Etruria, turned and interpreted against you. For what sacrifice is as ancient as this one, which came to us from the kings, coeval with this city? And what so secret as this, which excludes not merely the eye of curiosity but even a stray glance, into which error may not enter, let alone deliberate sin? Through all the centuries no one ever violated that sacrifice before Publius Clodius, no one ever approached it, no one made light of it, none of our sex but would have shuddered to behold it. It is performed by the Vestal Virgins, on behalf of the Roman People, in the house of a high magistrate, with a most elaborate ritual, to a Goddess whose very name no man may know. Clodius calls her "Good," in the persuasion that she pardoned his heinous offense. Ah, but believe me, she has *not* pardoned you. Perhaps you think you were pardoned because the jury let you go, relieved of every penny you had about you, found innocent by their verdict but guilty in the sight of all; or because you have not lost your eyesight, according to the cult belief. [38] But since no man before you had ever wittingly seen these rites, how would anybody know what punishment followed upon that crime? Would blindness of sight be worse for you than

---

61. A rather clumsy sarcasm. Clodius had perjured himself at the trial, but he had kept his word to the jurors whom he bribed, so to that extent "oath neglected" did not point his way.

62. L. Cornelius Lentulus Crus, Consul in 49.

blindness of lust? Don't you realize that your ancestor's[63] blinking eyes were better than your sister's lamps?[64] If you look closely, you will perceive that human retribution is still to come, yes, but the Gods have already punished you. *Men* defended you in a most ugly affair, men commended[65] you, disgraced and guilty as you were, men acquitted you in court when you almost confessed your offense, men did not resent the injury which they themselves suffered from your immorality,[66] some men put arms into your hands for use against me, others for use against our invincible fellow countryman.[67] I freely concede that you could not wish for greater boons than those which *men* have granted you. [39] But the Gods? What greater punishment can they inflict upon a human being than mental derangement, insanity? Or do you imagine that the characters in tragedies whom you see tortured and consumed by the pain of bodily wounds suffer the wrath of the Immortal Gods in a more horrible form than those who are brought upon the stage mad? The howls and groans of Philoctetes,[68] terrible as they are, are not so lamentable as the exultation of Athamas and the black moods of the matricides.[69] When you utter wild, whirling words at meetings, when you overturn the houses of fellow citizens, when you drive men of good will from the Forum with stones, when you hurl blazing brands into the dwellings of your neighbors,[70] when you set fire to sacred edifices, when you stir up the slaves, when you throw sacred ceremonies and games into turmoil, when you make no distinction between wife and sister, when you don't know which bedroom you are walking into: then you are raving mad, then you suffer the only

---

63. See p. 83, n. 148.
64. Clodia (wife of Q. Metellus Celer) had notably large, lustrous eyes (cf. *Cael.* 49), whence (partly) Cicero's nickname for her "Ox-eyes" (Boōpis, Homeric epithet of Hera).
65. I.e., gave witness to character in court (*laudatio*). This could be done in person or in writing.
66. Again alluding to Caesar and Caesar's wife.
67. Pompey.
68. In Sophocles' play of that name.
69. Orestes and Alcmaeon. All these legendary figures were the subject of tragedies by Sophocles and others.
70. I.e., Cicero himself.

punishment ordained by the Immortal Gods for human crime.

[40] But enough said about the various transgressions mentioned by the haruspices. Let us see what warning according to the same haruspices is now being conveyed by the Immortal Gods. They warn us, "Lest through discord and dissension among the optimates slaughter and danger be created for Senate and leaders, and they be bereft of divine help, whereby power may pass into the hands of one man and * * *.[71] These are the haruspices' words, every one; I add nothing of my own. Well, then, who is sowing dissension among the optimates? That same personage, not by dint of his own wit and policy, but because of a mistake on our part, which he easily perceived since it was sufficiently obvious. The sad plight of the Commonwealth is the more ignominious because of the character of her oppressor. She will not even seem to fall honorably, like a brave fighter wounded face to face by a brave opponent. [41] Tiberius Gracchus tore the community from its moorings; a man of serious purpose, a man of eloquence, a man of high standing. He would in no respect have fallen away from the eminent, exceptional qualities of his father and his grandfather Africanus but that he had parted company with the Senate. Gaius Gracchus followed: what intellect, what eloquence, what oratorical force and weight! Honest men grieved that such fine attributes were not put at the service of a better mind and purpose. Even Saturninus, ungovernable and half insane as he was, excelled as a pleader and was a past master at stirring up and inflaming ignorant minds.[72] And then, Sulpicius! So impressive an orator, so enjoyable, so fluent that he could lead the wise astray and shake the loyalty of the loyal. Those who guided the Commonwealth certainly did not enjoy clashing with these men and fighting every day for their country's good; but at least that irksome duty was not humiliating.

[42] But this fellow, of whom I myself am now speaking at such length—great heavens! What is he, what is he worth, what does he bring which could let us feel that, if our great community falls (which heaven forfend!), at least its destroyer is a man? After his

---

71. Text corrupt.
72. See Index I under Appuleius Saturninus.

father died, he put his tender young self at the service of wealthy men-about-town. When he had sated their intemperate desires, he wallowed in domestic vice with his nearest relations. A grown man, he went soldiering in the provinces, where he suffered the indignities of pirates,[73] satisfying the lusts of Cilicians and barbarians. Next, after most villainously tampering with the loyalty of Lucius Lucullus'[74] troops, he fled back to Rome and shortly after arrival struck a bargain with his kinsfolk not to put them in court and took a bribe from Catiline in return for a scandalous collusion.[75] From Rome he betook himself to Gaul with Murena.[76] In that province he forged dead men's wills, killed off minors, cooked up many nefarious bargains and partnerships in crime. Back in Rome once more, he monopolized a particularly rich source of profit, electoral corruption. So we find this people's man unscrupulously defrauding the people, this pattern of humanity brutally slaughtering the distributing agents of the various tribes in his own house.[77]

[43] Then came the Quaestorship, fraught with disaster for the Commonwealth, for rites and cults, for your collective authority and the public courts, in which he went on to outrage Gods and men, decency and chastity, the Senate's authority, human and divine law, statutes and courts. This step on the ladder, thanks to the wretched times and our stupid dissensions—this was the first step to political influence for Publius Clodius; his feet were now set on the upward path to demagogy. Tiberius Gracchus was hurt and frightened by the scandal of the Treaty of Numantia, to the signing of which he was a party as Quaestor to Consul Gaius Mancinus, and the Senate's stern disapproval of that treaty.[78] It was that circumstance which made that courageous and distinguished
+ man fall away from his father's high principles. A brother's death,

---

73. He was captured in 67 while serving in the fleet of his brother-in-law Q. Marcius Rex, governor of Cilicia.

74. Another brother-in-law. Clodius was on his staff in the East in 68–67 (Cicero inverts the order of events).

75. Cicero refers to this in a contemporary letter (*Att.* 1.2.1).

76. Governor of Narbonese Gaul in 64–63.

77. Presumably diverting to his own pocket the money which he was to have given them for the benefit of the candidates. This looks like a wild accusation.

78. See Index I under "Hostilius."

family affection, indignation, and a noble heart spurred Gaius Gracchus to avenge the blood of his house. We know that resentment made a people's man of Saturninus, because when he was Quaestor the Senate removed him from his charge of grain supplies during a shortage and gave it to Marcus Scaurus. Sulpicius' starting point was highly commendable: he opposed Gaius Julius' illegal candidature for the consulship. But the breeze of popularity carried him further than he wished to go. [44] Each of them
+ had a reason—not, indeed, a valid reason, for no reason for doing the Commonwealth disservice can ever be valid; but still a serious reason conjoined with the resentment of a manly spirit. But Publius Clodius—emerging from his saffron robe, his turban, his ladies' slippers and purple leg ribbons, his brassiere and lute,[79] his act of gross immorality, all of a sudden he became a people's man. If the women had not caught him so attired, and if by the courtesy of the slave girls he had not been let out of the place which he had no right to be in, the Roman People would not have their people's man nor the Commonwealth such a citizen.

Because of this act of madness, amid those very dissensions concerning which we are warned by the Immortal Gods in these recent portents, Clodius was snatched up to be the only patrician
+ eligible for the tribunate. [45] In the previous year his brother[80]
+ Metellus and a still united Senate, with Gnaeus Pompeius opening the debate, had ruled the thing out, hotly opposing it with one voice and one mind. But after that very split among the optimates on which we are now being warned, came confusion and reversal. What his brother as Consul had opposed, what his friend and marriage-connection[81] (that illustrious personage, who had *not* testified to his character at his trial) had ruled out, was accomplished amid the dissensions of our leaders by a Consul who ought to have been his mortal enemy;[82] and that Consul claimed to have acted on the prompting of one whom any man would be

---

79. All part of Clodius' disguise at the Bona Dea ceremony.
80. Metellus Celer, half-brother to Clodius and husband of Clodius' half-sister; cf. *AJAH* 2 (1977), 148f.
81. Pompey, whose former wife Mucia was half-sister to Clodius.
82. Another allusion to Clodius' affair with Caesar's wife.

proud to have as his prompter.[83] A lurid, sinister firebrand[84] was cast upon the Commonwealth, aimed at your authority, the dignity of our highest orders, the union of all honest men, in fact, the whole fabric of our society. For assuredly these *were* the targets, when the blazing torch of those days was thrown at me, their accredited defender. I let it come. I alone took the fire, for my country's sake. But the same flames surrounded you as you saw me, the first victim, struck and burning[85] on your behalf.

[46] The dissensions did not abate; indeed, the hatred among those who were thought to be defending me[86] grew even more intense. But then, at the instigation of the same persons, with Pompeius in the lead, I was restored. With his authority and even his entreaties he stirred up Italy, yourselves, and the Roman People for my recall. Italy was eager for it, you demanded it, the Roman People longed for it.

Let there at last be an end to strife. Let us rest from our protracted quarrels. That pest there will not hear of it. With his harangues, his agitation and troublemaking he tries to ingratiate himself with this group or that. It's not that anyone whom *he* praises feels flattered, but it makes them happy when he abuses people they dislike. I am not surprised at Clodius. What else is he to do? But I am surprised at those wise and weighty persons.[87] It surprises me that they are well satisfied to see any famous man,[88] who has often deserved excellently of the Commonwealth, assailed by the voice of a miscreant. It surprises me if they think any man's glory and dignity *can* be assailed by the vituperation of a ruined rascal (it would be by no means to their own advantage if such a thing were possible). Finally, it surprises me that they do not realize (though I fancy they already suspect) that his crazy, flighty aggressions could be turned against themselves. [47]

---

83. Pompey, as Augur in the adoption proceedings.
84. Clodius' adoption and consequent tribunate.
85. Lit., "smoking."
86. Pompey and the optimates. The manuscripts say "hatred against those," which makes nonsense.
87. Cicero never mentions them publicly by name. Certain leading nobles, especially L. Lucullus and Bibulus, were bitterly hostile to Pompey and so welcomed Clodius' attacks against him.
88. Pompey is in mind.

Through this unfortunate estrangement of certain persons from certain other persons,[89] darts are fixed in the flesh of the body politic, the same darts which used to stick in mine alone and which during that time I bore with difficulty, true, but somewhat more easily than now. He could never have persecuted me so cruelly and the Commonwealth so criminally if he had not first put himself at the service of those whom he thought to be averse to your authority, praised them to the sky with his flatteries (a fine encomiast!), threatened to bring Gaius Caesar's army (oh, it was an empty threat, but nobody gainsaid him)—bring that army, I say, with standards erect into the Senate-House, if he had not clamored that what he was doing was done with the aid of Gnaeus Pompeius and the backing of Marcus Crassus, and if he had not asseverated that the Consuls had made common cause with him—the one point on which he was not lying. [48] But later on, when he saw you beginning to breath again from your fear of massacre, saw your authority emerging from waves of servitude and recollection of me and desire to have me back reviving, he suddenly started to pay his hypocritical court to you.[90] Both here and at public meetings he said the Julian laws had been passed contrary to auspices—which included the curiate law[91] on which his whole tribunate was based, but he was too blinded by frenzy to
+ notice that. He used to bring forward Marcus Bibulus, that courageous gentleman, and inquire of him whether he had always been watching the heavens when Gaius Caesar passed his laws.[92] Bibulus would reply that he always had. Clodius would ask the Augurs whether legislation so passed had been properly passed. They would reply that such legislation was procedurally flawed. Certain honest gentlemen, to whom I am greatly indebted, but who, I imagine, were unaware of his insanity, used to make much of him. He went further still. He began to rail against Gnaeus Pompeius himself, the prompter of his own proceedings, as he used to

---

89. The optimates from Pompey.
90. With what follows cf. *Dom.* 40.
91. Sanctioning Clodius' adoption.
92. See Index I under "Calpurnius Bibulus." Bibulus' announcements of bad omens legally invalidated Caesar's legislation in 59, but Caesar took no notice; see p. 55, n. 52.

proclaim. That brought him favor in some quarters. [49] At that point he let himself hope that, having wickedly and feloniously savaged the civilian suppressor of domestic war,[93] he could bring down Pompeius too, the conqueror of Rome's enemies in wars abroad. Then it was that in the temple of Castor the nefarious dagger[94] which so nearly destroyed this empire was discovered; and the soldier against whom no hostile town was ever barred for long, who always broke through every obstacle by might and valor, however narrow the breach or high the wall, was besieged in his own house. What he saw fit to do cleared me of the imputation of cowardice cast by the ignorant. Gnaeus Pompeius, the bravest man ever born, did not see the sunlight so long as Clodius remained Tribune, never went out in public, put up with his threats, as when Clodius declared in public speeches that he would like to build a second portico in Carinae to match the Palatine.[95] If Pompeius' conduct evoked commiseration rather than contempt, then surely *my* leaving my house, however grievous in respect of private sorrow, was politically a thing to be proud of.

[50] You see this individual, therefore, long since an abject figure in himself, raised up from the dust by the mischievous quarrels of the optimates, whereas initially his crazy notions fed on the dissident policies of those who, at that time, seemed estranged from you.[96] In the remainder of his tribunate, now plunging to its close, and even after he went out of office, he found champions in *their* detractors and adversaries. They resisted the removal of this scourge of the Commonwealth, even his being brought to trial, even his remaining a private citizen. Could certain excellent persons actually cherish this poisonous, pestilent serpent in their bosoms and make a pet of him? What did he have to offer that could lure them? "I want there to be somebody on a platform to take Pompeius down a peg"—that is how they talk. Clodius take

---

93. Cicero himself, as having suppressed the Catilinarian uprising in 63.
94. To be used to assassinate Pompey (*Mil.* 37, etc.).
95. Pompey's town house was in Carinae. On Clodius' Palatine portico, see *Dom.* 103.
96. In the second part of the sentence, the Senate ("you") is distinguished from the "Triumvirs." In the first, Pompey, at least, is regarded as an optimate at variance with other optimates.

Pompeius down by abusing him? I hope the great man, who did so much for my restoration, will take this as I say it, at any rate I shall speak as I feel: upon my word, I thought Clodius was taking Pompeius' lofty prestige down a peg when he showered fulsome praise on him. [51] Did Gaius Marius' reputation shine more brightly when Gaius Glaucia was belauding him or subsequently when Glaucia angrily assailed him?[97] Did that madman, who had long since started on his headlong course to retribution and destruction, denounce Pompeius in fouler, more vulgar terms than he employed to vilify the entire Senate? It surprises me that such good citizens find the former activity so gratifying to their resentments that the latter does not distress them.

But these excellent persons must bid good-bye to that source of delectation when they read the speech I am talking about. In it he compliments Pompeius—or denigrates him? At all events, he sings his praises, he says he is the one man in our community worthy of Rome's imperial glory, professes the warmest regard for him and says they have made up their differences. [52] Well, I don't know about that, but I am clear about one thing: if he had really been a friend of Pompeius, he would not have praised him. For had he been Pompeius' bitterest enemy, what more could he have done to damage his reputation? Let those who rejoiced to see him Pompeius' enemy and for that reason turned a blind eye to all his abominable crimes, sometimes actually applauding his reckless, unbridled outbursts—let them see how quickly he has turned round. He is now praising Pompeius and inveighing against the people he used to court. What do you think he will do if a door to a reconciliation actually opens, when he is so ready to creep into the mere notion of one?

[53] What other "dissensions among the optimates" am I to suppose the Immortal Gods are indicating? Neither Publius Clodius nor any of his cronies and counsellors is designated by this word. The books of Etruria have certain terms, as you will shortly hear, which can apply to *that* category of citizens: they call persons whose minds and fortunes are ruined and quite alienated from

---

97. In his sixth consulship (100 B.C.), Marius turned against his "popular" allies, led by Saturninus and Glaucia.

the general welfare "the worser sort," "the rejected." So when the Immortal Gods warn of strife among optimates, they mean dissensions among our most illustrious and deserving citizens. When they portend danger and slaughter to leaders, they place Clodius out of harm's way, for he has as little to do with leadership as with
+ purity or religion. [54] It is you, my illustrious and excellent fellow countrymen, and your safety that they see in need of care and foresight. Slaughter of leaders is presaged. Then follows the inevitable sequel to a destruction of the optimates: we are warned lest power come into the hands of one man. If the divine warnings were not leading us in that direction, our own common sense and powers of inference would sweep us into such a fear. For when the famous and powerful fall out among themselves, it usually ends in one of two ways: universal destruction or the monarchical dominance of the victor. Lucius Sulla, a high-born and valorous
+ Consul, quarreled with the illustrious Gaius Marius. Each was defeated, and each in turn won the day and ruled. Cinna fell out with his colleague Octavius. Fortune, when kind, bestowed monarchical power on both; turned hostile, she gave them death. Sulla prevailed a second time. Then beyond any question he possessed monarchical power, though he had restored the Commonwealth.

[55] At the present time, there is a fund of only too evident ill-feeling, deeply engrained, seared in the minds of great men. Leaders are at loggerheads; hands are clutching at opportunity. Those not so strong in resources wait for some turn of fortune and circumstance, while others,[98] undoubtedly more powerful, are perhaps sometimes apprehensive of what their enemies are planning or may say in the Senate. Only let this strife be eliminated from the community, then all these portended fears will be extinguished and that viper, which now lurks in one quarter, now puts forth its head and moves to another, will be finally crushed to death.

+ The Gods also warn "lest harm come to the Commonwealth by occult designs." What designs are more occult than those of Clodius, who dared to say at a public meeting that we ought to declare a public holiday, adjourn the administration of justice,

---

98. Primarily, at any rate, Pompey.

close the Treasury, put the law courts out of action? You can hardly suppose that this idea of throwing the community into chaos could occur to him on the spur of the moment, as he stood in meditation on the Rostra. No doubt he is submerged in drink, debauchery, and somnolence, no doubt he is rash and reckless to the point of lunacy; but that holiday was pondered and prepared in the night watches, by a bunch of conspirators to boot. Remember, Members of the Senate, that our ears have been tested by this wicked word. We are now accustomed to the sound of it, and the road to mischief has been paved.

[56] Then we have: "Lest further honor accrue to the worser sort and the rejected." Let us see about "the rejected"—I shall show later on who are meant by "the worser sort," (it must be granted, however, that the phrase best suits one who is without question the worst of mankind). Who, then, are the rejected? Not, I think, candidates for office who have at some time or other lost an election by the fault of the community, not their own. That has happened to many of its best and most respected members. No, the rejected are those who have been repulsed, not only by strangers, but by their own folk, neighbors and fellow tribesmen, both city and country,[99] after going to all lengths, putting on illegal gladiator shows,[100] and practicing bare-faced bribery. It is they to whom the warning "lest further honor accrue" applies. We ought to be grateful for it, but in fact the Roman People provided against this threat on its own initiative, without any admonition from the haruspices. [57] "Beware of the worser sort." They are a numerous tribe,[101] to be sure, but Clodius is the captain and chief of them all. If a highly talented playwright wished to bring upon the stage a character stained with all the vices his imagination could muster, the last word in wickedness, he could surely find no infamy which Clodius does not share and he would overlook many that stick fast in the very core of him.

Nature attaches us first and foremost to our parents, to the

---

99. The four city and thirty-one country tribes.
100. Cf. *Sest.* 133–35.
101. A reference to Vatinius' phrase *natio optimatium* ("tribe of optimates")? Cf. *Sest.* 96, 132.

Immortal Gods, and to our country. At one and the same time we are welcomed into the light of day, grow with the breath of heaven, and are enrolled as members in a particular location of
+ citizenship and liberty.[102] Clodius smothered his paternal name,[103] hereditary rites, memory, and clan with the name of Fonteius. As for the Gods, he vitiated by an inexpiable crime their sacred fires, thrones, tables, hidden and interior hearths, occult ceremonies closed to the eye and even the ear of man. In the same spirit he set fire to the temple of the Goddesses who aid us against other fires.[104] [58] As for country, by armed violence and threats he drove from Rome a citizen whom you on many occa-
+ sions have declared the country's preserver, depriving him of all the protections the country could extend. Then, after overthrowing the Senate's fellow worker (that has always been *my* term; Clodius used to say "leader"), he subverted the Senate itself, the prime author of public welfare and public will, by violence, murder, and arson. He rescinded two most salutary laws, the Aelian and Fufian,[105] abolished the censorship, removed the right of veto, wiped out the auspices, armed the Consuls (his partners in crime) with the Treasury and provinces and armies, sold existing kings and proclaimed new ones, forced Gnaeus Pompeius into his house by armed force, overturned the monuments of generals, demolished his enemies' houses, and inscribed his name on your monuments. There is no limit to the crimes he has committed against his country. What of the individual citizens whose lives he has taken, the provincials he has plundered, the generals he has betrayed, the armies he has tampered with? [59] But then again, what crimes he has committed against himself and his family! No man ever had less mercy on an enemy camp than Clodius on any

---

102. I.e., become members of a particular free community.
103. In fact, Clodius did not change his name.
104. The Nymphs (water deities); cf. *Mil.* 73. J. Ramsey points out that their shrine was a repository for census records, the destruction of which gave opportunities for vote fraud. He refers also to C. Nicolet's suggestion (*The World of the Citizen in Republican Rome*, p. 199) that Clodius' express purpose was to destroy new lists, drawn up in 57 by Pompey as *curator annonae* (superintendent of the supply of grain to Rome), which excluded persons who had benefited under Clodius' grain distribution law of 58 (see *Sest.* 55).
105. See p. 10, n. 29.

part of his body. No public ferryboat was ever so open to all comers as Clodius' youthful bloom. No wastrel rolled so wantonly with his whores as Clodius with his sisters. The fancy of poets describes Charybdis and Scylla. But could they invent a Charybdis of such monstrous voracity as to compare with Clodius' engulfings of his Byzantine and Brogitarian plunder? Were Scylla's dogs so prominent and hungry as the dogs with whom you see him gnawing the
+ very Rostra[106]—a Gellius, a Cloelius, a Titius?

[60] Therefore, in the concluding words of the haruspices' response, take heed "lest the constitution of the Commonwealth be changed." Our society has already been shaken. It will not be easy, even if we prop up the fabric on all sides, no, it will not be easy to keep it together, resting on the shoulders of us all. This community of ours was once so steady and sturdy that it could tolerate senatorial negligence or even individual outrage. Not any more. The Treasury is gone, the tax-farmers do not get what they paid for,[107] the authority of our leaders has collapsed, the consensus of classes has been torn apart, the law courts are defunct, the voting tablets are kept by a small group,[108] the support of honest men will no longer be ready at a nod from our House, in future you will look in vain for anybody to confront unpopularity for the country's sake.[109] [61] So we cannot keep the constitution in its present shape, whatever may be thought of that, by any means but one—concord. Any *improvement* in our condition is past praying for, so long as Clodius goes scot-free. If it is to deteriorate, we can only fall one stage lower: either to destruction or slavery. The Immortal Gods are warning us lest we be thrust into that abyss, since human counsels have long since failed.

Members of the Senate, I should not have addressed you with words so somber and grave—not but that I should and could sustain such a character and role, given the honors of the Roman

---

106. A play on words, alluding to the beaks (*rostra*; see Glossary of Terms) of the ships from which Scylla seized her victims. Cf. *Att.* 6.3.6 "a certain Gavius . . . one of Clodius' dogs."

107. Allusion to Syria, where Gabinius was curbing the tax-farmers; cf. s 1.

108. Who would thus rig the voting in the assemblies; cf. *Att.* 1.14.5., "the voting tablets were distributed without any 'ayes'."

109. After what had happened to Cicero; cf. *Sest.* 1.

People and the many compliments you have paid me; all the same, I could easily have held my peace, while others held theirs. But all I have been saying is not my own advice, it is the voice of public religion. The words have been mine for the most part, but all they signify is from the haruspices. Either portents announced to us should not be referred to them, or we must needs take serious notice of their responses. [62] We have often paid heed to comparatively commonplace and trivial signs: surely the very voice of the Immortal Gods will deeply impress the minds of all. On the stage you often see a God descend from the sky to approach a gathering of us mortals, to move about the earth, and talk with human beings, but don't imagine that such things can happen in real life.

Ponder the nature of the sound reported by the Latinienses. Remember also something else that has not yet been referred to
+ us. A fearful earthquake accompanied by many specified alarming phenomena is reported as occurring about the same time at Potentia in Picenum. Hence you will surely dread the same impending calamities that I foresee. [63] For when the very world, the fields, the countryside tremble with strange movement and presage some event with a sound hitherto unheard-of, undreamed-of, this has to be considered the voice of the Immortal Gods, almost their spoken words. We must ordain rites of expiation and propitiation, as we are admonished. But prayers to those who freely show us the path to salvation are easy. It is for us among ourselves to allay our resentments and dissensions.

IN DEFENSE OF PUBLIUS SESTIUS
(*Pro P. Sestio*)

Along with Milo, Cicero's foremost champion among the Tribunes of 57 had been P. Sestius, who almost lost his life in an attempt to block Clodius' election as Aedile (s. 79). In February of the following year he was charged with *vis* (violence resulting in public danger), and the trial took place in early March under the presidency of the Praetor M. Aemilius Scaurus (son of the famous Leader of the Senate). Caesar's creature P. Vatinius seems to have been behind the prosecution, as also presumably was Clodius, who had brought a similar charge against Milo. It was initiated by a certain M. Tullius, but for reasons now unknown his place was taken by another nonentity, P. Albinovanus,[1] whom Vatinius, with or without foundation, accused of collusion with the defense.[2] Cicero wound up for Sestius, preceded by the orator-poet Licinius Calvus, Crassus, and Hortensius, while Pompey appeared as a defense witness, as did Milo and the young Lentulus Spinther—an impressive array of leading optimates within Cicero's definition of the term in s. 97. But Pompey's alliance with Caesar, temporarily under strain, was to be regalvanized at their meeting at Luca in the following month of April.

The speech is Cicero at his most discursive. An introduction and a brief sketch of Sestius' career down to his tribunate in 57 (ss. 1–14) is followed by a lengthy account of the events leading to Cicero's exile and the most elaborate justification yet of his flight (ss. 15–54). Ss. 55 ("but let me leave my own case now") through 71 cover the remainder of the year 58. In s. 71 he comes at last to Sestius' tribunate and matter directly related to the charge, but this is followed by invective against the Consuls of 58 and Clodius (ss. 93–95). Thence he passes to a survey of the Roman political scene,

---

1. *Q. fr.* 2.3.5. Hence the widespread belief that his name was M. Tullius Albinovanus. If it was, he must have been an Albinovanus adopted by a M. Tullius, since the former is a nomen, not a cognomen. But if the prosecutor had had a more distinctive name, Cicero would probably have used it in his letter.
2. *Vat.* 42.

"optimates" versus "people's men," as seen through the orator's eyes (ss. 96–127), leading into the glories of his restoration and the villainies of Vatinius. S. 136 ("but my discourse must have a finish") introduces a political exhortation to the young, followed by a "pathetic" peroration. Sestius was acquitted by a unanimous verdict.

Cicero had no great affection for the man, much as he knew he owed him. He wrote to his brother after the case (*Q. fr.* 2.4.1): "Our friend Sestius was acquitted on 14 March, and by a unanimous vote, which was politically of great importance as showing that no difference of opinion exists in a case like this. I have often noticed your anxiety lest I give a handle to a hostile critic who might accuse me of ingratitude if I did not put up with his unreasonableness in certain respects with the best of grace. Well, you may rest assured that my conduct in that trial has made me pass for a model of gratitude. By my defense I have more than discharged what was due to this peevish personage."

Catullus (44) caught a cold from reading a frigid speech of Sestius', and Cicero in 49 criticized Pompey for trusting him with the composition of an important letter ("I have never read anything more typically Sestian": *Att.* 7.17.2). His jokes were no better (*Fam.* 7.32.1). But he and Cicero remained good enough friends through the changeful years.

[1] Gentlemen of the jury, sometimes in the past it may have seemed strange that in so richly endowed a Commonwealth as ours and so majestic an empire citizens of high, unselfish courage, ready to put themselves and their civic existences at risk on behalf of constitution and common liberty, were found in numbers by no means sufficiently large. Well, from this time forward, it will be more surprising to see a brave and honest citizen than a self-server or a coward. You do not need to search your memories for what has happened to this individual and that. Survey the scene. You can see at a glance how the men who raised the Commonwealth from the dust and freed her from domestic banditry alongside the Senate and all honest men are standing trial, sad of countenance and dress, fighting for their lives, reputations, civic rights, fortunes, and children. Whereas those who violated, harassed, confounded, and overturned all things divine and human bustle

briskly and cheerfully about and actually stir up trouble for our best and bravest without any apprehensions on their own account. [2] A sorry spectacle from many points of view, but the sorriest part is that in their efforts to bring good citizens into jeopardy they are no longer using their own brigands, their beggarly, guilty desperados, but your good selves.[3] Having failed to wipe them out with stones, steel, and firebrands, with organized violence, they think to crush them with your authority, your sworn verdicts. As for myself, gentlemen of the jury, the voice I was expecting to use in rendering thanks and recounting what I owe to those who have deserved so well of me I am now forced to employ in averting their perils. But since the case stands thus, let this voice of mine serve first and foremost those through whose agency it has been restored to you and to the Roman People.

[3] My illustrious and eloquent friend Quintus Hortensius has pleaded Publius Sestius' case, leaving no word unsaid that needed saying, either by way of protest on behalf of the Commonwealth or of argument on behalf of the accused. None the less I propose to speak, for I should not wish it to appear as though my championship had been unavailable to the very man thanks to whose efforts it is *not* unavailable to the community at large. And I conceive, gentlemen of the jury, that in this case, as the last speaker for the defense, I have taken upon myself a role that has more to do with gratitude than with advocacy, more with protest than with eloquence, more with painful emotion than oratorical skill. [4] If I express myself more forcefully or more freely than those who have preceded me, I ask you to make allowances as I address you such as you may think proper to make for pain felt on behalf of a benefactor and for righteous anger. For no pain can be more closely linked to duty than this that I feel for the perilous predicament of a man to whom I owe so much; and no anger can be more laudable than the wrath that inflames me against the villains who have thought fit to declare war on all who espoused my

---

3. Roman juries at this time were chosen from three categories: Senators, Knights, and so-called Paymaster Tribunes (*tribuni aerarii*.) The two latter had a property qualification, so that "your good selves" implies respectable persons in good social and financial standing.

cause.

[5] Since others have replied to particular charges, I shall speak of Publius Sestius generally and comprehensively: of his style of life, his natural disposition, his habits, his extraordinary devotion to the honest men, his zeal for the preservation of the common welfare and tranquillity. So in this indiscriminate and all-embracing line of defense I shall endeavor, if only it lie within my power, not to let you feel that I have left out anything of relevance to your inquiry or to the accused or to the public interest. Fortune herself placed Publius Sestius' term as Tribune at a period of very grave political crisis, in the ruins of a stricken, prostrate Commonwealth. I shall approach these momentous matters of high politics only after I have described the beginnings, the foundations from which arose all the glory that he won amid great events.

[6] Publius Sestius, gentlemen of the jury, was the son of a man whom many of you remember as wise, upright and strict. He was elected Tribune in the good old days, in first place among competitors of the highest birth. Higher office he did not seek, but only to seem worthy of it. At his prompting, his son married the daughter of a highly respectable and distinguished gentleman, Gaius Albanius.[4] Their children are the boy you see here in court and a married daughter. My client won the approbation of these two pillars of society, men of the true ancient stamp; both of them loved him and were happy in him. The death of Albanius' daughter robbed him of the title of father-in-law, but not of the affection and good will appropriate to that relationship. How sincerely he cares for Sestius today you can easily judge for yourselves from his constant attendance, anxiety, and distress.

[7] While his father was still living, my client took a second wife, the daughter of a very estimable and very unfortunate gentleman, Lucius Scipio. Sestius' dutiful behavior to him attracted much approving notice. He set out for Massilia at once to see his father-in-law and to console him, a man cast out by political storms, a man stranded in a strange land, who should have been standing in the footsteps of his ancestors; and he brought his

---

4. On his name, see SB[4].

daughter to him, so that the unlooked-for sight and embrace of her might cause Scipio to lay aside his grief, or at least some part
+ of it. And my client rendered him other important and assiduous services, comforting his sorrow, as long as he lived, and his daughter's bereavement.

I could say much about my client's generosity, his private good offices, his service as Military Tribune,[5] his uprightness in his province while in that capacity; but the majesty of the Commonwealth is ever before me, she hurries me to her side and urges me to leave these lesser matters. [8] As Quaestor, Sestius was assigned by lot to my colleague Gaius Antonius, but in virtue of his partnership in my counsels he was mine. A scruple of ethics (as I look at it) prevents my setting forth how much Publius Sestius noticed when he was with my colleague, and conveyed to me, what foresight he showed. Of Antonius I say only this: in that time of acute alarm and danger for the community he never chose to remove by a denial either the general anxiety or the suspicion entertained by some of himself in particular nor yet to allay it by hiding his feelings.[6] I had to bolster my colleague and to govern him. If you used with reason to applaud my combination of indulgence toward him with vigilant care for the public interest, an almost equal share of the credit belongs to Publius Sestius, who served his Consul in such a manner as to appear a good Quaestor in *his*
+ eyes and an excellent patriot in the eyes of all honest men.

[9] After the conspiracy had burst out of the shadows where it lurked and moved freely in the open and in arms, my client conducted an army to Capua, a city offering many military advantages and on that account, we suspected, the object of designs by that band of traitors and felons. He threw Gaius Mevulanus, a Military Tribune of Antonius, head first out of Capua; this was a scoundrel, who had been pretty openly part of the conspiracy at Pisaurum and elsewhere in the Gallic Territory.[7] My client also had Gaius Marcellus expelled from the city. He had not only arrived there, but had thrust himself into a large school of gladiators

---

5. See Glossary of Terms under "Tribune."
6. I.e., he continued to manifest sympathy with Catiline and his associates.
7. *Ager Gallicus*, a strip of coastal territory north of Picenum.

under the pretext of studying armed combat. For that reason the assembly which was held in Capua in that period and which adopted me as their sole patron because I had saved their city during my consulship expressed to me their heartfelt gratitude to Publius Sestius. And at the present time the same people, though now called colonists and Decurions,[8] brave, loyal folk, have declared what they owe to Publius Sestius by a testimonial and passed a decree expressing their hope for his acquittal. [10] Lucius Sestius,[9] pray read out the decree of the Capuan Decurions; let your boyish voice give the foes of your family some inkling of how effective it is likely to become when it has gained the strength of maturity.

[Decree of the Decurions is read.]

I do not read you a decree evoked by some obligation of neighborhood, clientship, or public hospitality nor yet by a desire to win favor and approval. It embodies the memory of a past danger and the grateful acknowledgment of a benefaction; it is the voice of present gratitude, the testimony of time gone by.

[11] In that same period, when Sestius had removed the threat to Capua and the Senate and all honest men under my leadership had brought Rome out of the gravest peril with the arrest and suppression of the enemies in our midst, I wrote a letter recalling Publius Sestius from Capua with the army under his command. As soon as he read it, he at once hurried to Rome with extraordinary speed. So that you may recollect the terrors of those days, please hear the letter and put your memories to work. Think of the fear that has passed away.

[Consul Cicero's letter is read.]

P. Sestius' arrival slowed down the aggressive efforts of new Tribunes,[10] who were eager in the final days of my consulship to attack my achievements, and of the remnants of the conspiracy. [12] With our loyal and courageous Marcus Cato, then Tribune, defending the Commonwealth, it soon became apparent that by

---

8. Decurions were town councilors. Capua had gained corporate status as a Roman colony in 59.
9. Son of the accused.
10. Q. Metellus Nepos and L. Calpurnius Bestia.

themselves and without military support the Senate and People of
+ Rome could easily maintain their own majesty and the dignity of
those who at their own risk had defended the common safety. So
Sestius and his army by forced marches caught up with Antonius.
+ I need not tell you how the Quaestor roused the Consul to action,
spurred him on—a man desirous of victory, perhaps, but over-nervous of the inescapable hazards of battle.[11] The story is too long
to tell, but this much I will say in brief: if it had not been for Mar-
+ cus Petreius' outstanding spirit of patriotism, his exemplary political rectitude, his great reputation in the army, and his vast military experience, and if Publius Sestius had not been there to assist
in rousing Antonius, exhorting him, reproaching him, pushing
him, winter would have been allowed to take over that campaign.
And once Catiline had emerged from the frost and snow of the
Apennines and with the whole summer in front of him had
+ started to move at large among the byways and shepherds' cabins
of Italy, much blood would have been spilled and all Italy disastrously laid waste before he was brought down.

[13] Such then was the spirit which Publius Sestius brought to his tribunate—to leave aside his quaestorship in Macedonia and come to these more recent events. And yet, his remarkably upright conduct in the province deserves mention; not long ago I personally saw its traces in Macedonia, traces not lightly printed to earn a brief acclaim, but fixed for all time in the memory of that province. However, let us pass this by—but as we leave it let us give it a backward glance. Let us hasten full speed ahead and come to the tribunate, which all this while has been beckoning my speech, sucking it in, so to speak.

[14] Quintus Hortensius has so dealt with this topic that his speech seemed not only a defense against the charges, but a prescription to our younger generation, one they would do well to remember, of advice and rules of conduct as they enter public life. But Publius Sestius' entire tribunate was devoted to maintaining my name and cause, so I think I have no choice but to present the same happenings in greater detail, or, if not that, to deplore

---

11. *Communem Martem*, lit. "Mars common to both sides," i.e., impartial, an expression going back to Homer.

them with livelier indignation. If, in the course of my speech, I chose to inveigh against certain persons with some asperity, I imagine no one would deny me the right to censure with verbal freedom those whose criminal madness had done me injury. But I shall exercise restraint, and think of my client's situation rather than my own resentment. There may be some who secretly oppose my restoration: let them keep in hiding. Others may have done this or that in the past, but are now silent and inactive: let
+ me too forget. If any put themselves in my way or pursue me, I shall be patient with them, so far as patience is possible, and hurt no one who has not placed himself so squarely in my path that I shall not seem to have attacked him but to have run up against him.

[15] Before I begin to speak of Publius Sestius' career as Tribune, however, I must describe the entire political shipwreck of the previous year; for it will be found that his actions, words, and decisions all had to do with salvaging from the wreckage and reconsti-
+ tuting the common welfare. That year, gentlemen, was already a political disaster, when amid that great agitation and widespread terror a bow was levelled—at my single self, as the mass of the ignorant used to say, but in reality against the whole Commonwealth. I am referring to the translation to plebeian status of a crazy, desperate individual, who had a grudge against me but was
+ a much more bitter enemy to general tranquillity and welfare. That illustrious gentleman and very good friend of mine (though many tried to prevent his being so), Gnaeus Pompeius, had bound him by the most solemn pacts and pledges to take no action against me when he became Tribune. But that villain, that compound of every wickedness, not content with breaking his word, made the guarantor of another man's safety tremble for his own.

[16] This guilty, hideous monster was tied by auspices, bound by custom, fettered by the chains of inviolable laws.[12] Suddenly a Consul[13] released him by a curiate law, whether, as *I* suppose, induced by his own persuasions or, as some thought, annoyed

---

12. See p. 57, n. 63.
13. Caesar.

with me; at any rate, not knowing or foreseeing the dire crimes and evils that impended. As Tribune he succeeded in overturning the Commonwealth, not by any energies of his own—what energy could he have, leading the life he led? His vitality had been drained by brotherly outrage, sisterly debauchery, all manner of unheard-of vice. [17] No, it was surely by some kind of public fatality that this blind, demented Tribune lit upon—what shall I call them?[14] Consuls? Am I to accord that name to the subverters of this empire, the betrayers of your dignity, the enemies of all honest men, who thought they had been given their *fasces*[15] and other emblems of supreme rank and authority for the purpose of destroying the Senate, overthrowing the order of Knights, and extinguishing all our traditional rights and institutions? In the
+ name of the Immortal Gods, if you wish to recall their crimes and the wounds they burned into the flesh of the Commonwealth, picture their looks and manner. Their actions will come back to your minds more easily if you set their very faces before your eyes.

[18] Behold one of them:[16] reeking with perfume, his hair fresh from the curling tongs, scorning[17] his accomplices in vice
+ and the ancient troublers of his youthful bloom, displaying himself in his pride to the Well-Curb[18] and the flocks of moneylenders who once drove him to seek harbor in the tribunate, lest in that Scylla's strait of debt he should find himself stranded at the Column.[19] Despising the Roman Knights and threatening the Senate, he used to curry favor with the gangs, who, as he freely acknowledged, had snatched him from a trial for corrupt electioneering, and used to say that he expected a province at their hands, whether the Senate liked it[20] or no, and that unless he got it he thought he could not possibly survive as a citizen.

[19] And the other one! Gracious heavens, what a forbidding

---

14. Piso and Gabinius.
15. See Glossary of Terms.
16. Gabinius.
17. Or "looking back to" (*respiciens*); see SB^1 268f. and SB^2 148.
18. *Puteal Libonis*, in the Forum near the Praetor's tribunal, frequented by moneylenders.
19. *Columna Maenia*, also in the Forum, where malefactors were tried and the names of insolvent debtors posted.
20. Consular provinces were normally assigned by the Senate. See p. 48, n. 26.

air, how grim and terrible of aspect! You might think you were looking at one of our bearded forefathers, a typical ancient empire-builder, a portrait of antiquity, a pillar of the Commonwealth. Dressed roughly in our common plebeian purple, almost brown, he wore his hair bristling, as though he was set to remove Seplasia Street[21] from Capua, where he was at that time officiating as Duovir[22] with a view to the embellishment of his family portrait.[23] But what shall I say of his eyebrows? People did not think of them as eyebrows but as guarantees of the Commonwealth. So portentously grave was his eye, so furrowed his forehead that his year of office seemed to rely upon that brow as a pledge of security. [20] Everyone was saying: "At all events the Commonwealth has a grand, solid support. Here's a man to put against that foul disgrace.[24] For sure he'll wither his colleague's lust and levity with a look. This year the Senate will have a man to follow. The honest men won't want for counsel and leadership." They felicitated me in particular, because against that mad, reckless Tribune I should have a Consul who was not only a friend and relative[25] but a strong, responsible man to boot.

One of the pair disappointed nobody. Who could suppose that the helm of so great an empire could be grasped and the rudder of the Commonwealth guided in a long and stormy voyage by a fellow who had suddenly started up out of the shadows of brothel and debauch where he had spent so long? A man exhausted with wine, gluttony, harlots, and other men's wives? Placed against all expectation on this dizzy eminence by the resources which others[26] brought to bear on his behalf, he was too drunk to see the storm brewing or even to look at the daylight to which his eyes were unaccustomed.

[21] The other did disappoint a lot of people in every way, no doubt about it. His noble birth was in itself a recommendation to

---

21. Where perfumes were sold.
22. See p. 13, n. 43.
23. *Imago*, the wax death-mask which would hang in the hall of his house, with a label below giving his name and official career. This is doubtless irony.
24. Gabinius.
25. Through Cicero's son-in-law, C. Piso Frugi.
26. I.e., the "Triumvirs."

public opinion. Nobility has its seductive charm. We honest men are always predisposed in its favor for two reasons: it is good for the Commonwealth that the nobly born should be worthy of their ancestors, and the memory of famous men who have done the Commonwealth good service means much to us, even when they are no more. They saw him always gloomy and taciturn, with a rough, unkempt look about him. His name too[27] suggested frugality as in the family blood. So they favored the man and rejoiced and called on him by the hopes they placed in him to emulate the virtue of his ancestors, forgetting his mother's family.[28] [22] As for me, I shall be frank, gentlemen. I never thought there was so much villainy, audacity, and cruelty in him as I and the Commonwealth with me found by experience. That he was worthless, irresponsible, recommended from his young days by a deluded public opinion I did know. His heart was covered by his countenance, his vicious acts by his house walls. But such a screen is neither lasting nor so tightly drawn as not to offer a chink to curious eyes. We saw his way of life, his sloth and idleness. Those who came a little closer discerned his hidden vices. Finally, his conversation gave us clues to the secrets of his soul.

[23] As a person of erudition, he used to cry up some philosophers or other[29] —he could not give their names, but anyhow he used particularly to praise those who are said to be preeminently the advocates and eulogists of pleasure. He did not inquire into the which or the when or the how. The word was enough, and with every part of his mind and body he had devoured it. He used to say that the same philosophers had some fine doctrines to the effect that all a wise man's actions are for his own sake, that a person of sound mind ought not to engage in public affairs, that nothing is more desirable than a quiet life, filled to the brim with pleasures. As for people who say that a man should be zealous of his good name, take thought for the Commonwealth, pay regard in all affairs of life to duty, not personal interest, run risks and

---

27. One branch of the Piso family, though not the one to which this Piso belonged, bore the additional cognomen Frugi ("Worthy").

28. See p. 11, n. 35.

29. The Epicureans are meant, but Cicero does not wish to appear too conversant with such matters before a Roman jury.

receive wounds and give his life for his country—oh, he would call them crack-brained visionaries. [24] Such was his constant, daily talk. Hence, and because I saw what people he consorted with in the inner part of his house and because the house itself gave off a
+ potent odor suggestive of debauchery, I used to put him down as a negligible quantity, from whom nothing good was to be expected, but at any rate nothing bad to be apprehended. But this is the way of it, gentlemen of the jury: you may put a sword in the hands of a small boy or a feeble or crippled old man, and so far as his own efforts go he will harm nobody; but if he gets close to the naked body of even a very strong man, he might wound
+ him just with the sharp edge and the weight of the weapon. In the same way, when the consulship was given like a sword to worn-out debauchees who had never had the strength to stab anyone but themselves, once armed with the title of supreme authority, they cut the Commonwealth to pieces. They made a bargain with the Tribune, openly: he was to give them the provinces of their choice, with as large an army and as much money as they wanted, on condition that they should first hand over the Commonwealth to that Tribune, prostrate and in chains. The bargain, they said, could be sealed with my blood. [25] When this was revealed (for such a crime could not be disguised or hidden), the same Tribune promulgated two bills, one for my ruin, the other assigning provinces to the Consuls by name.

The Senate was alarmed, you Roman Knights were aroused, all Italy was in consternation. In fact, all citizens of every sort and class felt that the Commonwealth was at stake and the Consuls as the supreme authority should be called upon for help. But those two political tornados were the only citizens, except that crazy Tribune, who not only failed to come to their country's assistance as she plunged to disaster, but were sorry not to see her collapse more rapidly. Every day they were besieged by the protests of all honest men and the entreaties of the Senate as well, demanding that they take up my cause, do something, at any rate consult the Senate. Not only did they refuse, they assailed with mockery the most distinguished members of that House. [26] Suddenly a vast multitude from all over Rome and Italy assembled on the Capitol. All were in favor of putting on mourning and defending me by every means possible on private initiative, seeing that the Commonwealth had no official leaders. At the same time the Senate met in the temple of Concord[30] —the sacred building itself brought back the memory of my consulship. The entire House implored the ringleted Consul with tears—his bristly, austere colleague deliberately stayed at home. How haughtily that filthy pest rejected the entreaties of the august body and the tears of its most illustrious members! What scorn he had for me, that squanderer of his country—I won't say of his own fortune, which he lost when he was making money![31] You, you Roman Knights I mean, and all honest men with you, came to the Senate wearing mourning and threw yourselves at the feet of a foul pimp to plead for me. The brigand rejected your entreaties. Then Lucius Ninnius, in his extraordinary loyalty, high courage, and resolution, consulted the Senate on public affairs[32] and the Senate in large numbers voted to go into mourning for the sake of my preservation.

[27] Ah, gentlemen, that was a fatal day for the Senate and all honest men, a sorrowful day for the Commonwealth! For me it was heavy with private grief but glorious for my memory in time to come. What more splendid tribute is to be found in all history than this: that all honest men by private consent and the entire Senate by public resolution should have gone into mourning for the sake of a single citizen? The gesture was one of sorrow, not of intercession. Whom was there to intercede with, when all were in mourning and not to be in mourning was proof sufficient of rascality? So with Rome plunged into grief, wearing black—I say nothing of what that Tribune did, marauder of all things divine and human, who ordered young men of the highest birth, highly regarded Roman Knights, who were pleading for me, to appear before him and exposed them to the swords and stones of his

---

30. It was in this temple that the Senate met on the famous Nones (fifth) of December and doomed the arrested Catilinarians.

31. A paradox, alluding to Gabinius' alleged self-prostitution in his young days. *Quaestum (corpore) facere* ("make money with the body" or simply "make money") is particularly used of prostitutes. The word play *patriae . . . patrimonii* can hardly be brought out in English.

32. As Tribune, Ninnius had the right and took the initiative to consult the Senate since the Consul had refused.

gang: I speak of the Consuls, on whose loyalty the Commonwealth
+ should have relied. [28] * * * He[33] flees from the Senate in panic, his mind and his countenance as disordered as they would have been a few years previously if he had stumbled into a meeting of his creditors. He calls an assembly and makes a speech such as Catiline would never have made if he had won—he, a Consul. People, he said, were mistaken if they thought that the Senate still counted for anything in the Commonwealth. As for the Roman Knights, they should pay for that day during my consulship when they stood on Capitol Rise sword in hand. The hour of vengeance had arrived for those who had walked in fear—meaning, presumably, the conspirators. If he had only *said* such things, no punishment would have been too bad for him. For even words, mischievous words, from a Consul can shake the Commonwealth. But look at what he *did.* [29] In the assembly he banished Lucius Lamia from Rome, a gentleman with particular regard for me personally (his father and I were close friends), but who also was ready to lay down his life for the Commonwealth, ordering him in a public announcement to stay two hundred miles' distance from the city, because he had dared to intercede for a fellow citizen and one who had done good service, for a friend, for the Commonwealth.

What is to be done with such a fellow? For what fate is so unconscionable a citizen, or rather so villainous a public enemy, to be reserved? To say nothing of other wrongdoings which are joint and common to him with his foul monster of a colleague, he has this single one all to himself: he expelled from Rome, banished—I will not say a Roman Knight, a distinguished gentleman of excellent character, a most patriotic citizen, who at that very time was mourning the sad fate of a friend and of the Commonwealth, along with the Senate and all honest men; no, but a Roman citizen, casting him out of his country without form of trial by a public announcement as Consul.

[30] Our allies and the Latins[34] used to feel it as the worst of their grievances that, as very rarely happened, they should be

---

33. Some words have fallen out of the text.
34. See Glossary of Terms.

ordered by the Consuls to leave Rome. And yet they could return to their own communities and hearths. Furthermore, all suffered alike; no disgrace fell on any particular person by name. But this! Shall a Consul banish Roman citizens from their homes by an announcement? Drive them from their city? Pick out whom he pleases, condemn him, and cast him out by name? If he had expected that you[35] would ever be occupying your present position in the Commonwealth, if in fact he had believed that any image or semblance of law courts would be left in the community, would he ever have dared to remove the Senate from the Commonwealth, spurn the prayers of the Roman Knights, and cancel the rights and freedom of all citizens with novel, unprecedented announcements?

[31] Gentlemen of the jury, you have listened to me with the greatest attention and kindness. But I am afraid some of you may wonder what is the object of this lengthy discourse of mine, reaching far back in the past, or what the misdeeds of persons who harassed the Commonwealth before my client's tribunate have to do with his case. Now it is my intention to show that all Publius Sestius' designs and the purpose of his whole career as Tribune were directed to healing the prostrate and abandoned Commonwealth so far as he was able. If, as I set those wounds before you, I appear to say a good deal about myself, I ask your pardon. You and all honest men declared then that the calamity which befell me was the Commonwealth's worst blow. Publius Sestius is standing trial on my account, not his own. He spent the whole force of his tribunate in striving for my restoration, and so it must needs be that my cause in time past is bound up with his defense now.

[32] So the Senate was in mourning, the community likewise by public resolution had donned the dress of sorrow; there was no township, colony, or prefecture[36] in Italy, no revenue company in Rome, no college or council or association no matter what, but had passed in the most flattering terms a motion in my defense. Suddenly the two Consuls put out an announcement directing

---

35. Addressed to the jurors.
36. The towns of Italy are comprised in these three terms, connoting different historical origins. All were now communities of Roman citizens.

Senators to revert to normal dress. What Consul ever forbade the Senate to obey its own decrees? What tyrant ever prohibited the unhappy from mourning?

Is it not enough, Piso (never mind Gabinius), to have so grossly betrayed public expectation? You neglected the authority of the Senate, scorned the advice of its leading members, played traitor to the Commonwealth, brought low the name of Consul: would you also dare to publish an order forbidding men to mourn my misfortune and theirs and the Commonwealth's, and to signify their grief by their clothing? Whether the change of dress was an expression of their own sorrow or an appeal on my behalf, who ever had the cruelty to forbid anyone to mourn for himself or to supplicate for others? [33] Is it not customary to put on mourning spontaneously when a friend is in jeopardy? Will no one do that for you, Piso[37] —not even those Legates whom you chose yourself without any senatorial decree, in fact against the Senate's wishes?[38] Very well: those who so desire will perhaps mourn the calamity of an abandoned traitor; and shall not the Senate have license to mourn the peril of a citizen who enjoys the warmest regard of honest men and has done great service to his country, when his peril is bound up with that of the community? The same Consuls, if Consuls they are to be called—not a man but would like to see their names torn from memory, yes, and from the very roll of magistrates—after they had struck their bargain for the provinces, were introduced into an assembly in the Circus Flaminius by the country's demon and plague. There they approved by voice and vote amid loud groaning from you and your like all the measures which were being taken at that time against myself and against the Commonwealth. The same Consuls sat and looked on while a law was put through which provided that auspices be invalid, that declaration of contrary auspices or vetoing of a law be not allowed, that laws may be presented on all

---

37. Implying a threat of prosecution when Piso returned to Rome from his province.
38. See *Vat.* 35.

court-days,[39] that the Aelian and Fufian laws be invalid.[40] By that one bill (who fails to see it?) the entire Commonwealth was destroyed. [34] The same Consuls looked on while a levy of slaves was held in front of Aurelius' Platform[41] on the pretext of forming clubs.[42] They were enrolled street by street, assigned to sections ten apiece, incited to physical violence, murder, looting. Under the same Consuls arms were openly conveyed into the temple of Castor, the steps of the temple were torn up, armed men occupied the Forum and public meetings, there were killings and stonings. The Senate was no more, the other magistracies a cipher. One individual usurped the powers of all by arms and banditry, not by any strength of his own; but after withdrawing the two Consuls from the Commonwealth by a bargain on provinces, he established an insolent dominance, holding many by threats and fear, even more by hopes and promises.

[35] Such then was the situation, gentlemen of the jury. The Senate had no leaders; in their stead were traitors, or rather open enemies of the state. The order of Knights was cited by the Consuls to answer charges. The moral weight of all Italy was set at naught. Some were banished by name, others cowed by fear and danger. There were arms in the temples, armed men in the Forum. All this was not passed over by the Consuls in silence and affected ignorance, but approved both by voice and vote. All of us saw that, although Rome was not yet razed to the ground, it was already a captured city under enemy occupation. Despite all these adverse circumstances, I had so much support from the honest men, gentlemen of the jury, that I should have put up a fight, were it not that other fears, other anxieties and suspicions influenced my mind.

[36] Gentlemen, I shall explain today in full the reasons behind my conduct and decision. Your evident eagerness to hear and this great assemblage, greater than I ever remember at any court hearing, shall not go unsatisfied. I had a good cause, the

---

39. *Dies fasti*, on which, prior to Clodius' innovation, trials but not assemblies could be held.
40. See p. 10, n. 29.
41. See Index II.
42. See p. 21, n. 84.

Senate supported me warmly, the unity of all honest men was
+ amazing, the order of Knights was prepared, all Italy was ready for
any struggle. If I gave way to the fury of a Tribune, a despicable
creature, and feared the levity and unscrupulousness of two contemptible Consuls, I confess myself a coward without courage or
sense. [37] It was quite another matter with Quintus Metellus.[43]
Though all honest men approved his cause, the Senate had not
espoused it publicly nor any other class of persons separately nor
+ all of Italy by their decrees. He had been thinking of personal
glory rather than the evident welfare of the Commonwealth when
he alone refused to swear to observe a law passed by violence.
Finally, it was felt that his brave stand involved the sacrifice of his
love for his country in exchange for glory as a man of resolution.
+ Moreover, he was up against an invincible army, and Gaius Marius, the savior of the country, now in his sixth consulship, was his
enemy. He was up against Lucius Saturninus, Tribune for the second time, a keen politician on the democratic side, an extremist
perhaps, but at least he was popular and financially disinterested.
Metellus retired because he feared that if defeated by brave men
he would fall dishonorably,[44] whereas if he won it would cost the
Commonwealth many brave citizens.

[38] My cause had been espoused by the Senate openly, by the
order of Knights most ardently, by all Italy publicly, by all honest
men personally and vigorously. In my political actions I had not
been solely responsible, but a leader carrying out the general will.
Nor did they pertain merely to my personal glory but to the common safety of all citizens, one might say of all nations. The
circumstances were such that everyone had a lasting duty to
answer for what I did and defend it. Furthermore, I was not contending with a victorious army but with hired gangs, egged on to
plunder the city. For enemies I had, not Gaius Marius, the terror
of Rome's foes, the hope and help of his country, but two sinister
monsters, whose need, enormous debts, irresponsibility, and rascality had made them the helpless instruments of a Tribune. [39]

---

43. Numidicus.
44. Defeat would show that he had insufficient support and should not have made a fight of it; cf. p. 22, n. 86.

Nor was I up against Saturninus, a man in passionate pursuit of a
+ personal grudge, because the Senate had humiliated him by transferring control of grain from himself, as Quaestor for Ostia, to the leader of the Senate and the community, Marcus Scaurus. My adversary was a hired favorite of wealthy men-about-town, his married sister's lover, a priest of debauchery,[45] a poisoner, a forger of wills, an assassin, a brigand. If I had overcome these gentry by force of arms (it would have been easy to do, it needed doing, the best and bravest of my fellow countrymen were demanding it of me), I was not afraid that any man would blame me for answering violence with violence or shed a tear for the death of abandoned citizens, or rather enemies within the gates.

But other considerations weighed with me. In all his harangues that demon used to clamor that his actions against me had the backing of the illustrious Gnaeus Pompeius, who is now
+ and was then, so far as he was allowed to be, a very good friend of mine. The same evil creature gave out that the valiant Marcus Crassus, with whom I had every sort of friendly connection, was very hostile to my cause. Likewise, in speeches every day he used
+ to say that Gaius Caesar, to whom I had given some reason for estrangement, was bent upon my ruin. [40] He claimed that these three would be his advisers in planning and his helpers in action. He added that one of them had a large army in Italy, while the
+ other two, who were private citizens at the time, were dominant political figures and could get an army together if they wished, and would do just that. He threatened me, not with trial before the people or any legitimate contest or dispute or judicial process, but with violence, arms, armies, generals, camps.

Well, was I influenced by the words of an enemy, especially idle words, shameless slanders upon illustrious personages? No, not by his words but by the silence from the subjects of language so shameless. They had other reasons for keeping silent, but at that time it looked to people afraid of their own shadows as though their silence spoke and their failure to deny was an admission.

---

45. Clodius *was* a priest, a member of the College of Fifteen that had custody of the Sibylline books (cf. also *Dom.* 111 "our devout priest of Liberty"). But of course we are meant to think of the Bona Dea affair (cf. s. 66).

They[46] were alarmed by an apprehension they had—they thought that those proceedings and everything done the previous year were being called in question by the Praetors,[47] invalidated by the Senate and the leaders of the community. They did not want to alienate a democratic Tribune. They used to remark that their own dangers touched them closer than mine. [41] Even so, Crassus used to say that the Consuls ought to take up my cause and Pompeius appealed to them and said that as a private citizen he would not fail to support the cause, if it was publicly espoused. He was well-disposed to me and most anxious to preserve the Commonwealth, but certain persons who had been planted in my house for the purpose warned him to be more on his guard, said that I had set up a plot against his life in my own home. Some stirred up this suspicion of his with letters, others with emissaries, others in person to his face. The result was that, while Pompeius certainly feared nothing from me, he thought he should be on his
+ guard against others who might set something afoot in my name. Caesar himself, whom people ignorant of the truth thought to be especially angry with me, was at the gates holding military authority. His army was in Italy, and in that army he had given a command to the brother[48] of that very Tribune, my enemy.

[42] This then is what I saw, for it was not hard to see: the Senate, without which the community cannot survive, had been quite eliminated from the community. The Consuls, who ought to have been the leaders of our council of state, had seen to it that this council was by their means utterly abolished. The persons who had most power were presented at every public meeting as favoring my destruction—falsely, but still alarmingly. Speeches were being made against me every day. Nobody uttered a sound on my behalf and the Commonwealth's. The standards of the legions were thought to be threatening your persons and property—falsely, but so it was thought. The old forces of conspiracy, Catiline's sinister band, had reemerged from dispersal and defeat

---

46. The "Triumvirs." They were alarmed by moves to invalidate Caesar's consular legislation.
47. L. Domitius Ahenobarbus, and C. Memmius. See Suet. *Iul.* 23.
48. C. Claudius Pulcher, the second eldest of the three brothers.

under a new leader by an unexpected revolution of circumstances. Seeing all this, what was I to do, gentlemen of the jury? [43] I know that your support did not fail me at that juncture, but
+ that mine, one might almost say, failed you. Was I, a private citizen, to fight in arms against a Tribune? The honest men would have vanquished the rascals, the brave would have vanquished the cowardly. *He* would have been killed, the only medicine that would have relieved the Commonwealth of this pest. What then? Who could answer for the sequel? Was it to be doubted that the Tribune's blood, especially blood shed by no public authority, would find avengers and champions in the Consuls, when someone had said at a public meeting that I must either die once or conquer twice? What did that mean, "conquer twice"? Surely this, that if I fought it out with a demented Tribune, I should then find myself battling the Consuls and his other avengers. [44] As for me, even if I had to die instead of suffering a wound that was curable for me but lethal for my assailant, I should have preferred to die once, gentlemen, than to conquer twice. For the nature of that second conflict was such that, whether we won or lost, we could not have preserved the Commonwealth. Again, suppose I had been defeated in the first battle by tribunician violence and fallen in the Forum along with many honest men: would the Consuls have summoned the Senate, which they had totally erased from the Commonwealth? Would they have issued a call to arms, after not allowing the Commonwealth to be defended by dress?[49]
+ Would they have broken with the Tribune after my death, after electing that the hour of my destruction should coincide with the hour of their reward?

[45] One course remained to me: "thou shouldst have fought, fought back, and fighting met thy death,"[50] as perhaps some fierce, high-hearted man of mettle would put it. I call upon my country and her ancestral, domestic Gods to witness that it was for the sake of their dwellings and temples, for the sake of my countrymen's welfare, which was ever dearer to me than my life, that I fled from battle and carnage. Let us suppose that I was in a ship

---

49. See ss. 26–27.
50. Apparently cited from a play.

at sea with my friends, gentlemen of the jury. Let us suppose that many pirates issuing from various quarters threatened to sink that ship with their flotillas unless an individual, myself, was surrendered to them. Suppose then that my fellow passengers refused, preferring to perish by my side rather than hand me over to the enemy. In such a case, I would rather have thrown myself into the sea to save the rest than have brought people who thought so much of me into great and mortal danger, not to say certain death. [46] Well, this ship of the Commonwealth was adrift in the ocean amid tempests of sedition and strife. The helm had been torn from the Senate's hands. Many armed flotillas seemed about to rush upon her, unless I, I alone, was surrendered. Proscription, massacre, plunder were threatened. Some did not defend me because they feared the risk to themselves, others were motivated
+ against me by long-standing hatred of honest men, others were jealous, others thought I stood in their way, others wanted to work off some personal grudge, others hated the very Commonwealth, the peaceful establishment of honest men. For all those reasons they were demanding my single self. What was I to do? Fight it
+ out, and so bring—I won't say destruction but certainly the gravest danger upon you and your children, or single-handed on behalf of all take upon myself and undergo the fate that impended over all?

[47] The rascals, let us say, would have been defeated. But
+ they were countrymen and they would have been defeated in armed conflict by a private citizen, one who even as Consul had preserved the Commonwealth without arms. But if the honest men had been defeated, who would have been left? Do you not see that it would have come down to the slaves?[51] Or ought I myself, as some think, to have met death calmly? Was I avoiding death at that point? Was there anything I could have wished for more? When I was achieving all I achieved amid such a host of rascals, were not death and exile always staring me in the face? And at the time, in the course of action, did I not prophesy all this like an oracle? Was life worth keeping then for me, with my family in such dire distress, with the separation, the bitterness, the

---

51. See p. 77, n. 135.

spoliation of all that nature and fortune had given me? Was I so inexperienced, so ignorant, so lacking in sense or wit? Had I heard nothing, seen nothing, learned nothing by my own reading and inquiry? Did I not know that life is short, glory everlasting? That since death is determined for all, we should pray that our lives, the debt we owe to necessity, are seen as freely granted to our country rather than held back till nature takes them? It has been in dispute among the wisest of mankind, whether men's souls and senses are extinguished in death or whether the minds of the wise and brave are most actively conscious after they have left the body. So the one alternative, unconsciousness, is nothing to be shunned, whereas the other, a better form of consciousness, is actually to be desired. Did I not know this? [48] Finally, as one who had always made honor his yardstick in all things and believed that nothing in human life is desirable without it, would I fear death, which even girls in Athens, the daughters of King Erechtheus[52] as I remember, are said to have despised—I, a Consular, with a record of achievement such as mine? After all, I belonged to the community from which came Gaius Mucius, who entered Porsenna's camp alone and tried to assassinate him, knowing that it meant his own death, or Publius Decius—first the father, some years later the son, who inherited his father's valor and like him devoted himself and his life on the battlefield for the safety and victory of the Roman People. Countless other Romans have met death in various wars without a qualm, some to win glory, others to avoid disgrace. In this community I myself remember the father of Marcus Crassus here,[53] who shed his life-blood with the hand which had so often dealt death to the foes of Rome rather than live to see his enemy victorious.

[49] Thinking of all this and much else besides, I perceived that if my death gave a mortal blow to the public cause, no man in time to come would ever dare to champion the welfare of the

---

52. Legendary king of Athens. He was promised victory in battle if he sacrificed one of his three daughters. The youngest was chosen, and her two sisters killed themselves.

53. P. Licinius Crassus, Consul in 97 and father of the "Triumvir," committed suicide in 87, when Marius (probably the enemy referred to) and Cinna returned to Rome.

Commonwealth against bad citizens. Not only if I perished by violence but even if I were carried off by sickness, I reckoned that the example of preserving the Commonwealth would perish with me. For if I were not restored by the Senate and the People of Rome with such whole-hearted support from honest men (and if I had been killed, that obviously could not have happened), who, I asked myself, would dare to take any part in public affairs if it involved him in the slightest unpopularity?

Therefore, gentlemen of the jury, I saved the Commonwealth by leaving Rome. At the cost of pain and mourning to myself I lifted from you and your children the threat of massacre, devastation, fire, pillage. One man, myself, saved the Commonwealth twice, once to my glory, and a second time to my sorrow. For I shall never disclaim human feelings or boast that I did not suffer at the loss of my best of brothers, my dearest children, my faithful wife, the sight of my countrymen and my country, and the rank I hold. If I had not, what would you have to thank me for? I should merely have abandoned on your account things which were of no consequence to me. To my mind the surest proof of the great love I bear my country should be the fact that I could not be absent from her without deep pain, but preferred to endure that pain rather than let her be shaken by rascals.

[50] I remembered, gentlemen, how Gaius Marius, that extraordinary man who sprang from the same roots as myself [54] for the salvation of this empire, in extreme old age escaped from the violence of what might almost be called regular warfare to hide his aged person in the depths of a swamp; and after that,
+ how he threw himself on the mercy of very poor and humble folk, and then in a tiny vessel, avoiding all harbors and lands, made his way to the most solitary part of the African coast. He preserved his life lest he die unavenged, looking to a very doubtful hope and
+ to the undoing of the Commonwealth. Whereas, as many said in the Senate during my absence, a danger to my life was a danger to the Commonwealth,[55] and for that reason I was commended to

---

54. Both came from Arpinum, about sixty miles southeast of Rome.

55. Lit. "I lived at the risk of the Commonwealth." So *Flacc.* 41 *nostro periculo vivere tuos contubernales* ("that your fellow lodgers live at our risk").

foreign nations in a consular letter by desire of the Senate.[56] If I had thrown my life away, should I not have betrayed the Commonwealth, in which, now that I have been restored, there lives along with me an example of public good faith? If that example is kept intact for all time, who does not see that this community will be immortal?

[51] Foreign wars against monarchs, peoples, and nations have been extinguished long since. Those whom Rome lets live in peace[57] can count themselves fortunate. And a victory in such warfare has never, or hardly ever, entailed unpopularity at home. It is the evils in our midst, the designs of unscrupulous countrymen, that must often be resisted. These are the perils against which a specific must be kept in the Commonwealth. Gentlemen of the jury, you would have lost any such remedy if I had perished and the Roman People had been deprived of the power to express its grief at my loss. Therefore I admonish you young men, I counsel you as I have a right to do, you who care for prestige, for the Commonwealth, for glory: if some day a crisis summons you to the defense of the Commonwealth against wicked citizens, do not let the memory of what happened to me make you slow to respond and averse from courageous courses. [52] To begin with, there is no risk that anyone ever again will chance upon such Consuls, especially if they receive their just deserts. Secondly, never again, I expect, will any rascal declare that he is attacking the Commonwealth by the advice and with the assistance of honest men,[58] while they for their part hold their peace, or terrorize the civil population with the threat of an army under arms. Neither will a commander[59] sitting at the city gates have fair cause to allow the threat of his presence to be falsely bandied about and used as an obstruction. Nor will the Senate ever again be so crushed as to lack the power even to supplicate and mourn, or will the order of Knights be so much a prisoner that Roman Knights are banished by a Consul. Yet despite all this and much else of even greater

---

56. In 57, by the Consul Lentulus Spinther (cf. s. 128).
57. I.e., without annexing them to the empire.
58. Like the "Triumvirs"; see s. 40.
59. Like Caesar; cf. s. 41.

moment, which I deliberately pass over, you see that I have been recalled after a brief, unhappy interval to my old high place by the voice of the Commonwealth.

[53] Let me now return to what I have set out to show in all this discourse, namely that all manner of calamities overwhelmed the Commonwealth that year through the criminal behavior of the Consuls. And first, let me go back to that day, a day of doom for me and of mourning for all honest men, when I tore myself from my country's embrace and the sight of you my fellow countrymen and, fearing on your account, not my own, yielded to the fellow's fury, his villainy, treachery, weapons, and threats, and left the country I loved so well because of that very love. Not only men but the very dwellings and temples of Rome mourned my fate. It was so appalling, so overwhelming, so sudden. None of you wished to look upon the Forum or the Senate-House or the light of day. That very day—no, at the same hour, the same moment even, two bills were voted: one contained my ruin and the Commonwealth's, the other provinces for Gabinius and Piso. Immortal Gods, guardians and preservers of this city and empire, what monstrous, what villainous things ye saw done in Rome! A citizen had been driven out, one who had defended the Commonwealth by the Senate's authority along with all honest men; driven out, moreover, on that very charge and none other, driven out without a trial, by violence, stones, steel, and a stoked-up slave population. The bill had been put through in a waste and deserted Forum which had been given over to bravos and slaves; and the Senate had tried to prevent that bill's passing by going into mourning.

[54] In such a convulsion of the community the Consuls did not
+ let so much as a night intervene between my undoing and their plunder. No sooner had I been struck down than they hurried up to drink my blood and strip the body of the Commonwealth while it still breathed. I say nothing of the felicitations and feasting, the sharing out of the Treasury, the bounties, hopes, promises, booty, the joy of the few amid the general sorrow. My wife was harassed, my children searched for with murderous intent,[60] my son-in-law (and he a Piso) spurned as he lay in supplication at the feet of

---

60. Cf. *Dom.* 59.

Consul Piso, my property pillaged and carried off to the Consuls, my house on the Palatine in flames: the Consuls meanwhile were banqueting. Even if they rejoiced at my misfortunes, they might have shown some concern at the danger to Rome.

[55] But let me leave my own case now. Recollect the other disasters of this year. Thus you will most readily perceive what a quantity of various remedies the Commonwealth required from the succeeding magistrates. Remember the spate of laws passed or merely promulgated. The following were passed without opposition from the Consuls, or rather with their actual approval: a law abolishing the censorial cognizance,[61] that weighty judgment of a much revered magistracy; another authorizing not only the reconstitution of the old associations,[62] contrary to the Senate's decree, but the enrollment of countless new ones by a single gladiator; a third remitting the six-and-one-third asses[63] and so eliminating almost a fifth of our revenues; a fourth assigning Syria to Gabinius instead of his Cilicia, which had been the stipulated price for his betrayal of the Commonwealth, thus allowing that glutton the privilege of making up his mind twice on the same question and changing his province after one bill had been passed by the passage of another. [56] I pass over that law which by a single enactment swept away all ordinances in respect of religion, auspices, and magisterial powers, all the laws regulating the legality and timing of legislation.[64] I pass over all domestic destruction. We saw even foreign nations shaken by that year's madness. A tribunician bill expelled the High Priest of the Great Mother in Pessinus and stripped him of his priestly office. This very sacred and ancient religious foundation was sold for a large sum to Brogitarus, a dirty rogue unworthy of the sacred function, particularly as he sought it not to discharge but to profane it. The title of "king" was bestowed by the people on persons who had

---

61. See Glossary of Terms under "Censor." Clodius had not totally abolished the censorial *nota* but had restricted its use to persons accused before the Censors of specific misconduct.

62. See p. 21, n. 84.

63. Per *modius* (peck) of grain. This was the price previously charged by the state to citizens on the public dole.

64. Cf. *Red. sen.* 11 and n. 29 ad loc.

never asked for it, even from the Senate. Condemned exiles were brought back to Byzantium at a time when citizens unconvicted of any offense were thrown out of our community.[65] [57] King Ptolemy,[66] if he had not yet himself been declared an ally of Rome by the Senate, was brother to a king[67] who had already received that title in identical circumstances; he was of the same line, descended from the same ancestors, his ties of alliance with Rome were of equally long standing. Finally, if not yet an allied monarch, he was at any rate not a hostile one. In peace and quiet, relying on the empire of the Roman People, he was enjoying the royal estate of his father and ancestors in regal tranquillity. A bill was passed against this undesigning, unsuspecting ruler, by the votes of the same gangsters. Seated in his purple with sceptre and other royal insignia he was to be subjected to the public auctioneer. By command of the Roman People, whose practice has been to return their kingdoms even to kings conquered in war, a friendly king and all he possessed was put up to auction, no offense mentioned, no reparation demanded.

[58] Much that took place that year was painful, much was disgraceful, much was irregular. But next after the crime which the cruelty of these people committed against me I think we may fairly rank this episode. When our ancestors defeated Antiochus the Great, in a great war on land and sea, they made Mount Taurus the boundary of his kingdom and gave Asia, of which they deprived him, to Attalus,[68] to reign therein. Recently we ourselves waged a long and difficult war with King Tigranes of Armenia, whose aggressions against our allies practically amounted to an attack on Rome. He was himself no sluggard, and with the resources of his kingdom he defended the bitterest enemy of our empire, Mithridates, who had been driven out of Pontus.
+ Defeated by a great man and a great general, Lucius Lucullus, Tigranes remained as hostile as ever with the forces he had left. Gnaeus Pompeius, however, saw him at his feet, a suppliant in his

---

65. Allusion to Cicero's own exile.
66. Of Cyprus; see Index I.
67. Ptolemy XII Auletes ("the Piper"), king of Egypt (cf. *Dom.* 20).
68. Actually it was given to his successor, Eumenes II of Pergamum. See Index I under Attalus.

camp. He raised him up, replaced upon his head the royal diadem which Tigranes had discarded, and after imposing on him certain commands, told him to continue his reign. He thought the spectacle of a king established by himself on his throne redounded to Rome's imperial glory and his own no less than that
+ of a king in chains. [59] So Tigranes, who was himself an enemy of Rome and received her most bitter enemy into his realm, who fought us in pitched battle and almost disputed with us for empire, sits on his throne today and has obtained by entreaty the title of friend and ally which he had violated by arms. On the other hand, the unfortunate King of Cyprus, who was always our friend and ally, about whom no damaging suspicion was ever brought to the Senate or to our commanders in the field, was publicly sold up along with all his goods and chattels,[69] living and looking, as the saying goes. A fine encouragement to other monarchs to feel secure on their thrones, when they see by the precedent set in that year of disasters that a Tribune and a few hundred gangsters can deprive them of their possessions and strip them of all their royalty!

[60] Some tried to use that business to tarnish the fair fame of Marcus Cato. Little did they know the power of principle, integrity, high-mindedness—in a word, virtue. In the raging storm virtue is calm, in the darkness she shines, dislodged from her place
+ she yet remains, exiled she stays in her native land, her natural brightness is never dimmed by defilement from outside. These people were not minded to honor Marcus Cato but to banish him; they were not entrusting him with that business but saddling him with it. They said openly at a public meeting that they had plucked out Marcus Cato's tongue, which had always spoken out against extraordinary powers. They will soon find, I hope, that his
+ outspokenness is unabated, and even, if possible, greater than it was when he fought those Consuls with his indignant voice, even after he had given up hope of achieving anything by his authority, and when after my departure he harassed Piso in such terms, bewailing my fate and the Commonwealth's, that that most abandoned and shameless of mankind almost rued the day he got his

---

69. Lit. "with all he had to live on and to wear."

province. [61] Why then did Cato obey the bill? As though in the past he had not sworn obedience to other legislation which he held had been passed improperly![70] He does not present himself as a target to such recklessness, so as to deprive the Commonwealth of a citizen like himself with no patriotic object to be gained. As Tribune-Elect in my consulship he put his life in jeopardy. He made a motion[71] in the Senate knowing that he would have to answer for the hostility it provoked at the peril of his civic existence. He spoke energetically, took a strong line, made no secret of his views. He was a leader and an active supporter of those measures; not that he did not realize his own danger, but in such a national emergency he felt it wrong to think of anything but the dangers to the country.

[62] His own tribunate followed. What words can I find for his self-regardless courage? It was extraordinary, beyond belief. You remember the day when his colleague[72] had occupied a temple[73] and we were all in terror for the life of so admirable a man and citizen. Cato fearlessly entered the temple and quelled the shouts of the crowd by his authority and the fury of the rascals by his courage. He took a risk, but took it for a great cause, how great there is no need for me now to say. But if he had refused obedience to that villainous Cyprian bill, the disgrace would have stuck to the Commonwealth just the same, for the bill designating Cato by name was passed after the kingdom had already been confiscated. If he had rejected the mission, we cannot doubt that he would have been subjected to violence, for they would have felt that the validity of everything done that year was being put in question by Cato alone. [63] He saw something else as well: since that stain of the confiscated kingdom remained on the Commonwealth and nobody could now wash it out, it was expedient that whatever public good could come out of evil should be preserved by him rather than squandered by others. Even if some other pressure had been used to drive him out of Rome at that time, he

---

70. Caesar's agrarian law in 59, to which senators were required to swear obedience.
71. For the execution of the arrested Catilinarians.
72. Metellus Nepos, also Tribune in 62 (cf. Plut. *Cat. min.* 26).
73. Of Castor and Pollux.

would not have been sorry. He had kept out of the Senate the previous year, although if he had attended then he could at least have seen me there, a political ally; now that I had been expelled and the whole Senate and his own motion condemned in my name, could he calmly stay in Rome? No, he yielded to the same situation as myself, to the madness of the same individual, to the same Consuls, to the same threats, plots, dangers. My bitter cup was filled higher, but his heart grieved no less than mine.

[64] It was for the Consuls to protest against all these grievous injuries to our allies, to kings, and to free communities. Kings and foreign nations have always been in the tutelage of that magistracy. Was a sound heard from the Consuls at any point? And yet, who would have listened to a protest from them, however much they had wanted to make one? How could they protest about the King of Cyprus, when they had not only failed to defend me while I stood on my feet but had not even protected me as I lay on the ground—me, a fellow citizen, in trouble not from any fault of my own but on account of my country? I had yielded—to unpopularity, if you choose to think that the populace was unfriendly to me, which it was not; to circumstances, if everything seemed in convulsion; to armed force, if violence lay behind; to a bargain, if the magistrates made one; to the public interest, if my countrymen were in danger. [65] But why, when a bill of proscription was going through affecting the status of a citizen (I will not discuss what sort of citizen) and his property, although inviolable laws and the Twelve Tables[74] laid it down that legislation may not be enacted *ad hominem*[75] and that none which affects the status of a citizen may be proposed except in the Assembly of Centuries[76] —why was no sound heard from the Consuls? Why was it established that year, so far as lay in those two plagues of our empire, that any citizen might legally be forced out of the community by name through stoked-up gangs in an assembly called by a Tribune? [66] As for the promulgations that year, the lavish promises, written assurances, hopes, and dreams, what shall I say? What

---

74. See p. 57, nn. 63, 65.
75. See p. 19, n. 76.
76. See Glossary of Terms.

portion of the globe's surface had not been assigned to this beneficiary or that? What public commission could be thought of, desired, imagined, which had not been allocated and distributed? What sort of command, what province,[77] what method of minting money or raking it in was left undiscovered? Where was there a region or area on earth of any considerable size in which a kingdom was not set up? What monarch but thought fit that year either to buy what he did not have or to ransom what he had already? Who applied to the Senate for a province or money or a staff post? Restitution was being organized of persons condemned for violence, as was the candidature for the consulship of that same priestly demagogue.[78] The honest men were bewailing all this, the rascals were hoping, the Tribune acting, the Consuls assisting.

[67] Now at last Gnaeus Pompeius took a hand, later than he himself would have wished and much against the will of those who had turned that excellent and gallant gentleman's mind away from my defense by their designs and fictitious alarms. He roused into action his habit of good statesmanship, which was not indeed lying dormant but had been retarded by certain suspicions. This man, who by his valor and victory had subjugated villainous Romans and the most bitter enemies of Rome, great nations, kings, savage races we had never heard of, the numberless swarm of pirates, even revolted slaves—[79] this man who had extinguished all wars by land and sea and fixed the frontiers of the Roman People at the ends of the earth, did not allow the Commonwealth, which he himself had often saved not only by his measures, but by his blood, to be overturned by a handful of criminals. He joined the public cause, set his authority in opposition to what was to come, protested at what had already taken place. It looked as though matters were taking a more hopeful turn. [68] A well-attended Senate passed a decree for my return on the first of June without a single dissentient at the motion of Lucius Ninnius,

---

77. *Provincia* properly = "sphere of duty."
78. Clodius; cf. p. 155, n. 45. His candidature for the consulship at this time would have been grossly illegal.
79. Allusion to the suppression of the slave revolt led by Spartacus in 71.

whose loyalty and courage in my cause never wavered. An obscure individual, the man Ligus, an adjunct to my enemies, interposed a veto. The business, my cause that is, now seemed to have begun to raise its eyes and come alive. Whoever had touched any part of Clodius' crime[80] during my time of tribulation, wherever he went, whatever trial he had to face, was convicted. Nobody was found to admit to having cast a vote against me. My brother had returned from Asia. His dress was sad, his heart far sadder. As he entered Rome, the entire community turned out to meet him, weeping and wailing. The Senate began to speak more freely. The Roman Knights were rallying. My son-in-law Piso, who has been denied[81] the reward his loyalty deserved from me and from the Roman People, was demanding his father-in-law at the hands of his kinsman. The Senate refused to discuss any business until the Consuls had referred my case.

[69] It seemed as though success lay in my supporters' grasp. The Consuls, to be sure, had forfeited all independence by the bargain they struck for their provinces. When private citizens in the Senate demanded liberty to present their views on my case, they replied that they were afraid of the Clodian law. When they could not keep this up any longer, a plot was hatched to kill Gnaeus Pompeius. It was discovered and the weapon seized; Pompeius remained shut up in his house so long as my enemy was Tribune. Eight Tribunes gave notice of a bill for my return, thus
+ demonstrating that my friends had not deserted me in my absence, even in a situation in which some whom I had thought of as friends turned out otherwise, but that, while always bearing me the same good will, they had not always had the same liberty to show it. For of the nine Tribunes[82] whom I originally had on my side, only one fell away in my absence, a man who picked up a surname from the family portraits of the Aelii, with the result that he looked more like a Ligurian than an Aelius Ligus.[83] [70] So this

---

80. I.e., bought up any of Cicero's confiscated property; see *Dom.* 48–50.
81. By his death.
82. Of the year 59–58 (the Tribunes came into office on 10 December).
83. The Aelii Ligures were a consular family. According to the elder Cato, all Ligurians were tricksters (Serv. on Virg. *Aen.* 11.700), but Cicero in *Leg. agr.* 2.95 gives the national character as "dour and rustic." This Ligus was a blockhead (*Har.*

same year, after new magistrates had been elected and all honest men had pinned all hope of better things on their good faith, Publius Lentulus led the way with his authority and his voice in the Senate. Against the opposition of Piso and Gabinius he took up my cause and when the matter was put to the Senate by eight Tribunes,[84] made a splendid speech in my favor. He saw that from the standpoint of his own credit and the gratitude he would win from so important a service, it would be better that the case be kept open until he took office. Nevertheless he preferred that such an issue be settled sooner by others than later by himself.

+ [71] Meanwhile, gentlemen of the jury, Publius Sestius undertook a journey in order to intercede with Gaius Caesar for my restoration. He thought it important both for public harmony and as facilitating the attainment of the end in view that Caesar's attitude should not be unsympathetic. How he fared, what headway he made in this attempt does not concern this case. For my part, I
+ suppose that if Caesar was favorable to me, as I think he was, it accomplished nothing; if he was ill-disposed, not much. All the same it shows Sestius' sincere anxiety to be of service.

I come now to Sestius' tribunate, for he undertook the journey
+ earlier on, when Tribune-Elect, in the public interest. That year passed away. There seemed to be a general feeling of relief, with the hope, though not, as yet, the actuality of a restored Commonwealth. Those two vultures in general's uniform left Rome accompanied by evil omens and maledictions. I only wish that the imprecated disasters had fallen upon them personally. We should not have lost the province of Macedonia and an army[85] nor yet our cavalry and some fine cohorts in Syria.[86]

[72] The Tribunes enter office. All of them had made a firm promise to introduce legislation in my favor. The first to be bought by my enemies was he whom, laughing in their sorrow,
+ people used to call "Toothy,"[87] seeing that it was in the destiny of

---

resp. 5).

84. Of 59–58.

85. Not true; see R. G. M. Nisbet, *Cicero in Pisonem* (Oxford, 1961), pp. 175–80.

86. Gabinius had to suppress a rebellion in Judaea. Josephus (*Ant.* 14. 82–89; cf. 100–102) says nothing about Roman losses.

87. Brocchus ("projecting," applied to a person having prominent teeth), a

our community that this dormouse[88] pulled out from the brambles should try to gnaw at the Commonwealth. The other was Serranus; he did not come from any plough[89] but from the deserted
+ * * * of Gavius Olelus [?][90] grafted onto the Atilii Calatini. Having made his entries[91] in his accounts, he abruptly removed his name from the list.

The first of January arrives. You gentlemen should know what happened better than I, who only relate what I have heard—of the large attendance in the Senate, the public expectancy, the throng of delegates from all over Italy, the courage, conduct, and impressive bearing of Consul Publius Lentulus, and also the forbearance of his colleague in my regard. He said that political differences had made him my enemy, but that he would sink his quarrel for the sake of the Commonwealth. [73] Then Lucius Cotta, as first called upon, spoke in terms entirely worthy of the Commonwealth. He said that the steps taken against me were all contrary to justice, custom, and law. No man, he said, can be
+ removed from the community without trial. No judgment, no proposal even, concerning the status of a citizen can be made except in the Assembly of Centuries. What had happened was an explosion of violence, an outbreak of fire in a shaken Commonwealth, in times that were out of joint. In the absence of law and law courts, under the imminent threat of a great revolution, I had tacked a little and fled rough seas and tempests present in the hope of future calm. Therefore, since in my absence I had freed the Commonwealth from dangers no less grave than those I had averted on the spot, it was fitting that the Senate should not only restore me but do me honor. He also argued skillfully and at length that the matter in which that crazy, abandoned foe of modesty and morality had written what he wrote concerning me—the

---

nickname. His real name was Q. Numerius Rufus.

88. Dormice being reddish (Rufus = "red") and toothy.

89. According to tradition, an Atilius, possibly the Consul in 257, was called Serranus because he was found sowing (*serere*) his land when summoned to take command in war.

90. The text is very doubtful here.

91. Cicero makes untranslatable play with double senses of *nomen* ("entry," of a sum due, and "name") and *tabula(e)* ("ledger" and "writing tablet"), implying that Serranus had been bribed to take his name off the list.

words, the sense, the sentiments—was such that even if his bill had been lawfully passed it could have no validity. Accordingly, since I was absent under no law, I ought not to be restored by a law but recalled by resolution of the Senate.

[74] All agreed that Cotta was entirely right. However, the next speaker, Gnaeus Pompeius, while approving and applauding Cotta's speech, gave it as his opinion that the Senate's resolution should be accompanied by an act of favor towards me on the part of the Roman People. This would ensure that I should be left in peace and preclude any subsequent demagogic agitation. All present vied with one another in the emphasis and the amplitude of the terms in which they supported my cause, and a unanimous vote was being taken. Then, as you know, up stood this Atilius Gavianus. He had been bought, but he did not dare to cast a veto. He asked for the night to ponder in. There were shouts, protests, appeals. His father-in-law[92] went down on his knees. The Tribune gave his word that on the following day he would offer no hindrance. They believed him, and the sitting was adjourned. In the course of the long night that ensued, our ponderer's fee was doubled. There were only a few more days in January on which the Senate could meet; but my recall remained the sole item of business.

[75] The Senate's resolution was hampered by all manner of delay and mockery and chicanery. But finally the day arrived on which my case was to go before an assembly, the twenty-third of January. The leading sponsor of the bill, Quintus Fabricius, a very good friend of mine, took up his station on the Rostra some time before daybreak. Sestius, who now stands trial for violence, made no move that day. Active champion of my cause as he was, he took no initiative; he waited to see what my enemies would do. Now, what about those responsible for bringing Sestius into court? How do *they* conduct themselves? Having filled the Forum, the place of assembly,[93] and the Senate-House in the dead of night with armed men, many of them slaves, they rush upon Fabricius, a violent assault, killing some persons and injuring many. [76] They drive

---

92. His name was Cn. Oppius Cornicinus (cf. *Red. quir.* 12).
93. Comitium, at the northwest end of the Forum.

Tribune Marcus Cispius away by force as he enters the Forum, an excellent, resolute gentleman. They make a shocking slaughter in the Forum. All of them in every part of it, with swords drawn and bloody, look around for my brother and shout his name—my excellent, brave, devoted brother. So sorely did he grieve for me and miss me that he would gladly have offered his body to their weapons, not to fight back but to die, if he had not reserved his life against the hope of my return. Nevertheless, he underwent the brutality of those felonious brigands. He had come to plead with the Roman People for his brother's restoration; driven from the Rostra, he lay on the ground, covering himself with the bodies of slaves and freedmen. He protected his life on that occasion with darkness and flight, not with law or law courts. [77] You remember, gentlemen, how the Tiber was full of citizen's corpses, how the sewers were choked, how the blood in the Forum was soaked up with sponges. Yes, we realized that so lavish a display, such magnificent decor, came from a Praetor and a patrician,[94] not from a plebeian or a private citizen.

Neither in the foregoing period nor on this day of disorder itself does the prosecution have any charge against Sestius. They say that violence was rife in the Forum. So it was, never more so. We have frequently seen stone-throwings, swords less often, though more often than we liked. But such a slaughter, such heaps of piled-up corpses—who ever saw the like in the Forum unless it was on the day when Cinna fought it out with Octavius?[95] What popular excitement caused it? Often a clash originates from the pertinacity, or resolution, of a Tribune casting his veto, through the fault and misconduct of a proposer of legislation, who offers the ignorant some advantage or largesse; it originates from a dispute between magistrates; it originates by degrees: shouting comes first, then the meeting somehow splits into opposing camps; actual fighting comes at a late stage, if at all; it seldom happens. Who ever heard of a riot stirred up at night, without a

---

94. I.e., Appius Claudius Pulcher (Publius being now a plebeian), who seems to have lent Clodius his gladiators (cf. s. 85).

95. In 87, when the Consul Cn. Octavius drove his colleague L. Cinna out of Rome.

word previously spoken, when no meeting had been called and no law proposed? [78] Is it credible that any Roman citizen or free man went down to the Forum before daybreak carrying a sword to stop legislation in my favor except for those who have so long been fattened on the blood of the Commonwealth by that pernicious wretch?

Now I put it to the prosecutor himself, who charges that while he was Tribune Sestius went about with a crowd, a large bodyguard: did he have them that day? Assuredly he did not. And so the cause of the Commonwealth was defeated, and that not by auspices or a veto or voting but by armed violence. If the Praetor who had declared that he had watched the heavens had announced contrary auspices to Fabricius,[96] the Commonwealth
+ would have suffered a blow, but one which it could support. If one of Fabricius' colleagues had vetoed his proposal, he would have damaged the Commonwealth, but he would have damaged it
+ legally. But is it tolerable, Clodius, that you should send in newly fledged gladiators, substituted[97] by yourself in view of your prospective aedileship, and bravos released from jail? That you should thrust magistrates from their station, make a horrible
+ slaughter, clear out the Forum with swords? And after this orgy of armed violence, will you accuse a man who protected himself with a bodyguard, not to attack you, but to have the means of defending his own life?

[79] And yet it was not from that point on that Sestius decided to use his friends for protection so that he could discharge his office and play his part in public affairs with safety in the Forum. Relying on the inviolability of the tribunate, thinking that he was sufficiently armed by inviolable laws[98] not only against force and the sword but even against words and heckling, he came to the temple of Castor and announced contrary auspices to the Consul.[99] Suddenly the Clodian posse, with its triumphant record of

---

96. See p. 55, n. 52.
97. Bought up slaves, substituted for real gladiators? Cf. s. 157.
98. See p. 57, n. 63.
99. Probably the Consul Metellus Nepos, who as Clodius' half-brother later blocked an attempt to bring Clodius to trial early in 57 (s. 89). The measure Sestius sought to block is not known, but below the "fragments of fencing" (s. 79) will

civic massacre, raises a shout, works itself up, and charges. Some attack the unarmed, unprepared Tribune with swords; others with sticks and fragments of fencing. After taking many a blow, his battered, lacerated body collapsed unconscious. He escaped death only because they fancied him dead. When they saw him lying there, hacked about with numerous wounds, at death's door, bloodless, exhausted, they finally stopped beating him, more in weariness and error than in pity or because they thought enough was enough. [80] And is Sestius on trial for violence? How so? Because he is alive? That is no fault of his. That one *coup de grace*, which would have drained him of what life he had left, did not fall. Blame Lentidius. He failed to hit the vital spot. Scold Titius, the man from Reate in the Sabine country[100] for shouting so irresponsibly that Sestius was dead. But why accuse my client? Did he dodge the blades or fight back? Did he not receive the weapon, as gladiators are ordered to do? Perhaps it is an act of violence not to succeed in dying outright? Or the fact that he, a Tribune, stained the temple with his blood? Or that, as soon as he regained consciousness after having been carried away, he did not ask to be brought back? Where is the charge? What is it you censure?

[81] I ask you, gentlemen of the jury: if the Clodian clan had accomplished its purpose that day, if Publius Sestius, who was left for dead, had indeed been killed, would you not have taken up arms? Would you not have roused yourselves to emulate the spirit of your fathers, the valor of old Rome? Would you not at long last have demanded the Commonwealth back from the baleful brigand? Or would you even then have stayed passive, timidly procrastinating when you saw the Commonwealth trampled in the dust by ruffianly bravos and slaves? Very well, you would have avenged his death, that is if you had a mind to be free and to have a Commonwealth: can you hesitate about your duty to his living valor—what you should say and feel and think and determine?

[82] Even those murderers, whose unbridled fury is nourished by long impunity, were so horrified by the heinous thing they had

---

refer to the barriers (*saepta*) erected at voting assemblies to divide the voters into their voting units by tribes.
100. Home of the antique virtues.

done that if the belief that Sestius was dead had persisted a little
+ while longer, they were planning to kill that "Toothy" of theirs so
as to shift the charge over to us. Little peasant as he was, he had
his wits about him, and the rogues could not keep their mouths
shut; he got wind of the plan to quench the odium of this Clodian
atrocity in his blood. So he snatched up the muleteer's cloak in
which he had first come to Rome for the elections and clapped a
reaper's basket over his head. As some were looking for "Numer-
+ ius Quinctius"[101] and others just for "Quinctius," he was saved by a
double error of nomenclature.[102] You all know the fellow went in
mortal peril until it became known that Sestius was alive. If that
fact had not come to light somewhat sooner than I could have
wished, they would not indeed have succeeded through the death
of their hireling in shifting the odium to the quarter they desired,
but they would have palliated the infamy of an atrocious crime by
a crime which would have been in some measure welcomed. [83]
And if Publius Sestius on that occasion, gentlemen of the jury, in
the temple of Castor had given up the life that he only just
retained, I do not doubt that a statue would one day have been set
up in the Forum to this man, killed in defense of the Commonwealth—provided, that is, that there was a Senate in the Commonwealth and that the majesty of the Roman People had come back
to life. For none of those whose effigies you see placed on the
Rostra after their death by our ancestors could fairly have been
put above Publius Sestius, either for the tragic character of his
death or for his patriotism. Sestius had championed the cause of a
fellow countryman in distress, a friend, a good servant of the
Commonwealth, which was the cause of the Senate and Italy and
the Commonwealth. In obedience to the auspices and his religious duty he announced the contrary auspices which he had
observed; and in doing so he would have been slain by nefarious
creatures of evil in broad daylight, in the sight of Gods and men,
in a sacred temple, a sacred cause, and a sacred office. Will any

---

101. Alternatively spelled "Quintius." The pronunciation is the same.

102. With my text, the mistake lay in calling him Numerius (praenomen) Quinctius (nomen) instead of Quintus (praenomen) Numerius (nomen). See Appendix II and SB[1], 271.

man think it right to strip of its ornaments the life of one whose death you would have commemorated with an everlasting memorial?

[84] "You bought men," says the prosecutor, "assembled and organized them." With what object? To beleaguer the Senate?[103] To drive out citizens convicted of no offense? To plunder property, burn houses, demolish roofs? To set fire to the temples of the Immortal Gods? To drive Tribunes from the Rostra with weapons? To sell provinces, which he pleased and to whom he pleased? To recognize kings? To bring back men condemned on capital charges to free communities through the agency of Roman commissioners? To hold the first man in the community beleaguered in his house by armed force? Those, I suppose, were the objects Publius Sestius had in view when he got together his troop of loyal followers, objects which could by no possibility be realized without crushing the Commonwealth by force of arms. Will it be argued that the time was not yet ripe, that the facts themselves were not driving honest men to such means of self-defense? I had been expelled, not solely by Clodius' band, it is true, but not without it either. You, my countrymen, sat in silent sorrow. [85] The Forum had been captured the previous year, after the temple of Castor had been occupied by runaway slaves as a sort of stronghold; not a word! Everything was going through by violence, by a shouting mob of reckless, beggarly desperados: you submitted. Magistrates were driven from the temples, others were barred even from access to the Forum: nobody lifted a finger. Gladiators from the Praetor's entourage were arrested, brought before the Senate, and after confession thrown by Milo into jail: Serranus released them, and nothing was said in the Senate. The Forum was strewn with the bodies of Roman citizens in a nocturnal massacre: no new tribunal was set up, even the old ones had been put out of action.[104] You saw a Tribune lying on the ground at death's door with more than twenty wounds in his body.

---

103. See Plut. *Cic.* 31, where Clodius is said on one occasion to have been "in arms around the Senate-House."

104. Probably a reference to the obstruction that prevented Milo from bringing Clodius to trial in early 57 (s. 89).

Another Tribune, a true hero—I shall say what I think and what everybody thinks—yes, a hero, a man of extraordinary, unparalleled, unheard-of greatness of heart and commitment and loyalty, had his house assaulted by the Clodian army with weapons and torches.

[86] Even you,[105] sir, praise Milo at this point, as well you may. Have we ever seen courage so memorable? Looking for no recompense except the approval of honest men, nowadays considered a threadbare, despised commodity, he took upon himself manifold risks, most arduous ordeals, most dangerous conflicts and feuds. He alone of our citizens, I feel, has taught us by action, not words, what men of outstanding caliber *ought* to do politically, and what they *have* to do. They *ought* to counter the villainy of bold subversives by means of law and law courts; but if the laws are impotent and the law courts are non-existent, if the Commonwealth is held in subjection by arms, by the concerted violence of reckless men, then life and liberty must be defended with organized forces. To realize this takes good sense, to do it takes courage; both to realize and to do it is the very perfection and crown of civic virtue. [87] Milo appeared on the political scene as Tribune. If I say much in his praise, it is not because he himself prefers to have these things said rather than thought, nor because I take pleasure in giving him his meed of compliments in his presence (particularly as I cannot do him justice in words): it is because I calculate that if I can show that Milo's cause was commended by the voice of the prosecutor, you will take the view that Sestius' case in the present proceedings runs parallel. Well then, Titus Annius espoused the cause of the Commonwealth with the object of recovering for his country a citizen of whom she had been robbed. A simple cause, a consistent policy, commanding universal consent and agreement. His colleagues were ready to help. One of the Consuls was warmly enthusiastic, the other pretty well appeased. Of the Praetors, only one was unfavorable. The Senate's good will passed belief, the Roman Knights were roused in support, Italy waited for a signal. Only two individuals had been

---

105. The prosecutor, P. Albinovanus.

bribed to obstruct.[106] If those despised creatures proved unequal to such a task, Milo saw that he would have no trouble achieving his purpose. He had with him authority, judgment, our highest order,[107] the precedent of good and brave citizens. He gave careful thought to what was worthy of the Commonwealth and of himself, who he was, what his hopes should be, and what he owed his ancestors.

[88] The gladiator saw that if he went by the rules he could be no match for so impressive a personage. He and his army resorted to weapons, firebrands, daily killings, arson, and lootings. He began to attack Milo's house, meet his comings and goings, challenge and intimidate him with violence. Milo was too strong and resolute a man to be disturbed. But although indignation, his innate sense of liberty, and his ready, exceptional courage urged this gallant gentleman to break and rebuff force with force, especially as he was so often confronted with it, yet such was his moderation and good sense that he kept his feelings in check and did not pay Clodius back in his own coin. Instead he tried to lasso him with the law as he bounded and pranced amid so many public calamities. [89] He brought charges. Who ever accused anybody with a better personal right? He did it for the Commonwealth, without enmity or reward, without any public demand or even expectation that he would ever do such a thing. Clodius was cowed. With Milo prosecuting he despaired of repeating the scandal of his earlier trial. But lo and behold! A Consul, a Praetor, and a Tribune put out new announcements of a novel character to the affect that the accused must not appear or be cited or sought after, forbidding all persons so much as to mention juries or law courts. What was he to do, this man born for valor, honor, and glory, with the violence of criminals thus reinforced and the laws and law courts put out of action? Was he to present his neck—he a Tribune to a private citizen, a man of outstanding quality to an arrant profligate? Was he to throw aside the cause he had taken up? Or shut himself up in his house? He thought it dishonorable either to accept defeat or to be frightened off or to

---

106. The Tribunes Serranus and Numerius.
107. The Senate.

hide. Since he was not permitted to invoke the law against Clodius, he made sure that he did not have to fear his violence as threatening either himself or the Commonwealth.

[90] How then do you accuse Sestius on this score of raising a bodyguard when you applaud Milo? You agree that a man has the right to raise a bodyguard when he is defending his own home, driving fire and sword from his altars and hearths, wishful to secure his safety in the Forum or in a temple or in the Senate-House. What of one who is prompted by the scars he sees every day all over his body to protect his head and neck and throat and flanks with some sort of bodyguard, do you think he deserved to be prosecuted for violence?

[91] As we all know, gentlemen, it was in the course of nature that at one time, before either natural or civil law[108] had been mapped out, men wandered through the land dispersed at large, and they possessed just so much as they had managed to snatch or keep by main force, killing and wounding one another. Then there arose some men morally and intellectually superior to the rest. Seeing the potentialities of human teachability and intelligence, they collected their scattered fellows into one place and led them out of that wild state into the way of justice and civilization. They instituted what we call commonwealths for the common good and those gatherings of human beings which were later called communities. They discovered law both divine and human, and fenced round with walls those aggregates of dwellings that we call towns.

[92] Now the main difference between our way of life with all the refinements of civilization and the old savage way is the difference between law and force. If we don't wish to live by one of the two, we must live by the other. If we want force suppressed, the law must prevail, that is to say law courts, on which all law depends. If the law courts are unsatisfactory or non-existent, then force must needs be master. Everybody sees this; Milo both saw and acted. He repelled force in order to make trial of law. He wanted to use the latter, hoping that virtue would triumph over

---

108. The first being universal (*ius gentium*), the second special to particular communities.

audacity; and he was compelled to use the former to prevent audacity triumphing over virtue. Sestius' position was identical—not as to launching a prosecution, since there was no need for everybody to take a hand in the same operation, but at all events in the necessity of defending his life and raising a bodyguard against physical violence.

[93] Immortal Gods! Where do you show us a way out? What hope do you offer the Commonwealth? How few will be found with the courage to embrace good political causes, to devote themselves to the interests of the honest men, to seek glory that is solid and real, knowing the activities of Gabinius and Piso, those two all but ruinations of the Commonwealth! The former draws every day a mass of gold beyond reckoning from the treasures of
+ peaceful, opulent Syria. He wages war on the unoffending in order to pour their ancient, untapped riches into the fathomless vortex of his lusts. He is building a country house so enormous that it makes that other country house look like a cabin—the one whose picture he used to unroll at meetings when he was Tribune in order to bring one of our bravest and most eminent citizens[109] into odium—this paragon of purity and disinterestedness! [94] As for Piso, he started by selling peace for a huge sum to the Thracians and the Dardanians; after which he handed Macedonia over to them to harry and plunder, to enable them to raise the money. He divided the property of Roman creditors with Greek debtors. He extorted vast sums from the people of Dyrrachium, despoiled Thessaly, levied annual payments on the Achaeans.[110] And with all this, he left not a statue nor picture nor ornament in any public or religious location. Thus do they mock justice, these two, most richly as they deserve every possible pain and penalty: whereas these two whom you see before you face trial.

I leave aside Numerius, Serranus, Aelius, the offscourings of Clodian sedition—though they too are still active in our midst, as you see, nor will they ever fear for their skins so long as you are afraid for yours. [95] As for the Aedile himself, what am I to say?

---

109. L. Lucullus, owner and builder of the villa in question.
110. Cf. p. 64, n. 97. On Cicero's charges against Piso as governor of Macedonia, see R. G. M. Nisbet, *Cicero in Pisonem* (Oxford, 1961), Appendix I.

He has actually brought a charge of violence against Milo and accused him. No injustice will ever make Milo regret his courage and resolution in public affairs. But the young men who see what is going on, what conclusions are they to draw? Here on the one side is Clodius, who attacked or razed or burned public monuments, sacred edifices, and the houses of his enemies, a man who was always surrounded and guarded by a ring of bravos, swordsmen, and informers that crowd our streets nowadays, who stirred up a band of foreign ruffians, bought slaves to commit murder, and emptied the entire contents of the prison into the Forum when he was Tribune: a bustling Aedile, he prosecutes the man who in some measure repressed his effervescent folly. Here on the other side is Milo, who protected himself to the extent of defending his household Gods—his private concern—and the rights of the tribunate and the auspices—his public responsibilities: debarred by resolution of the Senate[111] from prosecuting with due restraint the individual by whom he is himself now villainously being prosecuted. [96] This, I suppose, is the drift of the question in your prosecuting speech which you addressed particularly to me: what is our "tribe of optimates?"—that was your phrase.[112] Well, that is a lesson which our younger generation can learn to their great profit and one not hard for me to teach. If I say a few words on the subject, gentlemen of the jury, I do not think they will be irrelevant to the best interests of my audience or to your duty as jurors or to the particular case of Publius Sestius.

In this community of ours those who have been eager to engage in public life and make their mark in it have always been divided into two classes: one group has chosen to be thought and to be in fact "people's men," the other "optimates." Those who wished their actions and words to please the multitude were put in the former catagory, those who set out to win the approval of the better sort in the latter. [97] So who are the "better sort"? If you ask their numbers, there is no counting. Otherwise our society could not survive. There are the leaders of our council of

---

111. Which apparently approved the announcements (*edicta*) mentioned in s. 89.

112. Cf. s. 132.

state, there are those who follow in their wake, there are members of the principal orders, to whom the doors of the Senate-House stand open, there are the men of the country towns and the countryside, there are men of business; even freedmen are optimates. The number of this species is widely and variously distributed, as I have said; but the whole category can be circumscribed in a brief definition, to remove any mistake: all those are optimates who are neither criminals nor born rascals nor out of their proper wits nor
+ involved in private embarrassments. The fact then is that the tribe, as you call it, consists of blameless, sane individuals, whose private affairs are in good order. Those who steer the Commonwealth in conformity with their wishes, interests, and views, defenders of the optimates and optimates themselves, are counted as our most distinguished citizens, leaders of the community. [98] What mark then do these helmsmen of the Commonwealth set before them to keep in view and guide their course? Why, that which is best and most desirable to all sane, honest, and well-to-do people: tranquillity combined with dignity.[113] All who want that are optimates, while those who bring it to pass are considered great men, preservers of society. For it is not proper that men be so carried away by the dignity which the conduct of public affairs confers as to take no thought for tranquillity nor yet that they embrace a tranquillity that is incompatible with dignity.

There are certain foundations on which this tranquil dignity rests, certain components which our leaders must maintain and defend with their lives: religious ordinances, auspices, magisterial prerogatives, the authority of the Senate, the laws, ancestral tradition, the law courts, jurisdiction, credit, the provinces, the allies, our imperial glory, the military establishment, and the Treasury. [99] To be protector and patron of so many great institutions calls for no ordinary degree of high-mindedness, talent, and resolution. For in so large a citizen body there is a great multitude who either seek change and revolution because they have guilt on their consciences and fear punishment, or who feed on civil strife

---

113. *Otium cum dignitate*, a Ciceronian cliché. *Otium* points to a peaceful existence, unthreatened from within the community, *dignitas* to personal prestige, especially as won by public activity and offices.

and sedition from some sort of innate mental derangement, or whose private embarrassments make them prefer to perish in a general conflagration rather than in one peculiar to themselves. Once these folk have found themselves protectors and leaders to further their vicious inclinations, rough seas are stirred up in the Commonwealth, and those who have claimed for themselves the helm of state must keep their eyes open. With all the skill and diligence at their command they must strive to stay on course and make that harbor of tranquillity and dignity, preserving the foundations and components I have just mentioned.[114]

[100] If I were to deny, gentlemen of the jury, that this is a rough and arduous road, full of dangers and pitfalls, it would be a lie. After all, not only have I always so understood, but I know it better than others from experience. The combatant forces attacking the Commonwealth are larger than those defending it. That is because reckless and abandoned individuals are set moving by a mere nod; often they stir themselves up against the Commonwealth without any prompting. The honest men, on the other hand, tend to be slow. They neglect trouble in its early stages, and it takes an emergency finally to arouse them. So it sometimes happens that by delay and tardiness, wanting to keep tranquillity even at the cost of dignity, they lose both through their own fault. [101] As for the would-be champions of the Commonwealth, if they lack staying power they fall away, and if they lack courage they fail to appear. Only men of a certain caliber stand fast and endure all things for the sake of the Commonwealth, men like your father,[115] Marcus Scaurus. He opposed all sedition-mongers from Gaius Gracchus to Quintus Varius, and no violence, threats, or unpopularity ever shook him. Or men like Quintus Metellus, your mother's uncle: as a Censor he put a mark against Lucius Saturninus, a thriving politician on the democratic side; he declined to register the false Gracchus, defying the violence of an excited mob; finally, he alone refused to swear obedience to a law which he judged to have been irregularly passed and preferred to

---

114. Ciceronian metaphors are sometimes mixed.
115. The Leader of the Senate (see Index I under Aemilius Scaurus), father of the presiding magistrate at this trial.

be forced out of the community than out of his decision. Or (to leave examples from long ago, which exist in abundance worthy of this glorious empire, and not to name any person now alive) men like the late Quintus Catulus, whom neither the blizzard of danger nor the breeze of favor could ever turn from his course, by hope or by fear.

[102] Let these be your models, by the Immortal Gods, you that seek honor, glory, and renown; great examples, marvellous, immortal, celebrated by fame, entrusted to historical records, handed down to posterity. There is toil, I don't deny it; great perils, I grant you. "Full many a snare is laid for honest men"; indeed a true saying. But he[116] adds:

Wouldst thou ask what many envy, many seek with all their will,
Ask, nor bear the toil and turmoil? Little of the world knowest thou.

A pity he said elsewhere "Let them hate me, so they fear me," a saying for rascals to catch hold of, for those were fine maxims he gave the young. [103] Not but what this line of political conduct used to be more hazardous in days when the inclinations of the populace or the interests of the people often ran counter to the good of the Commonwealth. Lucius Cassius proposed a law for voting by ballot.[117] The people thought their liberty was at stake. The leading men disagreed, fearing the rashness of the multitude and the license of the ballot in cases where the survival of optimates was involved. Tiberius Gracchus proposed an agrarian bill. The people welcomed it, for it promised the poorer folk financial security. But the optimates resisted, seeing it as a source of discord and reckoning that if the rich were turned out of lands they had been occupying for generations, the Commonwealth would be bereft of defenders. Gaius Gracchus proposed a grain law.[118] The people liked it, for it meant plenty of food without any work, but the honest men opposed it, seeing it as an invitation to common folk to exchange industry for idleness and a ruinous drain on the Treasury.

[104] Within our memory there have been many issues—I pass

---

116. Atreus, in Accius' tragedy of that name.
117. Cassius' law (137 B.C.) extended the use of the secret ballot to criminal trials other than high treason (*perduellio*).
118. Fixing a low maximum price.

them over advisedly—which set popular desires at odds with the policy of our leaders. Now it is otherwise. There is nothing to divide the people from the elite, the leaders. The people have no demands, they are not desirous of revolution, they take pleasure in their own tranquillity, the dignity of the better sort, and the glory of the Commonwealth as a whole. Our seditious troublemakers can no longer excite the Roman People by a largesse, for the common folk, after going through terrible seditions and civil conflicts, are in love with peace and quiet. So they hold assemblies packed with mercenaries. They don't care whether their speeches and proposals are such as their audiences want to hear, but make sure with hard cash that their audiences give the appearance of wanting to hear whatever is said. [105] Do you imagine that the Gracchi or Saturninus or any of those who were considered people's men in the old days ever had anybody in an assembly who was paid to be there? None of them did, for the proffered largesse and gain excited the crowd without any money down. So in those days the people's men fell foul of serious, respectable folk to be sure, but they enjoyed marks of popular approval in plenty, manifested in all kinds of ways. They were applauded in the theater, voted anything they wanted, their names, words, countenances, appearances were held in affectionate regard. The opponents of such figures were respected and admired, they had much influence in the Senate and more among the honest men, but they did not please the crowd. Votes often went against their wishes. As for applause, if one of them did get applauded once in a while, he was afraid he had done something wrong. And yet, if a matter of real importance came up, that same people listened to their advice most of all.

[106] Today, if I am not mistaken, we have a different situation. If we eliminate the hired gangs, it appears that all will be of one political persuasion. There are three locations especially in which the Roman People can give expression to their judgment and sentiment: the public meetings, the polls, and the games and gladiator shows. Well, during these years was there ever a public meeting—a real one, that is, not a hired one—at which the unanimity of the Roman People was not plain to perceive? That villainous gladiator held many meetings about me to which

nobody came unless bought and corrupt. No honest man could stand the sight of his ugly face or the sound of his madman's voice. Those meetings of blackguards had to be disorderly. [107] Publius Lentulus as Consul held a meeting, likewise about me. The Roman People attended in force. All classes, the whole of Italy, took part in that meeting. He put the case very impressively and eloquently; and from the silence and universal approval it appeared that nothing so popular had ever fallen upon the ears of the Roman People. He brought forward Gnaeus Pompeius,
+ who presented himself to the Roman People not merely as recommending my restoration but as pleading for it. Pompeius' speeches at meetings have always been impressive and well received, but I make bold to say that his views never carried greater weight and that his eloquence never pleased his hearers more. [108] When the other leaders of the community spoke of me, they were received with a like assenting silence.[119] I do not name them at this point, for fear my discourse might seem ungrateful if I said too little about this one or that, and unending if I said enough about them all. And now take the speech this same enemy of mine made on the same subject to the real people in Mars' Field.[120] Did anyone approve, or rather did not everyone think it an outrageous scandal that he lived and breathed, let alone spoke? Who but thought his voice a blot upon the Commonwealth and himself a criminal if he were to give it a hearing?

[109] I come to the polls, whether elective or legislative, as you will. We see bills proposed all the time. I leave aside such as are proposed in such a way that five persons per tribe (and the wrong tribe[121] at that) are found to cast a vote. That ruin of the Commonwealth says he carried a bill against me, whom he called "tyrant" and "depriver of liberty." Who will admit to having voted when the proposal against me was put to the assembly? But when another bill concerning me was put to the Assembly of Centuries under a senatorial decree, who does *not* claim to have been

---

119. Cf. *Red. quir.* 16f.
120. Cf. *Dom.* 90.
121. Suggesting that some voters voted in a tribe to which they did not belong in order to produce a quorum.

present and to have cast his vote for my restoration? So which of the two causes ought to be regarded as "popular"? That in which all the community's respectabilities, ages, and classes are as one or that in which incited demons flock, as it were, to the funeral of the Commonwealth?

[110] Or are we to say that everything is "popular" in which Gellius is concerned, a fellow unworthy of his brother,[122] our excellent and distinguished Consul, and of the order of Knights, of which he retains the name after having liquidated its appurtenances?[123] To be sure we are, for the man is devoted to the Roman People. I never saw anybody more so! As a young man he could have thriven in the high honors of his illustrious stepfather, Lucius Philippus, but he was so little of a people's man that he squandered his property all by himself. His was a debauched and truculent youth; but after he had brought his inheritance down from the riches such as laymen enjoy to the philosopher's pittance, he took a fancy to be thought of as a Greekling, a man of leisure, and suddenly plunged into literary study. His Athenian lectors, to be sure, were of no use to him, his books too were often pawned to buy wine. His insatiable belly remained, but his resources were running out. So he lived in continual hope of a revolution; in public peace and quiet he was pining away. Has there ever been a sedition in which he was not a ringleader, or a sedition-monger of whom he was not a familiar, or a disorderly meeting in which he was not an agitator? When did he ever have a good word to say of an honest man? A good word? Say rather, is there a good citizen whom he has not truculently assailed? He married a freedwoman, not, as I suppose, because he wanted her body, but to be seen as a little man's friend.[124] [111] He cast a vote against me, was present and participating at the banquets and felicitations of the betrayers of their country—well, at any rate he avenged me when he kissed my enemies with that mouth

---

122. I.e., stepbrother, L. Marcius Philippus, consul this year. Gellius was also brother to L. Gellius, Consul in 72.

123. I.e., the qualifying fortune, 400, 000 sesterces.

124. *Plebicola*, lit. "cultivator of the plebs." So in *Leg. agr.* 2.84. Probably no allusion to the cognomen Poplicola or Publicola, borne by a nephew of this Gellius (see Badian's article cited under Gellius, L. in Index I).

of his! He is my enemy simply because he is penniless, as though it were my fault that he wasted his substance. Did *I* rob you of your patrimony, Gellius, or did you squander it? When you were pouring your inheritance into the whirling depths of your profligacy, was I to have to take the consequences, so that if as Consul I defended the Commonwealth against you and your cronies you would want me out of the community? None of your family likes to see you, they all flee your approach, avoid talking or meeting with you. Your nephew Postumius, a responsible young man with the judgment of an old one, set a black mark against you when he left you out of a long list of guardians to his children. But the disgust I feel on my own behalf and the Commonwealth's (and I don't know which of the two the fellow hates more) has carried me away. I ought not to have said so much about this crazy, beggarly guzzler.

[112] To return to my point: in the proceedings against me, with Rome captive and crushed, the leaders and instigators of the mercenary bands were evil spirits like Gellius, Firmidius, and Titius; and the character of the proposer himself was quite in keeping with their disrepute, recklessness, and squalor. Whereas when the bill reestablishing my dignity was put to the vote, nobody thought ill health or advanced age an adequate excuse for absence, nobody but felt he was bringing the Commonwealth back home in my company.

[113] Now let us take a look at the elections of magistrates. We recently[125] had a board of Tribunes in which two were considered strong people's men, three quite the reverse. Of those who were *not* thought to be people's men and who could not take part in hired meetings of the sort to which I have referred, I observe that two have been elected Praetors by the Roman People. And so far as I have been able to make out from the talk of the common folk and the voting, the Roman People were declaring to all and sundry their approval of Gnaeus Domitius' splendid staunchness and Quintus Ancharius' good faith and fortitude; it appreciated their good intentions, even though they had been unable to get results. As for Gaius Fannius, we see how he stands in public estimation;

---

125. In 59.

nobody should have any doubt what verdict the Roman People will pass on him when he stands for office. [114] Now what about our two people's men? One of them[126] had kept in the background, proposed no legislation, merely adopted a political attitude other than what was generally expected of him—an honest, blameless man of whom honest men have always thought well. But because he apparently did not quite understand what the real people approved of and mistook the attendance at a meeting for the People of Rome, he missed the place he would have won easily enough if he had not hankered to be a people's man. The other[127] had made himself conspicuous as a "popular" politician, setting at naught the auspices, the Aelian law, the authority of the Senate, a Consul,[128] his own colleagues, respectable public opinion. He stood for the aedileship in competition with some honest men, persons of high standing but not especially well off in resources and influence. Well, he did not carry his own tribe and even lost the Palatina, the tribe which all these plagues used in their efforts to harass the Commonwealth; and all he got from the electorate was what honest men would have wished for him.[129] So you see, the people itself is no longer "popular," so to speak. It vigorously repudiates those who are considered "people's men" and judges the opponents of that species most deserving of its favors.

[115] Let us come to the games. When I see your minds and eyes fixed upon me, gentlemen of the jury, I feel that I may now permit myself to relax my tone. Demonstrations of feeling at elections and meetings are sometimes genuine, but sometimes they are vitiated and corrupt. Spectators at theatrical and gladiatorial shows are said, no doubt, to be in the habit of applauding in exchange for money, thinly and sporadically; for some of them are irresponsibles. But when that happens, it is easy to see how it happens and by whom, and what that part of the crowd which has not been tampered with is doing. No need to tell you now which

---

126. C. Alfius Flavus.
127. P. Vatinius.
128. M. Calpurnius Bibulus.
129. Rejection; cf. SB^1, 271.

persons and what type of citizens get applauded most. You all know. The thing may be a triviality, though it is not so very trivial
+ when it is accorded to the better sort; but if it *is* trivial, it is trivial to serious people, whereas someone who depends on trivialities, the captive and puppet of common talk and, as they themselves call it, popular favor—he must perforce see applause as immortality and a hiss as death. [116] Well then, Scaurus, I ask you in particular as the donor of most elaborate and magnificent games: did any of these people's men watch your games or dare to show his face in the theater before the Roman People? Even that prince of pantomimes—not only a spectator but an actor and artiste, who knows all his sister's "entr'actes,"[130] who is brought into a gathering of women as a female luteplayer[131] —he neither watched your games during that red-hot tribunate of his nor any other games except those from which he only just escaped with his life. Yes, once and once only did this people's man trust himself to the games: it was the day on which honor was paid to virtue in Virtue's temple, and the monument of Gaius Marius,[132] preserver of this empire, lent its space to the restoration of Marius' fellow townsman and the defender of the Commonwealth.

[117] On that occasion the feelings which the Roman People manifested were declared in two ways. First, when they heard the Senate's decree, all applauded the thing itself and the absent Senate; then, when they applauded individual Senators returning from the Senate to watch the spectacle. But when the Consul[133] who was holding the games took his seat, they stood up and stretched out their hands, thanking him and weeping for joy, thus declaring their good will and compassion toward me. But when that madman entered the theater in a characteristic fit of frenzy, the Roman People could hardly restrain themselves, they had difficulty in keeping their hatred from his foul, unspeakable person.

---

130. *Embolia* = entertainments between acts. There is doubtless an indecent double meaning, but I do not know what it is.

131. Clodius' disguise at the festival of Bona Dea.

132. He built the temple, and the Senate met there to pass a resolution commending Cicero's safety to all nations (*Planc.* 78).

133. Lentulus Spinther. These will have been extraordinary games, since the regular ones were not held by Consuls.

There was a universal volley of cat-calls and shaking of fists and shouting of insults.

[118] But why do I recall the manly spirit of the Roman People as they descried freedom at last after their long subjection, displayed as it was against a man whom the very actors did not spare as he sat in front of them, already a candidate for the aedileship?[134] A comedy was on the stage, I think it was called "The Pretender."[135] The entire cast shouted in unison full in the foul wretch's face, bearing down and haranguing him:

+   Such the beginnings, such the ending, Titus, of your most wicked life.[136]

He sat dumbfounded. Accustomed to fill his meetings with the shouts of his "choir,"[137] he was now being thrown out by the voices of actual performers.

While I am on the subject of games, I may as well remark that in all the variety of thoughts expressed by the poets, not a single passage containing some utterance which seemed to fit the contemporary situation escaped the public as a whole or was not brought out by the player himself. [119] And at this point, gentlemen, I beg you not to suppose that it is frivolity that makes me drift into an unconventional style of pleading if I talk in a courtroom about poets and actors and games. I am not so ignorant of judicial procedure, gentlemen, not so unused to public speaking as to cast around for oratorical material in every department, plucking and gleaning flowers of rhetoric from every quarter. I know what is called for by your dignity, by these friends of the defense,[138] by yonder assemblage, by the status of Publius Sestius, by the magnitude of his danger, by my age, and by my rank. But I have taken it upon myself at this point to instruct my juniors in the meaning of the term "optimate." In the course of my explanation I have to show that not all who are considered people's men

---

134. As Aedile, Clodius would be one of the supervisors of the *ludi*; the actors would offend him at their peril.

135. *Simulans*, by Afranius, second-century B.C. writer of comedies of which only fragments survive.

136. Text and meaning uncertain.

137. Plutarch (*Pomp.* 48) describes Clodius' supporters at a meeting as answering his questions "like a chorus."

138. *Advocatio*, denoting *advocati*, who were friends of a defendant present in court to give advice and moral support.

are really such. That aim I shall most easily accomplish by bringing out the genuine, uncorrupted judgment of the entire people and the innermost sentiments of the community.

[120] What did it mean, the behavior of a great artist,[139] one who in politics as in his dramatic roles[140] has always chosen the best, before a vast audience? When the first news of the Senate's decree passed in the temple of Virtue was brought to the games and to the stage, he wept for recent joy mingled with sorrow and regret for me. And he pleaded my cause before the Roman People in words more weighty than any I could have used myself. For not only his art but his emotion went into his rendering of the genius of a great poet:[141]

> He who with undaunted spirit lent the Commonwealth his aid,
> Gave support, stood by the Grecians—

he was saying that *I* stood by *you*; he pointed to your rows. Everybody kept calling for an encore.

> He, when danger loomed,
> Doubted not his blood to offer, aye, his life he freely gave.

[121] With what shouts of applause was this received as he delivered it! Miming was omitted; it was the poet's words, the actor's enthusiasm, and the prospect of my return that drew the applause.

> Best of friends in worst of warfare—

in the goodness of his heart the actor added this of his own making:

> man with wondrous wit endowed,

and perhaps the audience approved because they felt a pang of regret for what they had lost.

Then the passage a little later on in the same play[142] that begins "Father"—how the Roman People groaned as the player rendered it! It was I whose loss he thought so lamentable, yes, I,

---

139. The tragic actor Aesopus (cf. s. 123).

140. There is a play on two meanings of *partes*, "acting roles" and "side" or "party" in politics.

141. Accius (cf. s. 123). According to the scholiast, the quotation is from his play *Eurysaces*. It possibly refers to the Greek warrior Ajax.

142. The passage, often quoted, actually came from the *Andromache* of Ennius. It is supposed that Aesopus put it into his lines in Accius' play, altering it to suit the new context.

whom Quintus Catulus and many others in the Senate had so often called father of the fatherland.[143] How the tears flowed as he bewailed the father driven away, the fatherland struck down, the home burned and demolished—pointing to the burning and destruction of *my* property! After a portrayal of former prosperity he turned and cried,

All in flames I saw it,

so movingly that even enemies and ill-wishers wept.

[122] And another passage,[144] Immortal Gods, how he spoke it! The acting and the writing were such that I think it would have seemed eminently appropriate in the mouth of Quintus Catulus himself, if he had returned to life; for he was wont on occasion to mince no words in reprimanding or accusing popular rashness or senatorial misjudgment:

O ungrateful men of Argos, thankless Greeks, of memory void!

That was not true. They were not ungrateful, only unhappy, unable to save their preserver; and no man was ever more grateful to another than all of them were grateful to me. Be that as it may, an eloquent poet wrote for me and an excellent actor, yes, a cour<u>ageous</u> actor spoke with me in mind, as he pointed to all the classes, accusing the Senate, the Roman Knights, and the entire Roman People:

Aye, ye let him stay in exile, saw him banished, suffer it yet.

The universal demonstrations that ensued, the declaration of will by the entire Roman People in the cause of one who was no people's man—I only heard of it. Those who were present are better able to judge.

[123] And since my discourse has carried me thus far: so many times an actor bewailed my fate, pleading my cause with such emotion that his magnificent voice was choked by tears; neither did the poets, whose genius I have ever loved, fail me in my hour of need; and the Roman People approved with their applause, aye, and with their groans. Well then: was it for Aesopus or for Accius to say these things on my behalf, if the Roman People had

---

143. After the suppression of the Catilinarian plot.
144. This did come from the *Eurysaces* (see above, n. 141).

been free, or for the leaders of the community? In the *Brutus*[145] I was mentioned by name:

> Tullius,[146] who founded firmly freedom for his countrymen.

There were any number of encores. Was that not evidence enough that in the judgment of the Roman People I and the Senate established what abandoned citizens charge us with having subverted?

[124] But the judgment of the entire Roman People was most conspicuously manifested at a gladiator show. It was the gift of Scipio,[147] worthy of the donor and of the Metellus[148] in whose honor it was given. It was the kind of show that is thronged by all and sundry, every sort of people, the kind the public most enjoys. Into this assemblage entered Tribune Publius Sestius, whose sole official activity was to champion my cause. He entered and showed himself to the people, not because he craved applause, but to let even my enemies see the will of the entire people. He entered, as you know, from Maenius' Column[149] and applause broke out from every spot from which the show could be seen as far as the Capitol and the barriers of the Forum. It was said that never in any cause had a consensus of the entire Roman People found plainer or more overwhelming expression. [125] Where were they then, the moderators of meetings, the lords of laws, the expellers of citizens? Do the rascals have another people of their own, to whom I was an object of odium and hostility?

I suppose the people are never found in greater numbers than at the gladiators—neither at any meeting nor yet at any elections. So this countless multitude, this overpowering, unanimous demonstration by the entire Roman People at precisely the time when, as was thought, action was about to be taken on my case—what did it declare except that the welfare and dignity of our best citizens is precious to the whole Roman People? [126] As for that

---

145. Also by Accius.
146. I.e., Servius Tullius, sixth king of Rome.
147. See Index I under Caecilius Metellus Pius Scipio.
148. Q. Metellus Pius, son of Metellus Numidicus and adoptive father of Scipio. He had died several years previously.
149. Cf. p. 145, n. 19.

Praetor[150] who was in the habit of putting a question to his meetings, did they want me back or not (Greeklings do things that way, it would not have done for his father or his grandfather or *his* father before him, his entire ancestry in fact), and declaring "the Roman People is against it" when his hirelings feebly called back "no"—he used to watch the gladiators every day, but he was never seen coming in. He would creep under the boards and pop up all of a sudden, as though about to say, "Mother, I call thee";[151]
+ which is how that surreptitious route he took to watch the show became known as the Appian Way. But whenever he was sighted,
+ the volley of hisses alarmed not only the gladiators' horses but the gladiators themselves. [127] Do you observe, gentlemen, what a mighty difference there is between the Roman People and a meeting? The lords of the meetings are branded with every mark of popular disfavor, whereas those who could have no part in gang meetings are honored with every expression of the Roman People's approval.

You actually remind me of Marcus Atilius Regulus, who preferred to return voluntarily to Carthage and to his death without
+ the prisoners for whose recovery he had been sent to the Senate
+ rather than stay in Rome; and you say I should not have wished for a return brought about by organized bands of gladiators and armed men. I suppose it was I that craved for violence—I who could do nothing while violence ruled and whose position would have been impregnable but for violence! [128] Was I to reject a recall so flattering that I am afraid some may think I was out for glory and left just in order to come back in such style? What citizen except myself was ever commended by the Senate to foreign nations? For whose safety except mine did the Senate publicly thank our allies in the name of the Roman People? For me and only me the Senate decreed that governors of provinces, Quaestors, and Legates protect my life and welfare. In my cause and in no other's since Rome's foundation were all who desired the welfare of the Commonwealth summoned from all Italy by consular

---

150. Appius Claudius Pulcher.
151. From Pacuvius' play *Ilione*, in which the ghost of Polydorus appeared from below the stage and called on his mother Hecuba.

letters under a senatorial decree. To preserve a single individual, myself, the Senate thought fit to decree what it has never decreed even when danger threatened the entire Commonwealth.[152] Who was more missed in the Senate-House, more lamented in the Forum? Whom did the tribunals themselves regret in like measure? After I was gone, all was a dreary desert, silent, full of sorrow and mourning. Is there anywhere in Italy where zeal for my restoration and testimony to my standing is not placed on public record?

[129] Need I mention those wonderful decrees of the Senate concerning me? One, for example, was passed in the temple of
+ Jupiter Best and Greatest. The man who pacified three continents with three Triumphs and added them to our empire[153] bore witness in a speech read from script that I alone had saved our country. A crowded Senate supported his speech, one public enemy dissenting,[154] and that very fact was entered in the public records for all posterity to remember. On the following day it was decreed in the Senate at the prompting of the People of Rome and of those who had assembled from the country towns that no one should watch the heavens or cause any manner of delay; should any man act to the contrary, he would be an outright subverter of the Commonwealth, and the Senate would take a serious view. The decree provided that in such a case the Senate should be consulted immediately. By taking this strong line in full numbers the Senate put a brake on the criminal audacity of some individuals. However, it added that if no action concerning me had been taken during the five days in which action was possible, I should return to my country fully rehabilitated.

[130] At the same time the Senate decreed that thanks be rendered to those who had come together from all over Italy for my restoration and that they be asked to return for the resumption of business.[155] Such was the rivalry in enthusiasm for my cause that

---

152. The assumption of mourning dress.

153. Pompey, who celebrated triumphs for victories in Africa, Spain, and Asia in 81 (or 80), 71, and 61 respectively.

154. Clodius.

155. At the expiration of the period (probably twenty-four days) which had to elapse between the promulgation of a law and its passage.

the very people to whom the Senate addressed its request were themselves begging the Senate on my behalf. Only one individual was found in open dissent from the earnest desire of honest men. Even Consul Quintus Metellus, who had been an uncompromising enemy of mine as a result of major political conflicts, put the proposal for my restoration to the Senate. He was stirred to do it by the high authority and amazingly impressive eloquence of Publius Servilius, who practically summoned up all the bygone Metelli from the shades and turned his kinsman's mind from Clodian banditries back to the dignity of the family to which they both belonged, urging him to remember a family precedent in what happened—glorious or sad, as you will—to Metellus Numidicus. The noble gentleman whom he addressed, a true Metellus, was moved to tears and put himself entirely in Servilius' hands before he ended his speech. He could not long withstand such lofty earnestness, redolent of old Rome, from one of the same blood as his own, and reconciled himself with me in my absence by his good deed. [131] And I am very sure that, if the consciousness of great men survives death, his action was highly pleasing to all the Metelli, and above all to that bravest of men and finest of citizens, his brother,[156] who was my partner in my toils, my perils, and my counsels.

As to the manner of my return, who does not know it? You might say that the people of Brundisium stretched out the welcoming hand of all Italy and Rome herself to me as I arrived. It was the fifth of August, this day of my arrival and return; it was also the birthday of my beloved daughter, whom I saw again for the first time after the grievous sorrow of separation. Furthermore, it was the foundation day of that same colony of Brundisium and likewise of the temple of Weal.[157] The house of those excellent and learned gentlemen M. Laenius Flaccus and his father and brother which joyfully received me was the same house that had sorrowfully taken me in a year previously and defended me with its protection and at its peril. All along my way home, all the cities of Italy seemed to be holding carnival for my coming,

---

156. Q. Metellus Celer, Consul in 60. He died the year following his consulship.
157. Salus.

the roads were crowded with a throng of delegates from every quarter, my approach to Rome through an unbelievable multitude offering congratulations was a Triumph. My progress from the city gate, my ascent to the Capitol, and my return to my house[158] was such that in the plenitude of joy I grieved that so thankful a community should have suffered such unhappiness and oppression.

[132] Well, I have answered your question: Who are the optimates? They are not a "tribe," as you called them. I recognized the word. It is the property of Publius Sestius' principal assailant,[159] one who wanted this "tribe" cut to pieces, wiped out, and who often made a reproach and accusation out of Gaius Caesar's mildness and aversion to bloodshed, averring that Caesar would never have a carefree moment as long as this "tribe" survived. As regards the optimates as a whole, he made no headway, but he kept on hammering away at me, attacking me first through the informer Vettius,[160] whom he questioned at a meeting about myself and some illustrious personages—such in fact was the quality of those whom he implicated in the same charge and danger with myself that I was obliged to him for associating me with such great and gallant gentlemen. [133] Later, with no provocation on my part except my desire to stand well with honest men, he hatched all manner of villainous plots against me. Every day he brought some trumped-up story about me to those who would listen to him. He warned my very good friend Gnaeus Pompeius to fear my house and beware of myself. He had linked himself so
+ closely with my enemy that Sextus Cloelius, a fellow thoroughly worthy of his associates, used to say that this person was the board on which my proscription was inscribed, while he himself was the writer. Alone of our order[161] he openly exulted in my departure and your distress. He came plunging day after day, but I never said a word about him, gentlemen. I was under assault from all manner of artillery, from the violence of an army; I did not judge

---

158. Since the house (presumably a temporary residence; cf. p. 70, n. 115) was not the one Cicero left in 58, "return" is not strictly appropriate.
159. Vatinius.
160. See Index I.
161. Apart, that is, from the prime mover, Clodius.

it fitting to complain about a single sharpshooter. He says he does not approve of my measures. That is news to nobody. He is defying a law of mine which explicitly makes it illegal to give a gladiator show within two years before standing or intending to stand for office.[162] [134] I am really amazed, gentlemen, at his temerity. There he is, blatantly breaking the law, and he is not a person who can slide out of a trial on his personal popularity or go free by using his influence; nor does he have the resources and power to ride roughshod over laws and law courts. What makes him so unbridled? He must have come by a spectacular, celebrated team of gladiators, something to boast about. He knew the public's enthusiasm, he pictured the noisy crowds. Excited by anticipation, thirsting for réclame, he could not restrain himself from putting these gladiators on display—and himself the handsomest gladiator of them all![163] If that was why he erred, carried away by zeal for the people in return for the favor recently bestowed by the Roman People on himself,[164] even so, it was unforgivable. But as it is, he did not even take picked men from the slave market, but he bought them from the barracks[165] and stuck gladiatorial labels on them; it was a toss-up who should be Samnites, who Challengers.[166] Is he not afraid of where such license, such contempt for the laws, is going to end? [135] But he has two defenses. First he says "I am exhibiting beast-fighters, the law refers to gladiators." An amusing distinction! And here is an even smarter touch: he will say he is not exhibiting gladiators but just one gladiator and has put his entire aedileship[167] into the show. A fine aedileship!

---

162. The point of the distinction seems to lie in the fact that a man might be a candidate unofficially (*prensatio*) before formally presenting himself as such (*petitio*); cf. *Att.* 1.1.1. The law against electoral corruption was sponsored by Cicero during his consulship.

163. Vatinius was notably ugly.

164. He had been *defeated* in the aedilician elections for 56.

165. *Ergastula*, slave barracks in rural districts, where the inmates were kept under prison conditions.

166. Types of gladiators. The first is well-known. "Challengers" (*provocatores*) are mentioned elsewhere, but nothing is recorded of their characteristics.

167. I.e., the money he had collected in anticipation of being elected Aedile (cf. n. 164, above).

One Lion,[168] two-hundred beast-fighters. However, he is welcome to his defense. I want him to be confident in his case. When he isn't, he is apt to call upon the Tribunes and disrupt the trial by violence.[169]

It does not so much surprise me that he despises my law (after all, I am his enemy) as that he has decided to treat all consular laws without exception as null and void. He has defied the Caecilian-Didian law[170] and the Licinian-Junian.[171] What about Gaius Caesar's law on extortion,[172] Caesar, who, as he often boasts, was set up, protected, armed, by *his* law and favor?[173] Does he take that, too, for null and void? And they say other people are rescinding Caesar's measures when this excellent law is disregarded by that father-in-law[174] of his and this hanger-on! And the prosecutor has dared to urge you, gentlemen of the jury, to come down hard for once and to give the Commonwealth long-needed therapy! It is no therapy when the scalpel is applied to a sound and healthy organ; that is cruelty, butcher's work. The healers of the Commonwealth are those who cut out an evil, a wen[175] on the body of the community.

[136] But my discourse must have a finish if I am to come to the end of what I say before I come to the end of your patient attention. I shall therefore conclude my observations on the optimates and their leaders and the defenders of the Commonwealth. To you, young men, those of you who come of nobler stock, I shall say: "imitate your ancestors"; those of you who can attain nobility by your talents and energy I shall urge to the principles of

---

168. According to the Bobbio scholiast, commenting on this speech in the 4th/5th century A.D., a gladiator in Vatinius' troop was called Leo ("Lion").

169. The tactics used to thwart prosecution in 58 (see *Vat.* 33–34).

170. See p. 56, n. 60.

171. Requiring that copies of proposed laws be deposited in the Treasury.

172. *Lex Iulia de pecuniis repetundis*, pertaining to the regulation of provincial government; cf. *Vat.* 29.

173. The law that gave Caesar his command was proposed by Vatinius as Tribune in 59.

174. L. Piso, now governor of Macedonia. His daughter Calpurnia was Caesar's last wife.

175. *Struma*, an allusion to Vatinius' physical deformity; cf. *Vat.* 39.

conduct in which many "new men"[176] have covered themselves with honor and glory. [137] There is only one path, believe me, to praise and prestige and honor, and that is by gaining the commendation and esteem of honest men, men of wisdom, men of the right mould, and by knowing the distribution of functions most wisely ordained by our ancestors. When the power of the kings became intolerable, they created annual magistrates, but they also set a perpetual council over the Commonwealth: the Senate. Its members were chosen by the entire people. Access to the highest order was therefore open to the industry and energy of all citizens. They stationed the Senate as guardian, head, and
+ champion of the Commonwealth. They desired the magistrates to heed the authority of this order, to be, as it were, the servants of the august council, and the Senate itself to confirm the prestige of the orders next in rank and to protect and foster the freedom and interests of the commons.

[138] Those who defend these institutions to the best of their ability are optimates, to whatever class they belong. Those who
+ chiefly bear the heavy weight of such functions on their shoulders and sustain the Commonwealth have ever been accounted leaders of the optimates, promoters and preservers of the community. I admit, as I have said already, that persons of this description have many adversaries, enemies, ill-wishers. Many are the dangers they must encounter, many the injuries they must receive, formidable the ordeals they must experience and undergo. But all this while I have been addressing manhood, not sloth; honor, not pleasure; those who feel born to serve their country, countrymen, good name, and glory, not to sleep and feast and amuse themselves. Let the votaries of pleasure, self-abandoned to the temptations of vice and the blandishments of desire, say good-bye to honors, let them have nothing to do with public life, let them be content to enjoy the leisure they owe to brave men's exertions. [139] But they who look for fame among honest men, which alone can truly be called glory, should seek leisure and pleasures for others, not for themselves. Theirs to sweat for the common good, to incur enmities,

---

176. Men without senators in their ancestry. See Shackleton Bailey, "*Nobiles* and *novi* reconsidered," in *AJP* 107 (1986), 255–60.

often to brave storms for the sake of the Commonwealth, to contend with the bold and the bad, yes, and sometimes with the powerful.[177] Such is what we are told about the principles and actions of illustrious men by our teachers and our books. We see no praise go to such as at one time or another have incited the people to sedition, or blinded ignorant minds with largesse, or stirred up ill will against brave and famous men and good servants of the Commonwealth. Romans have ever held them for irresponsible, bad, mischievous citizens. But those who have repressed the onslaughts and attempts of such, who by their authority, good faith, resolution, and high-mindedness have resisted the designs of the unscrupulous—these have ever been accounted men of weight, chiefs, leaders, promoters of Rome's dignity and empire.

[140] Now in case what has happened to me and to others also causes any man to shy away from this course of conduct, among those who have done the Commonwealth fine service, Lucius Opimius is the only member of the community I can name who met with unmerited calamity. His monument[178] remains in the Forum, frequented by multitudes, but his tomb stands deserted on the coast by Dyrrachium. And yet, for all that feeling ran high against him on account of Gaius Gracchus' death, the Roman People themselves always freed him from jeopardy. It was a different sort of hurricane, an unjust trial,[179] which felled that noble citizen. The others, struck down by the sudden gales of popular violence, were called back to life and home by the people themselves; or else they passed their days without hurt or harm. On the other hand, those who neglected the Senate's advice, the authority of honest men, and the institutions of our ancestors and sought the favor of an ignorant or incited populace almost all paid for their offenses against the Commonwealth by death on the spot or dishonorable exile. [141] In Athens,[180] a city of Greeks far removed in character from our Roman gravity, statesmen were not lacking to defend their commonwealth against popular violence,

---

177. Cicero is thinking of the "Triumvirs."
178. The Basilica Opimia, near the temple of the Concord.
179. He was found guilty in 109 of receiving bribes from the Numidian king Jugurtha.
180. This excursion into Athenian history is largely travesty.

although all who did so were expelled from the community. The great Themistocles, the savior of his country, was not deterred by the condemnation of Miltiades, who had saved her only a little earlier, nor yet by the banishment of Aristides, traditionally accounted the most just of mankind. And later the great men of that community, whose names it is not necessary to mention, with so many examples of popular anger and levity before them, nonetheless defended that commonwealth of theirs. So what ought *we* to do—we who have been born in a community which I take to be the native soil of gravity and greatness of soul; who walk in such glory that all things human should seem of slight account; who have stepped forward to protect a commonwealth so majestic that to die in her defense is better than to gain supreme power as her assailant?

[142] The Greek statesmen whom I have just named were unjustly condemned and banished by their countrymen. Yet because they served their communities well, their glory today is such, not only in Greece, but here too and in all other lands, that the names of those who wrought their downfall are never mentioned and all prefer their calamity to the arbitrary power of their enemies.

What Carthaginian surpassed Hannibal in wisdom, valor, achievement—Hannibal, who for so many years contended with so many Roman generals for empire and glory? His own countrymen threw him out of his country.[181] We see him celebrated in our literature and memory, enemy though he was.

[143] Therefore, let us model ourselves on our great men—Brutus, Camillus, Ahala, the Decii, Curius, Fabricius, the Maximi, the Scipios, the Lentuli, the Aemilii, others beyond number who established this Commonwealth. For my part, I place them in the company and number of the Immortal Gods. Let us love our country, obey the Senate, work for the honest men. Let us disregard the prizes of the moment and think only of posterity; let "best" for us mean that which is most honorable; let us hope for what we want, but accept what comes; and let us reflect that the bodies of brave and great men are mortal, but the activity of their

---

181. Actually he fled under pressure from Rome.

minds goes on forever. We see that view enshrined in the sacred figure of Hercules, whose body was burned, but whose life and valor were received into immortality. Let us not doubt that those who augmented or defended or saved this great Commonwealth of ours by their counsels and trials have won glory everlasting.

[144] But, gentlemen, as I speak of the dignity and the glory of our bravest and most illustrious citizens and am set to speak yet more, I am suddenly checked in the very flow of my discourse by the sight of persons here present. I see Publius Sestius, defender, champion, promoter of my restoration, of your authority, and of the public cause, standing trial. I see his son in his boy's gown tearfully gazing at me. I see Milo, vindicator of your freedom, guardian of my safety, help of the prostrate Commonwealth, suppressor of internal brigandage, extinguisher of daily carnage, defender of temples and dwellings, bulwark of the Senate-House, dressed as a man with a charge hanging over his head. I see Publius Lentulus, whose father I call the guardian deity and parent of my fortune and name, of my brother and our children, in this sorry garb of woe. Last year he received this gown of manhood from his father and the purple-bordered gown by popular election.[182] This year in *this* gown[183] here he is appealing on behalf of that gallant and illustrious gentleman, his father, against the unlooked-for cruelty of an iniquitous bill.[184]

[145] I alone am the cause that so many citizens, and such citizens, are wearing these lugubrious garments, in sorrow and disarray, because they defended me, grieved for my sad fate, returned me to my sorrowing country, the call of Italy, the entreaty of you all. What is my heinous crime? What dire offense did I commit when I brought before you the depositions, letters, confessions concerning the plot for our common destruction, when I obeyed

---

182. Boys wore a purple-bordered gown (*toga praetexta*), men a plain white one, except for the magistrates and others. Young Lentulus had been elected to the College of Augurs.
183. The black of mourning.
184. To recall Lentulus Spinther from his province of Cilicia, put forward by a hostile Tribune at the beginning of February (cf. *Fam.* 1.5a.2). It did not go through.

your behest?[185] If it is a crime to love my country, I have paid pen-
+ alty enough. My house was torn down, my property dissipated, my children harassed, my wife dragged off, my excellent brother, the most brotherly and loving of brothers that ever was or could be, rolled in the dust at the feet of my worst enemies. I myself, driven from hearth and altar and household Gods, torn from my family,
+ lost the country which, to say the very least, I had surely loved. I bore the cruelty of the hostile, the villainy of the faithless, the perfidy of the jealous. [146] If this be not enough, since all these sufferings are felt to have been cancelled out by my return, then it is far better for me, yes, gentlemen of the jury, far better to fall back into my former evil plight than to bring such misfortune on my defenders and saviors. Could I stay in Rome when those who gave Rome back to me are driven out? I shall not, I cannot, gentlemen. Never shall this boy, whose tears declare his filial affection, lose his father on my account and see me myself a citizen in good standing. Nor shall he groan whenever he sets eyes on me and say he sees his own and his father's bane. No, in every condition, whatever shall come their way, I shall embrace it. No fortune shall ever divide me from those you see before you wearing mourning because of me, nor shall those nations to whom the Senate commended me and whom it thanked in respect of me see Sestius in exile on my account and without my company.

[147] But the Immortal Gods, who received me in their temples on the day of my homecoming, surrounded by these gentlemen[186] and Consul Lentulus, and the Commonwealth itself, the holiest thing on earth, have committed these matters to your discretion, gentlemen of the jury. It lies in your power by your ver-
+ dict to fortify the minds of all honest men and restrain the rush of the rascals, to make of these here present[187] excellent citizens, to give me back my strength, to revive the Commonwealth. Therefore I adjure and implore you: if you wished me restored, preserve those through whose agency you recovered me.

---

185. To execute the arrested conspirators. "Your" refers to the senators on the jury.
186. Sestius and Milo.
187. The young men addressed earlier in the speech (s. 136).

EXAMINATION OF THE WITNESS PUBLIUS VATINIUS
(*In P. Vatinium testem interrogatio*)

P. Vatinius was born about 95. Nothing is known of his family,[1] and aside from Cicero's allegations about an obscure but disreputable youth and a misconducted quaestorship in 63, followed by unspecified "misdemeanors and petty thefts" in Spain, he first comes into view as a Tribune in 59 and the Consul Caesar's most energetic adherent. It was Vatinius who about June in that year put through the popular assembly the fateful law conferring on Caesar his five-year command in Gaul. Having survived a prosecution in the year following, he stood unsuccessfully for the aedileship.

At Sestius' trial (which, according to Cicero, he had engineered) he gave evidence against the defendant. Cicero had attacked him during the process (s. 1: "perhaps I went too far a short while ago"). Vatinius replied next day, to be answered by Cicero with a continuous "interrogation," to which Vatinius was to reply *seriatim* (s. 10: "reply faithfully"). To do so he would obviously have needed a written copy. This might have been forthcoming, since speeches were sometimes taken down in shorthand. But on the whole it seems more likely that the speech as we have it was in the nature of a pamphlet, composed after the trial, though based more or less on things actually said in court. Writing to his brother about the case (see p. 138), Cicero adds: "I cut up his (Sestius') adversary Vatinius just as I pleased to the applause of Gods and men, which was what Sestius wanted more than anything. . . . In short that bullying ruffian left the court much disconcerted and unnerved."

His subsequent career, which included a consulship in 47 and a Triumph, need not much concern us, but it is noteworthy that, under pressure from Pompey, Cicero was reconciled with him and in 54 successfully defended him on a bribery charge. Vatinius was grateful. He was kind to Cicero at one point in the Civil War (*Att.* 11.5.4), and their extant correspondence in 45 (*Fam.* 5.9–11) shows them on friendly

---

1. See Shackleton Bailey, *Two Studies in Roman Nomenclature* (1976), p. 73.

terms.

Besides suffering Cicero's invective, Vatinius is the object of several unflattering references in Catullus' epigrams. But unpopularity, at least in conservative quarters, undistinguished origin, and physical ugliness did not prevent him from marrying well: first to Antonia, sister to Mark Antony and niece to L. Julius Caesar, Consul in 64, and a distant relative of the future Dictator; and later to a Pompeia, who was probably of aristocratic family, if not—as has been thought not unlikely—Pompey the Great's sister.

+ [1] If I had chosen to look only at what your unworthiness deserved, Vatinius, I should have taken the course which my friends here strongly favored and let you go in silence, seeing that your disreputable life and private turpitudes deprived your testimony of all weight. None of them thought it fitting to refute you as a serious opponent or to question you as a conscientious witness. But perhaps I went too far a short while ago.[2] My dislike of you prompted me—after the crime you perpetrated against me[3] I have better reason than anybody for that, though in fact almost everyone dislikes you more than I do. That is why, even though my contempt was equal to my dislike, I chose to have you leave this court harassed rather than merely despised. [2] You must not be surprised then that I do you the honor of interrogating you, a creature whom nobody cares to meet or approach or vote for, nobody thinks worthy to be a citizen or to breathe the common air. No motive would have induced me to do so except an urge to repress your insolence, quell your audacity, and slow down your flow of words by trapping you in a few of my questions.

Vatinius, even if Publius Sestius had suspected you wrongly, you should have forgiven me if I was disposed to comply with the needs and wishes of one to whom I was under a great obligation when he was in such jeopardy.[4] [3] But you lied in your evidence yesterday when you affirmed that you had never talked to

---

2. See introductory note.
3. In the Vettius affair (see *Sest.* 132 and Index I), followed by further hostility.
4. I.e., Vatinius should not take offense if Cicero treated him as being in league with the prosecutor as his client Sestius believed.

Albinovanus on any subject, let alone about prosecuting Sestius. You gave that away inadvertently just now, when you said that Titus Claudius[5] had communicated with you and asked your advice about prosecuting Publius Sestius and that Albinovanus, whom earlier you had said you scarcely knew, had come to your house and had a long conversation with you. Finally, you said you had given Albinovanus copies of public speeches made by Publius Sestius which he neither knew nor could have discovered and that these were read out in the course of his trial. Thereby you admitted that the prosecution had been furnished with material by you.
+ At the same time you exposed your own inconsistency, combined with irresponsibility and perjury too, alleging that a man whom you had described as quite a stranger to you had been in your house and that you had given a prosecutor whom you said you had thought from the first was in collusion with the defense the documents he requested for use in the case.

[4] Yours is too arrogant, too passionate a nature. You think it blasphemy if a word comes out of anybody's mouth which is not agreeable and flattering to your ears. You came in wrath against us all. I perceived that, foresaw it as soon as I set eyes on you, before you began to speak, while Gellius, that nanny of all sedition-mongers, was giving evidence before you spoke. For all of a sudden, like a snake from its lurking-place, you moved in, with starting eyes, swollen throat, bulging neck,[6] so that * * *

[5] * * * I defended my old friend (also, however, a friend of yours). In our society a defense is not as a rule adversely criticized, as an attack, such as you are now launching, sometimes is. But I put it to you: why would I not have defended Gaius Cornelius?[7] Had Cornelius proposed a law in contravention of auspices, had he disregarded the Aelian law or the Fufian?[8] Had he used violence against a Consul? Had he occupied a temple with armed

---

5. Otherwise unknown. On the speech, cf. Introductory note and p. 226, n.67.

6. The description suits the comparison with a snake striking and also pokes fun at Vatinius' physical deformity. The swelling of his neck was caused by the disease scrofula (cf. s. 10, *Sest.* 135).

7. See Index I. Vatinius will have charged Cicero with inconsistency in defending one "popular" Tribune and then attacking another (himself).

8. See p. 10, n. 29.

men? Had he by violence dislodged a Tribune[9] in the act of casting his veto? Had he profaned religious observances, exhausted the Treasury, plundered the Commonwealth? All that is in *your* department. Nothing of the kind was alleged against Cornelius. He was said to have read out a document. He replied, and he called his colleagues to witness, that he had not done so for the purpose of reading it but for the purpose of revising it. At any rate, it was established that Cornelius dismissed the meeting that day and complied with the veto. You do not approve of my defending Cornelius, but what about yourself? What sort of a case will you bring to your counsel—and what sort of a face? You are already telling them how much harm they will do to their reputations if they defend you when you think it is proper to reproach me with my defense of Cornelius among your other insults.[10] [6] But remember this, Vatinius: shortly after I had conducted this defense, which you say gave offense to honest men, I was elected Consul not only with the full support of the Roman People as a whole but also with the enthusiastic backing of the better sort—the greatest electoral triumph in memory. By living a decent life I attained all that you in your indecent vaticinations have often declared you hoped for.[11]

You bring my departure from Rome up against me, choosing to revive the sorrow and lamentation of these gentlemen,[12] to whom that day was the bitterest of their lives, as it was the happiest of yours. I have only this to reply: when you and your fellow plagues of the Commonwealth were seeking a pretext to take up arms, when you were eager to use my name in order to plunder the property of the well-to-do, to suck the blood of the leaders of our community, to satiate your cruelty and inveterate hatred of honest men, I preferred to break the force of your criminal fury by

---

9. Presumably one of the three colleagues of Vatinius in 59 opposed to Caesar; cf. s. 16.

10. "It is scarcely necessary to remark that Nemesis overheard and that Vatinius was successfully defended by Cicero in 54 B.C." (Pocock).

11. I.e., the consulship (cf. s. 11 and Catull. 52.3 "Vatinius foreswears himself by his consulship."). Some see *vāticinando* as a pun on Vătīnius, but the differing vowel quantities make that unlikely.

12. The jury and the people in court.

withdrawing rather than by putting up a fight. [7] So I beg you to forgive me, Vatinius, for sparing the country I had saved and to tolerate me, the preserver and guardian of the Commonwealth, if I tolerate you, her harasser and destroyer. Moreover, you are villifying the departure of one whom you see recalled by the sorrowing regret of all citizens and the mourning of the very Commonwealth. Oh, but you said it was not for my sake, but for the Commonwealth's that men were anxious for my return—as though any man who has embarked on public life with a high heart would think anything more desirable than to be loved by his countrymen for the sake of the Commonwealth. [8] No doubt I am a prickly sort of person, difficult to approach, heavy of countenance![13] I answer people arrogantly, rudeness is my habit! No one missed my society, my good nature, my advice, or my assistance! And yet, to say the least, regret for my loss brought sadness to the Forum and silence to the Senate-House. All cultivation of the liberal arts went into eclipse. But grant that nothing was for my sake. Let us acknowledge that those senatorial decrees, orders of the people, resolutions of all Italy, of all societies and associations were passed for the sake of the Commonwealth. How little you know of sterling reputation and true dignity! What greater distinctions could come my way? What more could I desire in order to perpetuate my glory and make my name remembered for all time to come than that all my countrymen should declare the welfare of the Commonwealth to be bound up with my individual welfare? [9] Well, I return your compliment. Just as you have said that I am dear to the Senate and People of Rome not so much for my own sake as for the sake of the Commonwealth, so I say that you, detestable though you are for your sinister and monstrous self, are hated by the community not so much on your own account as on the Commonwealth's.

But it is time I came to *you*, so about myself I shall say only this in conclusion: it does not very much matter what any one of us says about himself; but the judgment of honest men—that is of great weight and moment. [10] Two situations reveal the judgment of our countrymen concerning us: when it is a question of

---

13. Cicero was famous for being affable and easy-going.

an office and when it is a question of civic survival. To few have offices been granted by the Roman People with such hearty good will as to me, and none have been restored to their rights as citizens with such nationwide enthusiasm. The general feeling about *you* has already been tested when you stood for office;[14] we are waiting to see what happens when your survival comes into question. But to compare myself, not with the leaders of the community here present, but with your not only impudent but base and disreputable self, I put this question to your face, Vatinius, well knowing your arrogance and hostility to me: between the two of us, do you think it was better or more advantageous that I or you were born in this community—better for this community, for this Commonwealth, for this city, for the Treasury, for the Senate-House, for these gentlemen whom you see before you and for their property, estate, and children, for all citizens besides, yes, for the shrines of the Immortal Gods, the auspices, and the practice of religion? Your answer will either be so impudent that folk will barely be able to keep their hands off you or so mortifying that your swelling will at last burst.[15] Having given it, kindly reply faithfully to what I have to ask you concerning yourself.

[11] The murky period of your youth I shall leave in the shadows. So far as I am concerned, for what you did in your young days, as driving holes through walls, burgling your neighbors, beating your mother, you go scot-free. Let your unworthiness carry its reward, let the disgraces of your youth be veiled by your squalid obscurity. You stood for the quaestorship along with Publius Sestius. He talked only of the matter in hand, you used to say you were thinking about how to run your second consulship.[16] Tell me, do you remember how, after Publius Sestius had been elected by a unanimous vote, you just managed to stick to the last place, against everybody's wishes and not by the people's favor but

---

14. The aedileship. He was defeated; cf. s. 16.
15. See p. 209, n. 6.
16. A joke. For Vatinius to aim at the consulship at all was gross presumption in Cicero's eyes. At the time of this speech nobody since Sulla had held the office more than once, though Pompey and Crassus were about to do so in the year following. But that was not yet known.

by the Consul's?[17] [12] When in that magistracy you were assigned by lot to Coastal Control amid loud protests,[18] do you recall that as Consul I dispatched you to Puteoli to forbid the export of gold and silver from the port? In that charge you thought you had been sent, not as a watchdog to keep the traffic down, but as a customs officer to split the receipts. You subjected the houses, storerooms, ships of all and sundry to a thievish scrutiny. You entangled businessmen in iniquitous lawsuits, terrorized traders as they left their ships, held them up at embarkation. Do you remember that during these operations you were physically assaulted at a meeting in Puteoli and that complaints from the townspeople were laid before me as Consul?

After your Quaestorship did you go to Further Spain as Legate to Proconsul Gaius Cosconius? The journey to Spain is normally made by land, or if anyone wants to go by sea, there is a standard route. Did you go to Sardinia and then from there to Africa? Were you in Hiempsal's kingdom,[19] which you had no right to enter without a senatorial decree? Were you in Mastanesosus'[20] kingdom? Did you travel to the Straits by way of Mauretania? And did you ever hear of a Legate for Spain going to the province by such a route?

[13] You were elected Tribune—I shall not trouble to interrogate you about your Spanish misdemeanors and petty thefts. First I ask you in general terms whether there is any sort of rascality and wrongdoing that you failed to commit in that office. And I warn you from now on not to mix up your own baseness with the celebrity of illustrious names.[21] All the questions I ask shall concern you personally. I shall drag you from your own obscurity, not from the heights of a great man's reputation. My shafts shall all be directed against you, and nobody else shall be wounded

---

17. No doubt L. Caesar, Consul in 64, whose niece Antonia Vatinius had married.
18. Vatinius' assignment included supervision of the grain port of Ostia; hence the concern.
19. Numidia. Vatinius may have gone there on some business of Caesar's, who had opposed Hiempsal in a lawsuit in 62 (Suet. *Iul.* 71).
20. The latter half of the name of this unknown monarch may be corrupt.
21. Caesar's.

through your body, as you like to put it. They will lodge fast in your lungs and entrails.

[14] The Immortal Gods are the starting point from which all great things proceed. You like to call yourself a Pythagorean, using the name of a very learned personage[22] to cloak your monstrous, barbarous practices. You have engaged in strange and wicked rituals, you are by way of raising the souls of the dead, of offering up the entrails of children to ghosts. Tell me: what mental perversion, what madness led you to despise the auspices by which this city was founded and on which our whole Commonwealth and empire depend? Why did you give notice to the Senate at the outset of your term as Tribune that the responses of the Augurs and the arrogance of that College would not hamper your proceedings? [15] Next question: were you as good as your word? Were you ever delayed from calling an assembly and presenting a law by the knowledge that the heavens had been watched that day?[23] And since this is the one point you say you have in common with Caesar, I am going to separate you from him, both for the Commonwealth's sake and for Caesar's own, lest his prestige may seem to have taken a stain from your utter despicability. First, I ask whether you let the Senate be your judge, as Caesar does.[24] Then, what respect can we have for a man who uses someone else's action, not his own, to defend himself? Then—the truth will out of me at last and I shall say what I feel without mincing words—even suppose Caesar had gone too far in some respect or other, even suppose that the magnitude of the conflict, his thirst for glory, his outstanding spirit, his exalted birth had urged him to behavior which was to be tolerated at the time in such a personage and to be obliterated by his subsequent great achievements: is a scamp like you to claim such a license and shall the voice of Vatinius, a sacrilegious brigand, be heard demanding that

---

22. Pythagoras himself. He and his followers were popularly associated with occultism.
23. See p. 55 n. 52.
24. According to Suetonius (*Iul.* 23), when early in 58 the validity of Caesar's measures as Consul was called in question, he laid the matter before the Senate. If that is what Cicero refers to, he might have been expected to use the past tense, *fecit*. But the present, *facit*, in the manuscripts makes a better rhythm.

he be given the same latitude as Caesar?

[16] Let me put it to you this way. You were Tribune (detach yourself from the Consul),[25] you had nine stout colleagues. Among them were three[26] whom you knew to be watching the heavens every day, whom you laughed at, calling them private citizens. You see two of them sitting here in purple-bordered gowns; whereas *you* have sold the purple-bordered Aedile's gown which you had had made up to no purpose. As for the third, you know that from his beleaguered and battered tribunate the young man acquired the prestige of a Consular. That leaves six, of whom some were definitely on your side, while others steered a middle course. All had laws announced; among them many sponsored by my friend Gaius Cosconius, acting too on my advice—a member of this jury, whose status as an Ex-Aedile makes you burst with envy. [17] Kindly tell me, out of the entire Board did any man except yourself dare to present a law? Where do you come by this audacity, this violence? What your nine colleagues thought proper to respect, only you, a product of the gutter, by far the lowest among them in every way, thought proper to scorn and despise and ridicule. I ask whether you know of any Tribune since the foundation of the city having transacted business with the people when it was established that the heavens had been watched. [18] At the same time, please answer the following: when you were Tribune the Aelian and Fufian laws[27] were still in force, laws which have often tempered and checked tribunician excesses and against which nobody but you has attempted to act; laws which in the following year, with two—not Consuls, but traitors and scourges of the community,[28] sitting on the Rostra, went up in flames along with auspices and vetos and all public law. Well, did you ever hesitate to transact business with the people and convoke an assembly in contravention of those laws? Of all seditious Tribunes in the past, have you heard of one so reckless as to convoke an assembly in contravention of the Aelian or the Fufian law?

---

25. Caesar.
26. Cn. Domitius Calvinus, Q. Ancharius, and C. Fannius. The first two are referred to in the next sentence. Cf. *Sest.* 113.
27. Abrogated by Clodius in 58 (*Sest.* 33). See p. 10, n. 29.
28. Piso and Gabinius.

[19] I further ask you whether in the course of that insufferable brigandage of yours (I won't say "tyranny,"[29] for that is what you want to hear) you tried or wished or even conceived the notion (for the thing is so outrageous that if it so much as entered your mind everyone would judge you deserving of any torture) to take Quintus Metellus'[30] place as Augur, thus giving whoever set eyes on you double cause to grieve and groan—the loss of an illus-
+ trious and gallant countryman and an honor envisaged for an infamous rascal. The Commonwealth was shaken by your tribunate, the community tottered, but did you think this city so totally captured and overturned that we could tolerate Augur Vatinius? [20] At this point let me ask: suppose your wish had come true and you had been elected Augur—an idea which we who loathed you found almost too painful to endure, whereas those who doted on you could hardly stop themselves from laughing—but let me ask: if, on top of the other assaults under which you thought the Commonwealth was foundering, you had dealt this lethal blow, your augurate, would you have determined, as all Augurs have done from Romulus down, that when Jupiter sends lightning it is unlawful to transact business with the people; or, to be consistent with your own constant practice, would you as Augur have abolished auspices?

[21] I shall say no more about your augurate. I mention it reluctantly to recall how the Commonwealth fell; you did not imagine you would ever become an Augur so long as the majesty of this people,[31] or even the city itself still stood. At all events, to leave your dreams and come to your crimes, let me have your answer to this: Consul Marcus Bibulus was—I won't say a loyal citizen or I might incur your formidable displeasure, since you were at loggerheads with him: but, at any rate, a man who was not moving in any particular direction or pushing any political plan, but who simply did not care for your proceedings. When you were sending him, the Consul, to prison and your colleagues issued an

---

29. But see s. 23.
30. Q. Metellus Celer, Consul in 60, died in 59.
31. Lit. "of these" (*horum*); Cicero waves his hand toward the people crowding the court. "The majesty of the Roman People" is a stock phrase.

order from the Tabula Valeria[32] for his release, did you raise a gangway in front of the Rostra with benches set end to end in order that he be led down this gangway not to prison but to a cruel death, a Consul of the Roman People, a very moderate man and a very steadfast one, cutting off all succor, excluding his friends, inciting the violence of desperate men, a spectacle sorry and shameful to behold? [22] I ask whether any man before you was wicked enough to do the like, so we may know whether to set you down as an imitator of old misdeeds or an inventor of new ones. Furthermore, by such designs and outrages, in the name of Gaius Caesar, a most mild and estimable personage, but out of your own cruel audacity, you drove Marcus Bibulus from the Forum, the Senate-House, the temples, all public places and kept him shut up in his house. The Consul's life was protected, not by the majesty of his office or the sanction of the laws, but by the guard at his door and the sentries at his walls. Did you send a constable to drag Marcus Bibulus from his house by force? For private
+ persons a man's house has always been his sanctuary; was that not to hold good for a Consul when you were Tribune? [23] At the same time tell us whether you, who call us tyrants who joined together for the common safety, were not yourself no Tribune but an intolerable tyrant, a tyrant out of the gutter, out of the dark. First, you tried to overthrow a commonwealth which was established with the discovery of auspices by abolishing those same auspices. Second, you and you alone trampled under foot and set at naught those most sacrosanct laws, the Aelian and the Fufian, which had survived the fury of the Gracchi, the audacity of Saturninus, the chaos of Drusus, the strife of Sulpicius, the bloodbath
+ of Cinna, even the arms of Sulla.[33] You, a Tribune, brought a Consul face to face with death, shut him up and besieged him, tried to drag him from his home—you, who not only emerged from beggary in that office, but are now intimidating us with your wealth.

[24] Were you so savage as to attempt to remove picked men,

---

32. Headquarters of the Tribunes, to the west of the Senate-House, so called from a fresco commemorating M. Valerius Messalla's naval victory in the First Punic War. See Shackleton Bailey on *Fam.* 14.2.2.

33. On these names, see Index I. On the Aelian and Fufian laws (cf. s. 18), see p. 10, n. 29.

leaders of the community, and destroy them with a bill? You brought Lucius Vettius before a meeting, who had confessed in the Senate to carrying a weapon and designing to assassinate the great and illustrious Gnaeus Pompeius with his own hand. You placed him on the Rostra as an informer, in the hallowed spot where other Tribunes have been accustomed to bring forward leaders of the community to seek their counsel. There you wanted the informer Vettius to lend his tongue and voice to your criminal lunacy. Did Lucius Vettius at your meeting, when questioned by you, name as his backers and instigators and partners in the crime men without whom, if they were removed from the community, as was your plan at the time, the community could not survive? I refer to Marcus Bibulus, whom not content with incarcerating, you had tried to kill, had stripped of his consulship, and were now eager to deprive of his country; Lucius Lucullus, of whose achievements in war you were mighty jealous, having yourself, of course, been ambitious of military glory from boyhood; Gaius Curio, perennial foe of all rascals, conspicuously outspoken as an adviser of our state council[34] in defense of our common liberties, together with his son, one of our leading young men, whose politics are sound, sounder even than was to be expected from one so young.[35] [25] You sought to destroy Lucius Domitius, whose
+ standing and prestige no doubt dazzled your eyes, whom you hated as part of your general hatred of honest men, and whom, looking some way ahead, you feared because of the hopes we all had and have of him.[36] By the same information of Vettius you sought to crush Lucius Lentulus,[37] sitting here on the jury, Flamen of Mars, because he was at that time running for office[38] against your friend Gabinius; had he defeated that scourge, that bane, which through your villainy he was not allowed to do, the Commonwealth would not have been defeated. You tried to

---

34. The Senate.

35. The younger Curio's past had not all been to Cicero's liking. He seems to hint that he is none too sure of the young man politically; still, he was doing well enough at present, better even than might have been expected at his age.

36. As likely to bring Vatinius to justice.

37. Lentulus Niger.

38. The consulship.

associate the son in his father's destruction on the same deposition and charge. Into the same information of Vettius, the same group, you brought Lucius Paullus, who was Quaestor in charge of Macedonia[39] at the time—Paullus, a fine man and a fine citi-
+ zen, who had tried to remove two wicked traitors[40] by process of
+ law, a man born for the salvation of the Commonwealth. [26] As for myself, why complain? I really should thank you for deciding that I ought not to be set apart from this group of courageous citizens. But you pushed your folly even further. When Vettius had finished what you had told him to say, slandered the community's leading lights, and stepped down from the Rostra, you suddenly called him back and talked to him while the Roman People looked on, then asked him whether he could give any other names. Did you force him to name my son-in-law, Gaius Piso, who in all our abundance of fine young men has not left his like for self-restraint, manliness, and sense of family duty? Likewise Marcus Laterensis, whose thoughts turn day and night on glory and
+ the Commonwealth? Did you, foul, reckless enemy of the people
+ that you are, announce a bill for a special court to try all these distinguished persons and for a lavish informer's reward for Vettius? And when this was universally rejected—hooted down in fact—did you break the same Vettius' neck in jail for fear information of false information be forthcoming and a special court be demanded to try you yourself for that crime?

[27] You often claim that you carried a law providing for the alternate rejection of juries.[41] In order to make it clear to everybody that even when you did something right you could not help doing wrong, I ask this: You had announced this equitable law at the beginning of your term of office and subsequently carried many others; did you wait until Gaius Antonius was charged[42] before Gnaeus Lentulus Clodianus and, immediately after the
+ charge was laid down, did you present your law specifying "whosoever should be charged subsequent to this law," to the end that

---

39. Left there by the outgoing Proconsul, C. Octavius.
40. Catiline and Cethegus, according to the scholiast.
41. The provisions of this law, which evidently favored defendants, are unknown.
42. Perhaps with *lèse-majesté*, for misconduct as Consul and Proconsul.

this unfortunate Consular should be deprived by a fraction of time of the benefit and equity of your enactment? [28] You will say that you were a personal friend of Quintus Maximus. A fine way to defend your misdeed! As for Maximus, he was perfectly within his rights in refusing to allow an enemy a more advantageous method of rejection, after enmity had been declared, the case undertaken, the president and court selected. Maximus did nothing inconsistent with his own fine character or those illustrious names—Paulli, Maximi, Africani—whose glory we hope to see, indeed already see, renewed in him. The dirty trick, the wrongdoing, the crime—that what you announced in the name of compassion you postponed until it served your cruelty—is yours. And now Gaius Antonius' only consolation in misfortune is that it was easier for him to hear of than to see his father's and his brother's portraits and his brother's daughter[43] established not in a family but in a prison.[44]

[29] Since you despise other people's money and brag insufferably of your own affluence, please answer me this: did you, a Tribune, make bargains with committees and monarchs and tetrarchs? Did you with your laws pay out money from the Treasury?[45] Did you snatch shares,[46] very highly priced at the time, partly from Caesar, partly from the tax-farmers? All of which being so, I ask you whether from a very poor man you became a wealthy one that very year in which an extremely severe law concerning extortion was enacted, from which it was obvious to one and all that you despised not only *my* measures (after all, you call me a tyrant) but your very good friend's law.[47] You are in the habit of calumniating me to him, though my feelings toward him are most friendly; but you insult him grossly every time you claim to be a connection of

---

43. Vatinius' wife Antonia, Mark Antony's sister.
44. I.e., a foul place because it was inhabited by the criminal Vatinius. There may be a further double-entendre intended in the word *familia* ("family"/"gladiatorial establishment"). See Pocock.
45. To the Consuls of 58. Cf. p. 47, n. 20.
46. In tax-farming companies, which were indebted to Vatinius for a law revising an unfavorable contract.
47. The *lex Iulia de pecuniis repetundis* of 59 on provincial administration covered acts of extortion. On Cicero's law, see p. 200, n. 162 and s. 37.

his.[48]

[30] I should also like to ask you what design or object you had in view when you took your place at my friend Quintus Arrius' banquet in a dark gown. Have you ever seen or heard of such a thing? Where was your precedent, what usage were you following? You will say that you did not approve of that Thanksgiving.[49] Very good. Suppose there was no Thanksgiving—you see, don't you, that my questions do not relate to what took place that year nor to anything that might seem to involve you jointly with exalted personages, but only to your own peculiar offenses. Well, suppose there was no Thanksgiving: tell me, who ever dined in a black gown? It was a funeral feast, true; but while the function of such a
+ feast is to celebrate a death, the feast itself is an occasion of good cheer.[50]

[31] But leave aside the fact that it was a feast of the Roman People, a festal day with plate and fabrics, the whole outfit a sight to see: who ever dined in a dark gown when in private mourning for a death in the family? Who was ever handed a dark gown as he came out of the bath, except you? When so many thousands were at their tables, when the master of the feast, Quintus Arrius, was
+ in white, you and Gaius Fidulus (also in black) and the other evil spirits entered the temple of Castor in funeral attire. Who but groaned to see it and grieved for the plight of the Commonwealth? Was there any topic of conversation at that banquet except the subjection of this great, majestic community to your mockery on top of your madness? [32] Did you not know the custom? Had you never seen a feast? As a boy or young man had you never been one of the cooks?[51] Had you not only a short while previously sated your inveterate appetite at a magnificent banquet given by a young nobleman of the highest quality, Faustus? Before

---

48. Through his mother-in-law Julia, a distant relative of the future Dictator.

49. According to the scholiast, this was in honor of C. Pomptinus, who had suppressed a revolt in the Roman province of Gaul. From what Cicero says, the banquet appears to have been somehow connected with the Thanksgiving, an additional reason for putting on a cheerful appearance. "Ah, but I didn't approve of that Thanksgiving." Very good, says Cicero, leave the Thanksgiving out of it.

50. I translate *hilaritatis* (SB^3) for the transmitted *dignitatis* ("dignity"), which makes no apparent sense.

51. An insulting remark: cooks were invariably slaves.

+ the banquet you had seen the master[52] and his friends in black gowns, but you did not see them dressed so at dinner.[53] What fit of lunacy took possession of you to think that unless you commit-
+ ted sacrilege and violated the temple of Castor and the omen of the feast and established custom and the dignity of your host you would have failed to demonstrate sufficiently your opinion that the Thanksgiving was invalid?

[33] I must also question you about a private offense, in which you certainly will not be able to claim that your cause is bound up
+ with that of an illustrious personage.[54] Were you charged under the Licinian-Junian law?[55] Did Praetor Gaius Memmius issue a notice according to the law requiring your appearance in thirty days' time? Did you appeal to the Tribunes to stop your standing trial—which is putting it too mildly, though even that would have been unprecedented and intolerable—did you appeal by name to that year's plague, the country's evil spirit, the Commonwealth's
+ blizzard, Publius Clodius? Since, however, he could not hold up the trial by law or custom or prerogative, he resorted again to his accustomed reckless violence and gave his services as captain to your troops. So that you may not think I have attacked rather than questioned you, I shall not impose on myself the burden of giving evidence; I shall hold in reserve what I see I shall soon have to say from where you now stand, and not prove you guilty but merely interrogate, as I have done in other matters. [34] I ask you, Vatinius, whether any man in this community since the foundation of the city has appealed to the Tribunes to prevent his standing trial. Has any man mounted the tribunal of the magistrate trying his case, driven him down by force, thrown the benches helter-skelter, scattered the voting urns, in fact committed all these actions in breaking up a trial which trials were instituted to prevent? Do you know that Memmius then fled, that your accusers were rescued from the hands of you and your following, that the jurors in other courts were ousted from the adjacent tribunals, that in the

---

52. The host. The feast was in memory of his father, the Dictator Sulla.
53. "In black gowns . . . dinner": a conjectural supplement (SB³).
54. Caesar.
55. See p. 201, n. 171.

Forum, in broad daylight, in full view of the Roman People,
+ courts, magistrates, traditional customs, laws, jurors, defendant, penalty were eliminated? Do you know that, thanks to Gaius Memmius' diligence, all these facts were set down and attested in the public records? One further question: After you had been charged, you returned from your post as Legate[56] so as to scotch any notion that you were avoiding the courts, and you used to say that, having a free choice, you preferred to stand trial; how was it consistent, having decided not to use the refuge provided by your post, to betake yourself to a nefarious kind of help by way of a most improper appeal?

[35] Since your post has been mentioned, I should like to hear from you under what decrees of the Senate you were appointed. I see your response from your gesture: under your own law, you say. Are you not then the most arrant of traitors? Was it your intention that the Senate be totally eliminated from the Commonwealth? Would you not leave the Senate even what no one ever took away, namely that Legates be chosen on the authority of that body? Did you think so meanly of the council of state, did the Senate seem so cast down, the Commonwealth so distressed and prostrate that the Senate could not, according to traditional practice, choose messengers of peace and war, envoys, intermediaries, advisors in military operations, assistants in provincial administration?[57] [36] You had deprived the Senate of its power to assign a province, discretion in choosing a military commander, control over the Treas-
+ ury, although the Roman People never sought these functions or tried to transfer to itself the directive authority of the supreme deliberative body. But I will grant that in other matters some of all this has precedent. It is rare for the people to choose a commander, but it has happened. But who ever heard of Legates without a senatorial decree? Nobody did that before you, though Clodius straight away did the same in respect of two public portents.[58]

---

56. It appears that Caesar had appointed Vatinius one of his Legates (lieutenants) in Gaul: so Pocock, pointing to "your own law" in the next section. Vatinius' law setting up Caesar's command will have authorized him to name his own Legates.
57. The term *legatus* might cover any of these.
58. Piso and Gabinius. They named their own Legates (*Sest.* 33) and were evi-

That makes you all the more worthy of condign punishment: you injured the Commonwealth by your example as well as by your act, you were not only a rascal yourself but you have tried to teach rascality to others. On all these accounts do you know that you were censured by the verdict of your fellow tribesmen, the strict Sabines and the brave Marsi and Paeligni, and that since the foundation of the city no member of the tribe Sergia ever lost that tribe except yourself?

[37] I should also like to hear from you the reason why you do not recognize as valid the law on electoral corruption which I carried under senatorial decree, carried moreover without violence and without violating the auspices and the Aelian and Fufian laws, especially as I comply with your laws, no matter how *they* were carried. My law explicitly forbids any person to give a gladiatorial show within two years before standing or intending to stand[59] for office, except on a day previously fixed under the terms of a will. How could you be mad enough to give a show while actually a candidate? Would you suppose that a Tribune can be found, like that thorough-paced gladiator of yours, to intervene against your standing trial under my law?

[38] If you scorn and despise all this because you have persuaded yourself, as you often say openly, that you will get everything you want in despite of Gods and men through Gaius Caesar's extraordinary partiality for you, have you heard, has anyone told you what Gaius Caesar said at Aquileia recently when certain names cropped up? He said he was very sorry that Gaius Alfius had been passed over,[60] having found him thoroughly honest and trustworthy, and that he also took it hard that someone who had opposed his own interests[61] should have been elected Praetor. Somebody then asked him how he felt about Vatinius. He replied that Vatinius had done nothing in his tribunate without getting paid for it. Having made money his sole object, he ought not to mind doing without honors. [39] Now if the very person who, to

---

dently empowered to do so under Clodius' bill assigning them their provinces.
59. Cf. p. 200, n. 162.
60. In the praetorian elections (*Sest.* 113).
61. Domitius Calvinus or Ancharius? Cf. s. 16, *Sest.* 113.

raise his own standing, was willing to see you plunge headlong, at your risk and without any culpability on his part, none the less judges you quite unworthy of any honor; if your neighbors, family connections, fellow tribesmen dislike you so heartily that they looked on your defeat as their triumph; if nobody looks at you without a groan or utters your name without a curse; if they avoid you, flee your presence, don't want to hear of you, and when they set eyes on you, call upon the Gods to avert the evil omen; if your kinsmen reject you, your fellow tribesmen execrate you, your neighbors fear you, your marriage-connections blush for you; if the very wens have moved from your rascally countenance and taken up their quarters elsewhere;[62] if you are the general bugbear of the people, the Senate, all manner of men, town and country: why should you hanker after a praetorship rather than your death? After all, you want to be a people's man[63] and you could do nothing that the people would appreciate more.

[40] But it is time for us to hear how fully you answer my questions. So I shall now wind up my examination and in conclusion ask you a few things about the case itself. I put it to you: how do you come to be so frivolous and irresponsible as to praise Titus Annius at his trial in such terms as honest men and good citizens are wont to praise him, when the other day, before an assembly into which you were introduced by that same horrible demon,[64] you eagerly gave false witness against him? Or is it perhaps a matter of your choice and discretion, so that when you see Clodian gangsters, a band of desperate criminals, you say, as you said at the meeting, that Milo held the Commonwealth down with gladiators and beast-fighters, whereas when you come before gentlemen such as these, you don't dare abuse so outstandingly courageous, loyal, and resolute a citizen? [41] Since, however, you praise Titus Annius so warmly and with your eulogy cast some aspersion on that illustrious gentleman—Titus Annius prefers to be numbered with those whom you abuse—well, let me ask:

---

62. I.e., as swellings on his neck (see p. 209, n. 6).
63. See Glossary of Terms.
64. I.e., Publius Clodius, who as Aedile in 56 initiated criminal proceedings against Titus Annius Milo before the popular assembly on charges arising from Milo's tribunate in 57.

Seeing that in Milo's public actions Publius Sestius has been party to his every move—and that is a fact declared by the judgment not only of honest men but of rascals too; both are on trial for the same reason and on the same charge, one prosecuted by an individual[65] whom you sometimes recognize as your sole superior in rascality, the other by your devices but with his assistance—well, let me ask how you separate in your evidence those whom you tie together in your charge.

[42] The final point on which I should like an answer from you is this: you have said[66] a good deal against Albinovanus about collusive prosecution: Did you say that you did not approve of Sestius' being prosecuted for violence, that it was wrong, that he would better have been prosecuted under any other law, any other charge? Did you also say that our gallant Milo's case is thought to
+ be bound up with this one? That what I have done for Sestius is welcome to honest men? I am not convicting the inconsistency between your speech and your evidence[67] —though the activities of my client which you say were approved by honest men were the same which you denounced at length in your evidence, whereas you praise in the highest terms the person whom you tie up with Sestius' cause and jeopardy; no, my question is whether you think Publius Sestius ought to be found guilty under a law under which you say he should never have been prosecuted in the first place.
+ Or else, if you object to a witness being asked for his opinion, and not wishing to appear to be attaching any weight to your views, I ask whether you gave evidence regarding violence against a person whom you say should never have been standing trial for violence in the first place.

---

65. Clodius.
66. In giving evidence.
67. Since he was neither under prosecution nor prosecuting, the speech was presumably made with the court's indulgence; cf. s. 4.

APPENDIX I

DIVERGENCES FROM THE OXFORD TEXT

In this list the readings of Peterson's Oxford Text are followed by those which I prefer and translate, including some that do not affect the translation. My conjectures are marked by asterisks. "(M)" and "(C)" indicate that the divergent reading has already been adopted by Maslowski and/or Cousin respectively. For "SB[1]" etc., see Bibliographical Note.

The numbering is by section of speech followed by line of Oxford Text. Variant spellings are not noticed.

Post reditum in senatu

1.10 parentes / -tem* (SB[3])   **3.18** non est permissa / facta non est (M)   **4.28** *I translate a conjectural supplement:* promulgavit; <sed in illa lege ita scriptum erat>* (SB[2])   **4.2** idemque / atque   **8.17** proscriptionem / p- <vim>* (SB[3])   **9.24** fuit / est (M)   **9.29** numquam / n- post Romam conditam (M)   **9.1** in / e* (SB[1])   **9.1–2** de duobus consulibus] *delete*   **9.2** non] *delete*   **9.8** fuisset [inimicus] / f- i-   **11.30** quod / quo (M)   **12.26** diceret / intercederet (M *on his own conjecture*)   **13.10–11** non consilium, non dicendi copia, non rei militaris / non iuris <notitia>, non dicendi vi<s, non scien>tia r- m- (M)   **17.5** comitiis / c- tuis (M)   **18.18** de Palatio / in P- (SB[2])   **23.19** indicem / non in- (M. cf. SB[1])   **25.1** omnibus, sed / o- sane (M)   **26.2** unum / summum (M)   **26.4** cum / cum vos (M)   **27.16** qui impedisset / qui id im-, vos (M)   **27.22** quid? denique illo die / quid denique ille dies (M)   **28.28** eo / quo (M)   **33.8** in / ii   **33.21** mecum etiam / mecum, etiam* (SB[3])   **33.23** et / aut*   **35.14** <consors> / <particeps>   **36.23** divinorum / duorum (M)   **36.24** nam / nam et (M)   **37.10** tamen] *delete*

Post reditum ad quirites

1.13 desideriumque / <ac> desiderum (M)   **2.17** <namque> / <etenim>*   **2.7–8** tanta voluptate . . . quanta / tantae voluptati . . . quantae (M)   **5.30** vestram] *delete*   **7.11** auctoritas / pietas   **10.19** <consule>] *delete*   **11.26** cum / <neque solus

neque> cum* (SB²)   11.30 infrenati / irretiti (M)   12.11 *I mark a lacuna before* noctem *following A. Klotz* (M).   12.12 deliberatio] *delete** (SB²)   14.6 flumine / <et> f-* (SB²)   16.19 me] *delete* (M)   18.11 <causam>] *delete* (M)   19.25 <omne> / et (M)   20.2 tum / <non> tum* (SB¹ . M)   20.14 <oratione> / <verbis> (M *on his own conjecture following Sydow*)   21.17 permittit / -ttet*   21.26 facinora / facinora <eor>um (M)   21.5 rationem repetendo / -ne -da (M)   23.16 utique / <nisi> utique* (SB¹)   23.19 in eo <consilium> aperte laudatur / bono rumore fere utitur(*) (cf. M)   23.23–24 pecuniae debitae / et pecunia debita (M)   24.4–5 <nec tantum> dum anima exspirabo mea, sed . . . <illa> monumenta / <nec eam> cum anima e- mea; sed . . . monumenta (M)

De domo

7.30 hostem / hospitem* (SB¹ . M)   **8.4** his / iis (M)   **8.5** ipsum] *delete*   **10.21** illis / illa (M)   **10.21** ob / per   **11.6** senatus . . . potuit / -um . . . oportuit   **12.12** inlatum / obl- (M)   **12.19** consulis / -lum*   **13.10** in / <iniecta> in (M)   **15.27** illam rationem / aliam rationem (M)   **20.25** patrocinium / praeconium* (SB¹ . M)   **21.6** atque / neque (M)   **21.7** quem / qui in ipso Catone, quem (M)   **21.7** ea <re> / eo <negotio> (M)   **21.8** produceres . . . subduceres / producebas . . . subducebas*   **25.13** Clodio / Cloelio (M)   **26.20** Clodi / Cloeli (M)   **27.6** est / <non> esset* (SB³)   **30.22** <sententiam> / <senatus probasset quae>   **34.7** exheredabit / -arit (M)   **37.7** dicere / d- <se>   **37.14** vellet / velit* (SB²)   **38.27** pontificum / -cium   **40.24** *In the lacuna I translate my supplement:* <Caesaris acta rescissa volentis qui>* (SB²)   **46.13** nobiles] *delete*   **47.25** Clodius / Cloelius (M)   **48.4** Clodium / Cloelium (M)   **48.4** faceret / -re (M)   **49.21** alienae / <assecla> alienae* (SB²)   **50.23** quam quisque / aliquam quisquis* (SB³; cf. SB²)—cf. *Sest.* 68   **50.28** RETTULERIT / -LIT*   **50.5** sortitore / sortitu (M)   **50.6** perbonus / † in bonis †   **50.8** Decumis / † Decumis †   **50.9** Clodiis / Cloeliis (M)   **51.15** num / num <non>* (cf. SB²)   **52.27** dedisset / -sses (M)   **53.11** iacti / <non> iacti*   **57.18** tam turpis / obscura*   **58.28–29** ne, mihi praesenti si multa inrogaretur] *delete*   **62.13** scilicet eos consules / sic eos*

DIVERGENCES FROM THE OXFORD TEXT

63.25 discordiarum] *delete** (SB³)   **64.12** dubitarem / d- <me devovere>   **64.13** esse] *delete**   **65.19** ut / <nisi> ut (M)   **65.19** amoribus / honoribus* (SB¹)   **66.6** hostem / hospitem* (SB¹ . M)   **68.23** dissensione hominum et caede / discriptione h- ad caedem (M)   **71.15** ad administrandam civitatem] *delete*   **72.23** nomen / <id> n-* (SB³)   **75.23** ipse / i- <se> (M)   **76.5** <excitanda> / emenda   **76.6** exussit / excu-   **76.13** non negant / censent* (boni censent, *Koch*)   **77.24** libertatem / sui potestatem (M)   **79.18** municipiis / <multis> mu-* (SB²)   **79.27** Fidulio / Fidulo*   **80.7** Fidulii / Fiduli*   **80.11** <praetorum decreta> / <res iam iudicata> (M)   **81.17** Anagninis / A-, <hominibus> ornatissimis* (SB²)   **82.20** Fidulius / Fidulus   **82.22** amplexeris / -xaris (M)   **82.2** <C.> Gracchus / G- (M)   **83.8** Clodio / Cloelio (M)   **87.28** sempiternam / -ni   **87.4** <alieno> / <praetore>   **89.20** optent / <qui>* optant   **91.13** vis / virtus   **91.13** <Graccho> / <Graccho, tribuno pl.,>   **91.15** re / re publica   **92.19** res publica / res* (SB³)   **93.6** ipso / ipsum   **98.7** adsis / <feras> et sis   **99.15** <pestis> / <pestis patriae> (M)   **100.4** virtutis] *delete* (M)   **101.26–27** exstinctor . . . auctor et dux fuisse videar / -ores . . . -ores et duces f- videamur (M)   **102.3** Fulvi / <M.> F- (M)   **105.22** dicat se / se d- (M)   **107.6** <nisi sit> honesta / n- h- sit*   **107.6** ut / cum   **107.7** atque / aut   **107.8** <iustum aut honestum> arbitrere / <fas esse> arbitrare   **108.22** praedae, societatis, emptionis / p- s- <vel> e-* (SB²)   **108.26** ista / <immo vero> ista*   **110.10** tu /eam tu (M)   **112.11** istorum / i- <licentiae>   **116.5** tam variam / <tantam>, tam v- (M)   **120.15** pontifex / <et> p-   **121.22** scirem / scirem, <me scire>* (SB³)   **121.25** templi] *delete* (SB²)   **122.4** dicerem / concederem* (SB²; cf. SB³)   **123.16** aeque] *delete**   **125.11–12** <verba> prisca / p- <v-> (M)   **127.28** orationem] *delete** (SB²)   **128.19** ipsi <ei> loco / i- l- (M)   **129.10** senatus ne quid / senatui ne quid <praesidi>* (SB²)   **130.15** tali / t-, <etiam honestae>* (SB²)   **131.9** curia/curia <Concordiae effigiem>* (SB²)   **131.12** licentiae / l- <tuae>*   **132.13** si quid / si quid <privati consili>* (SB²)   **132.15** vetere / v- <rem> (M)   **133.9** exsultare / † et scelere † (*I translate:* in scelere et patriae parricidio <subvenire>*)   **134.14** etiam] *delete*   **134.17** delicto / <alieno> delicto   **136.12** Flaminio / Flaminino

(M) 136.18 <tractaverit> / <egerit> (*after* diligentia senatus)
(M) 136.19 cognoscetis / c-. <recita senatus consultum.
SENATUS CONSULTUM.> 138.18 ex senatu consulto, ex
lege] *delete* (M) 140.8–9 delata tum sunt <ea> . . . celebrata /
delatum est . . . celebratum (M) 143.22 fructum / f- ipsum
(M) 143.26 si] *delete* (SB²) 144.8 qui / <vosque> qui* (SB¹)
145.14 ut] *delete* 146.4 usu / visu 147.15 vim / speciem (M)

De haruspicum responsis

Title responso / responsis (M) 4.3 inquam, tum / tum,
inquam* (SB²) 7.16 tacens / stans* (SB²) 7.17 initium /
metum (SB³) 8.27 et] *delete* 11.5 Clodi / Cloeli (M)
15.11 sedibus / aed- 16.27 cum sint / quae sunt 17.9 me]
delete* 17.13 litterate / <vix> 1-* (SB¹) 18.24 his / iis
21.16 celebrantur / -rentur* (SB²) 24.22 loquar quos / loquar?
quos* 27.7 Q. / Quinta 29.8 quod] *delete** (SB³) 30.21
<et> aras] *delete* (M) 30.23 res, quod / res, quam 30.24 vos
/ nos 32.14 neglegimus / -gamus 33.2 tollam / t- <etiam>*
(SB¹) 36.31 quid sequatur / quod sequitur (M) 36.4 haec
/ h- <etiam> * (SB³) 37.8 responsum / -nso* (SB³) 40.10
DIVINI NUMINIS / DIVINITUS (M) 40.10–11 UNUM
IMPERIUM PECUNIAE REDEANT / UNIUS IMPERIUM RES
REDEAT (M) 40.11–12 APULSUS DEMINUTIOQUE
ACCEDAT] *obelize* (M) 41.3 brevitas / ubertas* (SB²; cf. SB³)
43.7 patrum / patria* (SB²) 44.15 omnibus / o- causa (M)
44.26 non] *delete* 45.27 senatus, senatus / s-, (M) 46.16 in /
inter* 48.20 quam / quod 54.2 carissimi / cla- 54.10
Mario / <C.> Mario* (SB²) 55.26 enim / autem* (SB³)
57.30 parentum / paternum* (SB³) 58.5 omnibus / <orba-
tum> omnibus 59.30 Clodiis / Cloeliis (M) 62.1–2 quibus-
dam † multis / m- q-

Pro Sestio

1.5 ex / is ex 2.23 qua / <quoniam> qua (M) 2.2 <ut>]
delete (M) 4.17 ullius / ullus (CM) 6.12 Albini / Albani*
(SB⁴; cf. SB². M) 6.15 Albino / Albanio* (SB⁴; cf. SB². M)
7.19 uxorem / <alteram> u- 7.26–1 <pro illa necessitudine stu-
diis et> / <praeterea assiduisque> (C) 8.19 nobis / bonis (CM)

12.2 maiestate sua / -tatem suam   **12.6** consulem / c- quaestor (CM)   **12.10** et amor / amore (CM)   **12.17** praeoccupare / peragrare   **14.20** offerunt, / o- <aut>*   **15.28** fuerat ille annus tam / funestus erat ille a- iam <tum>* (SB³)   **15.3** acrius / -ioris* (SB³)   **17.1** nondum] *delete*   **18.7** inflatus] *I translate:* inflatus <se ostentans>* (SB²)   **19.18** aspere / asper erat* (SB³)   **22.27** hominem] *delete** (SB³)   **23.9** <viribus> / <partibus> (CM)   **24.20** eius <consorti>onis / helluationis* (SB³)   **24.26** cum / <sic>, cum   **25.18** his / iis (C)   **26.7** vos / vos, <vos>   **28.1** examinatus / * * * e-*   **28.9** se / sui (M)   **32.9** audebas /-eas (M)   **36.5** <populo> / <equestri ordine> (C)   **37.14** <respiciens rem gesserat> / spectarat (C)   **37.17** C. Mari] *delete* (C)   **39.11** sciebat / suscensebat* (SB³)   **39.22** et quoad / et <tum> quoad*   **39.25** nullo / nonnullo* (SB¹)   **40.2** <populo Romano> / <rei publicae>   **41.26** illis / aliis* (SB¹)   **43.17** vestro / vobis* (SB²)   **44.8** interitum / i- <meum> (CM)   **46.1** bonorum / b- <in me>   **46.6** summo *after* cum / *after* sed (SB³)   **47.10** cives / c-, <at armis> (M)   **50.20** Minturnensium] *delete* (C)   **50.24** <interitum> / <casum> (C)   **54.23** <interitum> / <casum> (CM)   **58.26** pulsus animo tamen hostili / superatus [animo tamen hostili]   **59.6** qui / * * * qui (C). *I translate Lambinus' supplement:* Tigranes igitur, qui   **59.14** em / en (CM)   **60.22** atque / a- <exsul>   **60.28–29** hoc . . . quod / ea . . . qua* (SB¹)   **69.28** crevisse / defuisse   **71.16** designatus] *delete* (CM)   **71.21** ab] *delete* * (SB¹)   **71.24** primum / prius* (SB³)   **72.5** Gracchum / Brocchum (C)   **72.8–9** deserta Gavi Oleli area calatis / deserta G- O- † orea calatis †   **73.22–23** ferri, sed ne iudicari / iu-, sed ne f-   **78.17** gemere / gerere* (SB¹.M)   **78.18** <tribunicio>] *delete* (M)   **78.21** forum / forum <ferro>   **79.13** extremo / <in> extremo* (SB¹)   **82.12** Gracchum / Brocchum (C)   **82.18** Numerium / N- <Quinctium>* (SB¹)   **85.8** divini / d-, <inquam, et>*   **89.29** umquam / u- <quemquam>*   **89.11** adfligeret / abiceret (CM)   **89.12–13** <et clam eripi: id egit> / <et latere. perfecit> (CM)   **91.6** sunt / s-, <instituerunt>   **92.13** ut / <qui>, ut* (SB²)   **93.26** pacatissimis atque opulentissimis / -mae atque -mae (C)   **97.30** esto / est (CM)   **100.4** aut / atque   **106.2–3** de <re publica>] *delete*   **107.18** <praebuit> / <professus est>   **110.29**

BACK FROM EXILE

Actaei / Attici (CM)   **110.1** pro vino etiam / e- pro v-   **113.14** gratum / -tam (C)   **114.1** dicebantur / † dicebantur † (*I translate*: conabantur*)   **114.2** quod boni viri vellent nisi repulsam / nisi quod b- v- vellent* (SB¹)   **115.16** quoniam / cum* (SB²)   **118.22–23** huic . . . vitae / † huic . . . vitae †   **126.26** latebrosior / -sa   **126.28–29** gladiatores sed equi ipsi gladiatorum / equi gladiatorum sed ipsi gladiatores* (SB³)   **127.5** quam] *after* erat (6) (CM)   **127.6** a / de   **129.2** notavit / pacavit* (SB³)   **131.16** reditusque / -que <qui> (C)   **131.17** idem] *delete**   **133.23** quam adiuvabat, Sex. Clodius / Sex. Cloelius   **134.10–11** iste nimia gloriae cupiditate] *delete* (C)   **137.4** voluerunt] *delete*   **138.9** munia / m- <ferunt>* (SB³)   **143.29** magnorum / -umque (CM)   **143.4** aut laboribus / ac l-   **145.1** vexatae, dissipati / dissipatae, vexati* (SB²)   **145.5** protexeram / dilexeram (CM)   **147.25** improborum / -rum <impetum>

In Vatinium

1.1 indignitas / i- <tua>   **3.1** <die> / <die te> (C)   **3.12** refellisti / praetulisti   **7.3** cum / quod (C)   **9.5** quid dicant / <quid> iudicent (C)   **10.16** his templis] *delete* (SB²)   **19.9** clarissimi / c- et fortissimi (C)   **22.19** id] *delete*   **22.20** exsilium / asylum* (SB²)   **23.1** consulem / consulem <tribunus pl.>*   **25.26** Vatini / tuos   **25.10** exterminarat / -are voluerat* (SB²)   **26.12** ergo / ego   **26.23** impurissime / i- et perditissime (C)   **26.24** amplissimis] *delete* (C)   **27.3** in eum 'qui / 'quicumque (C)   **28.7** summa laus / summum ius* (SB¹)   **30.12** dignitatis / † dignitatis † (*I translate*: hilaritatis* [SB³])   **31.19** Fibulo / Fidulo*   **32.28** convivium? / c- * * *. *I translate*: < videras, cenantis non item> (SB³)   **32.1** nomen / o-* (SB³)   **33.6** clarissimis viris causam / -mi viri causa   **33.14** Clodium / <P.> C-   **34.2** quaestionem / -nes   **34.6** arbitretur / -traretur (C)   **36.25** senatui / † aut †   **36.25** auferre / ad se transferre   **39.13** rusticanorum / <urbanorum> rusticorum* (SB¹)   **42.14** hoc / hac* (SB²)   **42.21** ne / <et> ne (SB²)

APPENDIX II

ROMAN NAMES

A Roman bore the name of his clan (*gens*), his *nomen* or *nomen gentilicium*, usually ending in *-ius*, preceded by a personal name (*praenomen*) and often followed by a *cognomen*, which might distinguish different families in the same *gens*: e.g., M. Tullius Cicero. The *nomen* was always, and the *cognomen* usually, hereditary. Sometimes, as when a family split into branches, an additional *cognomen* was taken: e.g., Gaius Calpurnius Piso Frugi. Other additional *cognomina* were honorific, sometimes taken from a conquered country as Africanus or Numidicus, or adoptive (see below). Women generally had only the one clan name (e.g., Tullia), which they retained after marriage.

Only a few personal names were in use and they are generally abbreviated as follows: A. = Aulus; Ap(p). = Appius; C. = Gaius; Cn. = Gnaeus; D. = Decimus; K. = Kaeso or Caeso; L. = Lucius; M'. = Manius; M. = Marcus; N. = Numerius; P. = Publius; Q. = Quintus; Ser. = Servius; Sex. = Sextus; Sp. = Spurius; T. = Titus; Ti. = Tiberius (I omit a few rarities which do not occur in this text). The firstborn son was customarily given his father's *praenomen*. The use of the *praenomen* by itself in address or reference is generally a mark of close intimacy, real or affected (as when Cicero addresses the abhorred Sex. Cloelius as *Sexte noster* ["my good Sextus"]), but in the case of a rare, distinctive *praenomen*, as Appius or Servius or Faustus, this no longer holds. Such a *praenomen* is often used instead of *nomen* or *cognomen*.

Adoption of males was very common in Rome. According to traditional practice, the adopted son took the father's full name and added his former *gentilicium* with the adjectival termination *-ianus* instead of *-ius*: thus C. Octavius adopted by C. Julius Caesar became C. Julius Caesar Octavianus. But in Cicero's time the practice had become variable. Sometimes the original name remained in use.

A slave had only one name, and since many slaves came from the East, their names were often Greek. If freed, he normally took his master's *praenomen* and *nomen*, adding his slave name as a *cognomen*: thus Tiro, when freed by his master Cicero, became M. Tullius Tiro.

Much the same applied to Greek or other provincials on gaining Roman citizenship. Such a man retained his former name as a *cognomen* and acquired the *praenomen* and *nomen* of the person to whom he owed the grant: thus the philosopher Cratippus became M. Tullius Cratippus after Cicero had got Caesar to grant him citizenship.

In official documents, the *praenomen* of a man's father (and sometimes of his grandfather) and the tribe to which he belonged were included as part of his name, and placed between the *nomen* and *cognomen* (e.g., Cn. Pompeius Cn. f. Sex. n. Clu. Magnus = Gnaeus Pompeius Magnus, son of Gnaeus, grandson of Sextus, of the tribe Clustumina).

The use (at any rate Cicero's use) of the three components, *tria nomina*, and the order in which they were placed was partly conventional, sometimes with social implications. For example, members of the noble families (with certain exceptions) are generally referred to by *praenomen* plus *cognomen*. (See *Onomasticon*, pp. 3–8; also, on adoptive names, *Two Studies in Roman Nomenclature* [American Classical Studies 3, 1976], pp. 81–99.)

INDEX I
PERSONS, DEITIES, LAWS

References enclosed within parentheses indicate that the person is referred to but not named. Similarly, parentheses are put around the names of persons to whom Cicero alludes in these speeches without mentioning them by name. References introduced by "cf." usually indicate that the person, although not named, fits the description given but that the language is too general to make possible a positive indentification or to exclude other persons. An asterisk indicates nobility (see Glossary of Terms).

Accius, L. (*RE* 1): last of the three major Latin writers of tragedy. Cicero knew him in his old age. His works are lost except for some fragments. — *Sest.* (120, 122), 123.

Acilius Glabrio, M'. (*RE* 38): Consul 67. Pontifex. — *Har. resp.* 12.

Aelian and Fufian laws: cf. *RE* XII.2320. — *Red. sen.* 11 (see note). *Har. resp.* 58. *Sest.* 33. *Vat.* 5, 18, 23, 37. Aelian law: *Sest.* 114.

Aelii: — *Sest.* 69.

Aelius Lamia, L. (*RE* 75): hereditary friend of Cicero's. As a prominent Knight, was banished from Rome in 58 by Gabinius for championing Cicero's cause. Later entered the Senate, becoming Aedile in 45 and probably Praetor in 43. — *Red. sen.* 12, (32). *Sest.* 29 (f., 52). His father: *Sest.* 29.

(*?)**Aelius** Ligus (*RE* 83): as Tribune in 58 allied himself with Clodius. He seems to have been adopted into the Aelius Ligus family, which had produced a Consul in 172. — (*Red. sen.* 3). *Dom.* 49. *Har. resp.* 5. *Sest.* 68 (f.), 94. Cf. *Red. sen.* 4, 8.

***Aemilii:** — *Sest.* 143.

***Aemilius** Lepidus, M. (*RE* 68, suppl. I and XV.381f.): Consul 187, 175. Pontifex Maximus. — *Dom.* 136. Cf. *Sest.* 143 (Aemilii).

***Aemilius** Lepidus, M. (*RE* 73): Consul 46, 42. Triumvir 43–38, 37–36. Pontifex, later (44–12) Pontifex Maximus. His important role in the Civil War and the triumviral period need not be described here. — *Har. resp.* 12.

***Aemilii** Paulli (i.e., L. Aemilius Paullus [*RE* 114], Consul 182, 168, conqueror of Macedonia): — *Vat.* 28.

*[**Aemilius** Paullus, L. (*RE* 81): Elder brother of the Triumvir. Consul 50, allegedly bought by Caesar. Probably neutral in the Civil War, he was proscribed by the Triumvirs, but escaped to end his days in Miletus. — *Vat.* 25.

***Aemilius** Scaurus, M. (*RE* 140): Consul 115. Leader of the Senate (*princeps senatus*) and a major figure in Roman political life until his death ca. 90. A hero to conservatives like Cicero, depicted by Sallust as crafty and corrupt. —

Dom. 50. *Har. resp.* 43. *Sest.* 39 (101).

Aemilius Scaurus, M. (*RE* 141): son of the foregoing. Praetor 56. Pontifex. In 54 successfully defended by Cicero on a charge of extortion in his province, but found guilty on a subsequent bribery charge and disappeared into exile. — *Har. resp.* 12. *Sest.* 101, 116.

Aesopus: see Clodius Aesopus.

Ahala: see Servilius Ahala.

(Albania) (cf. *RE* Albinius 1): — (*Sest.* 6).

Albanius, C. (*RE* Albanius; cf. *RE* Albinius 1): senator, father-in-law of Sestius. Cf. SB⁴. — *Sest.* 6.

Albinovanus (*RE* 1): prosecutor of Sestius, perhaps identical with the following. — (*Sest.* 78, 80, 84, 86f., 90, 96, 135). *Vat.* 3, 42.

Albinovanus, P. (*RE*): Pontifex minor. — *Har. resp.* 12.

Albinus: see Postumius Albinus.

(Alcmaeon): mythical matricide. — (*Har. resp.* 39).

Alfius Flavus, C. (*RE* 7): Tribune 59. — (*Sest.* 113f.). *Vat.* 38.

(Ampius Balbus, T.) (*RE* 1): Praetor 59. — (*Dom.* 23). Cf. *Onomasticon.*

Ancharius, Q. (*RE* 3): Praetor 56. — *Sest.* 113. (*Vat.* 16). Cf. *Vat.* 5, 38.

Annius Milo, T. (*RE* 67): Tribune 57. Praetor 55. A Papius adopted by a maternal grandfather, T. Annius; see *Onomasticon.* As Tribune championed Cicero's recall and raised armed bands against Clodius. Was condemned for Clodius' murder in January 52, and retired to Massilia. In 48 returned to Italy to take part in a rising against Caesar's regime, and was killed. — *Red. sen.* 19, 30. *Red. quir.* 15. *Har. resp.* 6f. *Sest.* 85–92 *passim,* (94), 95, 144. *Vat.* 40–42.

Antiochus (III, "the Great") (*RE* 25, suppl. I). Seleucid king of Syria, lost war against Rome 191–189. — *Sest.* 58.

(***Antonia**) (*RE* 111): daughter of M. Antonius "Creticus" and Julia, married to Vatinius. — (*Vat.* 28).

***Antonius** ("Hybrida"), C. (*RE* 19): son of the following. Consul 63, having previously been expelled from the Senate for rapacity and insolvency. Governor of Macedonia in 62–60. Condemned after his return to Rome (Cicero defending), went into exile but lived to become Censor in 42. Mark Antony was his nephew. — *Dom.* 41. *Sest.* 8f., 12. *Vat.* 27f.

(*?)**Antonius,** M. (*RE* 28, suppl. I): Consul 99. Celebrated orator. — *Red. quir.* 11. (*Vat.* 28).

(***Antonius** "Creticus," M.) (*RE* 29): son of foregoing, father of Vatinius' wife Antonia and Mark Antony. Praetor 74. — (*Vat.* 28).

Apollo: — *Har. resp.* 18.

Appuleius Saturninus, L. (*RE* 29): Tribune 103, 100. "Popular" leader, killed in his second tribunate after the Senate passed its "Ultimate Decree," calling on the Consuls "to see that no harm come to the Commonwealth." In his history of Roman oratory (*Brut.* 224), Cicero says that he was considered the most eloquent speaker since the Gracchi, though he owed his reputation to his appearance, gestures, and dress rather than to oratorical talent. — *Dom.* 82. *Har. resp.* 41, 43. *Sest.* 37, 39, 101, 105. *Vat.* 23.

Aristides (*RE* 1): Athenian statesman, known as "the Just," ostracized ca. 484. — *Sest.* 141.

Arrius, Q. (*RE* 7, 8): Praetor 73. Friend of Cicero, who, however, thought him a traitor in 58, and henchman of M. Crassus. — *Vat.* 30f.

Athamas: legendary king of Thebes who killed his son in a fit of madness. — *Har. resp.* 39.

Athenio (*RE* 6): leader of the Sicilian slave revolt from 103–101. — *Har. resp.* 26.

*****Atilii** Calatini (or Caiatini): — *Sest.* 72.

(*****Atilius** Regulus, C.) (*RE* 47): Consul 257, 250. Possibly the first Atilius to adopt the cognomen Serranus. — Cf. *Sest.* 72.

*****Atilius** Regulus, M. (*RE* 51): Consul 267, 256. Captured by the Carthaginians in the First Punic War, he was sent to Rome to arrange an exchange of prisoners. His return to Carthage to face torture and death is the subject of one of Horace's best known odes (3.5) — *Sest.* 127.

Atilius Serranus, Sex. (not in *RE*): adoptive father of the following (but the reference may be to the son). — *Har. resp.* 32.

*****Atilius** Serranus Gavianus, Sex. (*RE* 70): Quaestor in Cicero's consular year (63). As Tribune in 57 he at first supported a move to recall Cicero, who claims to have done him important favors, but then changed sides, allegedly bribed by Clodius. No more is heard of him after 57, and there is reason to believe that he was dead in 54 (see Shackleton Bailey on Q. *fr.* 3.6 [8].5). — *Sest.* 72, 74, 85, (87, 89), 94. Cf. *Har. resp.* 32 (Sex. Serranus).

Atinius Labeo Macerio, C. (*RE* 10): Tribune 131. — *Dom.* 123.

Attalus (I, King of Pergamum) (*RE* 9): apparently confused by Cicero with his son and successor, Eumenes II. — *Sest.* 58.

Aufidius, Cn. (*RE* 6): Praetor 107 (?). — *Dom.* 35.

*****Aufidius** Orestes, Cn. (*RE* 32): an Aurelius Orestes (a consular family) adopted by the foregoing. Consul 71. — *Dom.* 35.

*****Aurelius** Cotta, L. (*RE* 102): Consul 65. Censor 64. A relative of Caesar's mother, he took no part in the Civil War and lived on after it, but retired from public life after Caesar's murder in 44. — *Dom.* 68, 84. *Sest.* 73f.

Bibulus: see Calpurnius Bibulus

Bona Dea: see Good Goddess.

Brocchus: see "Toothy."

Brogitarus (*RE* and suppl. VII): Galatian, son-in-law of King Deiotarus. Clodius made him High Priest of Cybele ("The Great Mother") at Pessinus. — *Dom.* 129. *Har. resp.* 28f, 59. *Sest.* 56.

Brutus: play by Accius. — *Sest.* 123.

Brutus: see Junius Brutus.

Caecilius Cornutus, C. (*RE* 43): Praetor 57. — *Red. sen.* 23.

(*****Caecilia** Metella) (*RE* 134): wife of the elder Scaurus and Sulla. — (*Sest.* 101.)

*****Caeciliae** Metellae: daughters of Metellus Macedonicus. — *Red. sen.* 37. *Red. quir.* 6.

Caecilian-Didian law: — *Dom.* 41 (see note), 53. *Sest.* 135.

*****Caecilii Metelli:** one of Rome's greatest families (plebeian), especially prominent in the latter half of the second century and the first half of the first. — *Red. sen.* 25. *Red. quir.* 6. *Sest.* 130f.

(*****Caecilius** Metellus, L.) (*RE* 74): son of Metellus Caprarius. Consul 68. — (*Red. sen.* 37. *Red. quir.* 6).

*****Caecilius** Metellus Baliaricus, Q. (*RE* 82): Consul 123. — *Dom.* 136

*****Caecilius** Metellus Caprarius, C. (*RE* 84): Consul 113. Censor 102. *Red. sen.* 37. *Red. quir.* 6.

(*****Caecilius** Metellus Celer, Q.) (*RE* 85): son of Metellus Diadematus? Tribune 90. — Cf. *Red. sen.* 37. *Red. quir.* 6.

*****Caecilius** Metellus Celer, Q (*RE* 86, suppl. I): as generally supposed, son of Metellus Nepos, Consul 98, adopted by the foregoing. Consul 60. As Praetor in 63 cooperated with Cicero. Died in 59. His wife was the notorious Clodia. — (*Red. sen.* 25). *Har. resp.* 45. (*Sest.* 131.) *Vat.* 19.

*****Caecilius** Metellus Creticus, Q. (*RE* 87, suppl. XV.391): son of Metellus Caprarius. Consul 69. Pontifex. Gained his honorific cognomen by conquering and annexing Crete (68–65). — (*Red. sen.* 37. *Red. quir.* 6.) *Dom.* 123. *Har. resp.* 12.

*****Caecilius** Metellus Diadematus, L. (*RE* 93): son of Macedonicus. Consul 117. — *Red. sen.* 37. *Red. quir.* 6.

*****Caecilius** Metellus Macedonicus, Q. (*RE* 94, suppl. I and III): Consul 143. Censor 131. A highly successful general in Macedonia and Greece (148–146). — *Dom.* 123.

*****Caecilius** Metellus Nepos, Q. (*RE* 95): son of Metellus Baliaricus. Consul 98. — *Red. sen.* 37. *Red. quir.* 6.

*****Caecilius** Metellus Nepos, Q. (*RE* 96, suppl. III): son of the foregoing. Consul 57. As Tribune in 62 agitated against Cicero and was suspended from office. As Consul, however, refrained from opposing Cicero's recall and finally supported it. Thereafter they were on friendly terms (see his letter, *Fam.* 5.3). Died soon after 55. He and his brother Celer were half-brothers to Clodius. — *Red. sen.* 5, 9, 25 (f. *Red. quir.* 10, 15). *Dom.* 7, 11, 13, 70, (87). *Har. resp.* 13. *Sest.* (11, 62, 72, 79, 87, 89), 130. See Consuls.

*****Caecilius** Metellus Numidicus, Q. (*RE* 97): nephew of Macedonicus. Consul 109. Censor 102. Commanded successfully against the Numidian king Jugurtha until superseded by Marius in 107. In 100 went into voluntary exile because he refused to take an oath to uphold legislation by Saturninus, and was brought back the following year. — *Red. sen.* 25, 37f. *Red. quir.* 6, 9(f.), 11.

Dom. 82, 87. *Sest.* 37, 101, 130.

*Caecilius Metellus Pius, Q. (*RE* 98): son of the foregoing. Consul 80. Pontifex Maximus. The cognomen Pius ("dutiful") referred to his efforts on behalf of his father's recall. In 79–71 fought against the anti-Sullan Sertorius in Spain, where Pompey joined him in 76, with final success. — (*Red. sen.* 37. *Red. quir.* 6). *Sest.* 124.

*Caecilius Metellus (Pius) Scipio, Q. (*RE* 99, suppl. I, III, and XV.393): previous to his adoption by the foregoing, P. Cornelius Scipio Nasica. Consul 52. Pontifex. After the death of his son-in-law Pompey, led the republican forces in Africa and committed suicide after Thapsus. — *Dom.* 123. *Har. resp.* 12. *Sest.* 124.

Caecilius Rufus, L. (*RE* 110): City Praetor 57. — *Red. sen.* 22.

Caepio: see Servilius Caepio.

"Caesoninus Calventius" (i.e, L. Calpurnius Piso Caesoninus): — *Red. sen.* 13. See Calventia.

Calidius, M. (*RE* 4, suppl. III): Praetor 57. Distinguished orator. — *Red. sen.* 22.

(*Calpurnius Bestia, L.) (*RE* 24): Tribune 62, hostile to Cicero. — (*Sest.* 11).

*Calpurnii Pisones: — *Red. sen.* 15. (*Sest.* 21).

*Calpurnius Bibulus, M. (*RE* 28, suppl. I): Consul 59. Opposed his colleague Caesar's legislation, shutting himself in his house and "watching the skies." Died of overstrain while commanding Pompey's fleet in 48. — *Dom.* 39f., 69. *Har. resp.* 48. *Vat.* 21f., (23), 24.

*Calpurnius Piso Caesoninus, L. (*RE* 90, suppl. I and III): Consul 58. Censor 50. As Consul took a line unfriendly to Cicero, who in 55 delivered a violent attack, the extant speech *In Pisonem.* Governor of Macedonia 57–55. As Censor tried to moderate the harsh measures of his colleague Appius Claudius. Neutral in the Civil War (Caesar was his son-in-law), he opposed Antony in 44, but in 43 tried to promote a settlement. — *Red. sen.* (10, 13–15), 16, (17f., 32, 38. *Red. quir.* 11). *Dom.* 23, 55, (60, 62), 66, 70(f.), 102, 112. *Har. resp.* 2, 32, (35). *Sest.* (19–24, 26, 29), 32f., 53f., 60, (68), 70, 93(f., 135). See Caesoninus Calventius, Consuls.

*Calpurnius Piso Frugi, C. (*RE* 93, suppl. I and III): Cicero's son-in-law. Quaestor 58. Worked hard for Cicero's recall, but died before it took place. — *Red. sen.* (15, 17), 38. *Red. quir.* 7. *Sest.* 54, 68. *Vat.* 26.

(Calventia) (not in *RE*): mother of L. Piso — (*Sest.* 21).

Calventius: see Caesoninus Calventius.

Camillus: see Furius Camillus

Capitolinus (i.e., Jupiter of the Capitol): — *Dom.* 144.

Cassius Longinus, C. (*RE* 55): Consul 171. Censor 154. — *Dom.* 130, (131f.), 136 (f.)

Cassius Longinus Ravilla, L. (*RE* 72, suppl. I): Consul 127. Censor 125. — *Sest.* 103.

Cassius Vecellinus, Sp. (*RE* 91): Consul 502, 493, 486. Put to death (by his father according to one account) for plotting to make himself king. — *Dom.* 101.

Castor, temple of: — *Dom.* 54, 110. *Har. resp.* 28, 49. *Sest.* 34, 79, 83, 85. *Vat.* 31f.

Catiline: see Sergius Catilina.

Cato: see Porcius Cato.

Catulus: see Lutatius Catulus.

Ceres: — *Dom.* 125.

Cestilius, C. (*RE*): Tribune 57. — *Red. sen.* 21.

Cethegus: see Cornelius Cethegus.

Charybdis: mythical monster or whirlpool infesting the Straits of Messina, between Sicily and the toe of Italy. — *Har. resp.* 59.

Cinna: see Cornelius Cinna.

Cispius, M. (*RE* 4): Tribune 57. — *Red. sen.* 21. *Sest.* 76. His father and brother: — *Sest.* 76.

*****Claudia,** Quinta (*RE* 435): Her story is told in Ov. *Fast.* 4.305-344 and elsewhere. — *Har. resp.* 27.

*****Claudius,** L. (*RE* 21): King of Rites (*rex sacrorum*). — (*Dom.* 127). *Har. resp.* 12.

Claudius, T. (not in *RE*): — *Vat.* 3.

(*****Claudius** Caecus, App.) (*RE* 91): Consul 307, 296. His censorship in 312 is memorable for, among other things, the construction of the Appian Way from Rome to Capua (cf. *Sest.* 126) and of Rome's first aqueduct. — (*Dom.* 105. *Har. resp.* 38).

*****Claudius** (?) Marcellus, C. (*RE* 215): Catilinarian. — *Sest.* 9.

(*****Claudius** Marcellus, M.) (*RE* 229): Consul 51. — Cf. *Dom.* 42.

(*****Claudius** Pulcher, App.) (*RE* 295, suppl. III): Consul 143. — (*Dom.* 84. *Sest.* 126).

*****Claudius** Pulcher, App. (*RE* 296, suppl. I): son of the foregoing. Consul 79. — (*Dom.* 83f.) *Har. resp.* (2), 26, (42. *Sest.* 126).

*****Claudius** Pulcher, App. (*RE* 297, suppl. I): brother of P. Clodius. Consul 54. Censor 50. As Praetor in 57 at enmity with Cicero, but later reconciled. Supported Pompey in the Civil War but died before Pharsalia. — *Dom.* 40, (87, 111f. *Har. resp.* 31. *Sest.* 77f., 85, 87, 89, 126). Cf. *Dom.* 26, 83. *Har. resp.* 42. *Sest.* 16.

(*****Claudius** Pulcher, C.) (*RE* 300): Consul 177. — (*Sest.* 126).

*****Claudius** Pulcher, C. (*RE* 302): Consul 92. — (*Dom.* 118). *Har. resp.* 26.

(*****Claudius** Pulcher, C.) (*RE* 303): brother of Appius and P. Clodius. Praetor 56. — (*Dom.* 118). Cf. *Dom.* 26, 83. *Har. resp.* 42. *Sest.* 16.

(*****Clodia**) (*RE* 66): half-sister of P. Clodius, wife of Metellus Celer, cos. 60; probably the "Lesbia" to whom Catullus wrote his love poems. — (*Dom.* 25, 83, 92. *Har. resp.* 27, 38f. *Sest.* 39, 116). Cf. Clodiae.

(*****Clodiae**): (*RE* 6, 67, 72): sisters of P. Clodius. — (*Dom.* 26. *Har. resp.* 9, 42, 59. *Sest.* 16).

Clodian (Claudian) clan: — *Dom.* 34, 116, (127. *Har. resp.* 57). *Sest.* 81.

Clodii: — *Dom.* 116.

Clodius Aesopus (*RE* 16): tragic

actor — (*Sest.* 120–22), 123.

*****Clodius** Pulcher, P. (*RE* 48): Tribune 58. Curule Aedile 54. In 58 drove Cicero into exile and remained his arch-enemy. From then on until his death in 52 in an affray with Milo, he was a power in politics through his popularity with the city mob and organized rowdyism. — *Red. sen., Red. quir., Dom., Har. resp., Sest. passim. Vat.* 33, 36, 40.

Cloelius, Sex. (*RE* Clodius 12, suppl. I): principal lieutenant of P. Clodius. Traditionally known as Sex. Clodius after an error in inferior manuscripts. — *Dom.* 25f., 47f., 50, 83, (129). *Har. resp.* 11, 59. *Sest.* 133. See Sextus.

Concord: — *Dom.* 130f., 136f. Temple of: — *Dom.* 11. *Sest.* 26.

Consuls (Piso and Gabinius): — *Red. sen.* 3f., 10, (31). *Red. quir.* 13, (21). *Dom.* 5, 24, 58, 62, 82, 91, 96, (98), 99, (103), 113f., (119) 122, 129, 131, 143, 146. *Har. resp.* (3f.), 47, 58. *Sest.* 17, (24), 25, 27, 33f., (38), 41–44, 52–55, 60, 63–66, 68f., (71). *Vat.* 18, (36).

Consuls (Lentulus Spinther and Metellus): — *Red. sen.* 18. *Dom.* 9, 11–13, 68. (*Har. resp.* 15).

(*****Cornelia**) (*RE* 416): second wife of Sestius. — (*Sest.* 7).

Cornelius, C. (*RE* 18): Tribune 67. Prosecuted for his proceedings in office and assailed by senatorial leaders, he was successfully defended by Cicero in 65. — *Vat.* 5.

Cornelius, Q. (*RE* 51): Pontifex minor. — *Har. resp.* 12.

*****Cornelius** Cethegus, C. (*RE* 89): conspirator, put to death in 63. — *Red. sen.* 10. *Dom.* 62. Cf. *Vat.* 25.

*****Cornelius** Cinna, L. (*RE* 106): Consul 87–84. Expelled from Rome in 87, he reestablished himself by force of arms and, after Marius' death in January 86, remained at the head of affairs until his own death in 84. —*Red. sen* 9. *Dom.* 83. *Har. resp.* 18, 54. *Sest.* 77. *Vat.* 23. Cf. *Sest.* 48 and *Onomasticon.*

*****Cornelii** Lentuli: — *Sest.* 143.

(*****Cornelius** Lentulus, L.) (*RE* 196): son of L. Lentulus Niger. — Cf. *Vat.* 25.

*****Cornelius** Lentulus Clodianus, Cn. (*RE* 216): Consul 72. Censor 70. — *Dom.* 124.

*****Cornelius** Lentulus Clodianus, Cn. (*RE* 217): son of the foregoing. Praetor 59. — *Vat.* 27.

*****Cornelius** Lentulus Crus, L. (*RE* 218): Consul 49. — *Har. resp.* 37.

*****Cornelius** Lentulus Marcellinus, Cn. (*RE* 228): Consul 56. — *Har. resp.* 2, 11, 13(f., 15), 21f.

*****Cornelius** Lentulus Niger, L. (*RE* 234): Flamen of Mars. — *Har. resp.* 12. *Vat.* 25.

*****Cornelius** Lentulus Spinther, P. (*RE* 238): Consul 57. Pontifex. Played a leading part in Cicero's restoration. Governor of Cilicia 56–54. Supported Pompey in the Civil War and was put to death in Africa, perhaps by Caesar's orders (46). — *Red. sen.* 5, 8f. (24–26), 27f. *Red. quir.* 11, 15(f.), 17f. *Dom.* 7, 30, 70f., 75, (87). *Har. resp.* 12f. *Sest.* 70, 72, (87), 107, (117), 144, 147. Cf. *Red. sen.* 7. *Red. quir.* 14. See Consuls.

*Cornelius Lentulus Spinther, P. (*RE* 239): son of the foregoing. Quaestor 44. —(*Red. sen.* 24). *Sest.* 144.

*Cornelii Scipiones: — *Sest.* 143.

*Cornelii Scipiones Africani: — *Vat.* 28.

*Cornelius Scipio Aemilianus Africanus, P. (*RE* 335): Consul 147, 134. Destroyer of Carthage. — *Har. resp.* 6.

*Cornelius Scipio Africanus, P. (*RE* 336): Consul 205, 194. Leading figure in the Second Punic War and after. — *Har. resp.* 24, 41.

*Cornelius Scipio Asiaticus / Asiagenes, L. (*RE* 338): Consul 83. Marian. Deserted by his army, which went over to Sulla, he was allowed to retire to Massilia. — *Sest.* 7.

*Cornelius Scipio Nasica, P. (*RE* 350, suppl. I): Consul 191. According to tradition, he was selected as the most virtuous living Roman to bring the image of the Mother of the Gods from Pessinus to Rome in 204. — *Har. resp.* (22), 27.

*(Cornelius Scipio Nasica, P.) (*RE* 351): Praetor 93 (?). — Cf. *Red. sen.* 37. *Red. quir.* 6.

*Cornelius Scipio Nasica, P.: see Caecilius Metellus (Pius) Scipio.

*Cornelius Scipio Nasica Serapio, P. (*RE* 354): Consul 138. Killer of the revolutionary Tribune Ti. Gracchus in 133, as a result of popular odium was sent by the Senate in 132 on a special mission to Asia, where he died after a short time. — *Dom.* 91. (*Har. resp.* 22).

*Cornelius Sulla, Faustus (*RE* 377): son of the Dictator. Quaestor 54. Killed in Africa after Caesar's victory at Thapsus in 46. — *Vat.* 32.

*Cornelius Sulla Felix, L. (*RE* 392): the Dictator. Held supreme power in Rome from 82 until his retirement in 79. Died in 78. — *Dom.* 43, 79. *Har. resp.* 18, 54. *Vat.* 23.

Cornutus: see Caecilius Cornutus.

Coruncanius, Ti. (*RE* 3): Consul 280. — *Dom.* 139.

Cosconius, C. (*RE* 4): Praetor 63. — *Vat.* 12.

Cosconius, C. (*RE* 5): Tribune 59. — *Vat.* 16.

Cotta: see Aurelius Cotta.

Crassus: see Licinius Crassus.

Curio: see Scribonius Curio.

Curii, i.e., M'. Curius Dentatus (*RE* 9): Consul 290, 275, 274. Censor 272. Often adduced as an example of old Roman virtue. — *Sest.* 143.

Curtius Peducaeanus, M. (cf. *RE* 8 and 23): son of Sex. Peducaeus (q. v.), adopted by a M. Curtius. Tribune 57. Praetor 50. — *Red. sen.* 21.

Decius, P. (*RE* 10): see † Decumus.

Decii, i.e., P. Decius Mus and his son: — *Dom.* 64. *Sest.* 143.

Decius Mus, P. (*RE* 15): Consul 340. — *Sest.* 48. See Decii.

Decius Mus, P. (*RE* 16): son of the foregoing. Consul 312 etc. Censor 304. — *Sest.* 48. See Decii.

† Decumus (not in *RE*): satellite

of Clodius. The name seems to be corrupt (for Decius?) — *Dom.* 50.

Deiotarus (I, King of Galatia) (*RE* 2, suppl. III): a staunch ally of Rome until his death ca. 40. He chose the wrong side (first Pompey, then Brutus) in two Roman civil wars, but still managed to retain his kingdom. A speech made by Cicero in his defense before Caesar in 45 is extant. — *Har. resp.* 29.

Diadematus: see Caecilius Metellus Diadematus.

Diana: — *Har. resp.* 32.

*****Domitius** Ahenobarbus, L. (*RE* 27): Consul 54. Originally a supporter of Cicero, but later disliked by him. A bitter enemy of Caesar, he was killed at the battle of Pharsalia in 48. — *Vat.* 25.

(*?)**Domitius** Calvinus, Cn. (*RE* 43): Tribune 59. Consul 53, 40. Probably condemned for bribery in 52 and recalled from exile by Caesar. Held high commands in the war, and a second consulship and Triumph after Caesar's death. — *Sest.* 113. (*Vat.* 16) Cf. *Vat.* 5, 38.

Epicurean(s): — *Red. sen.* 14. (*Sest.* 23f.).

(**Equitius,** L. [the false Gracchus]) (*RE* 3): an impostor, pretending to be the son of Ti. Gracchus. — (*Sest.* 101).

Erechtheus: mythical king of Athens. — *Sest.* 48. His daughters: — ibid.

(**Eumenes** [II, King of Pergamum]) (*RE* 6): see Attalus.

*****Fabii** Maximi: one of Rome's greatest patrician families. — *Sest.* 143. *Vat.* 28.

*****Fabius** Maximus Sanga, Q. (*RE* 108 and 143, suppl. III—separated for no good reason): supported Cicero's recall (*Pis.* 77). Supported Caesar in the Civil War, who made him Consul Suffect in 45. Died in office. — *Vat.* 28.

(*****Fabius** Maximus Verrucosus, Q. [Cunctator]) (*RE* 116): Consul 233 etc. Censor 230. Dictator 221 (?), 217. Hannibal's great adversary in the Second Punic War. — Cf. *Sest.* 143.

Fabricius, Q. (*RE* 7): Tribune 57. — *Red. sen.* 22. *Sest.* 75, 78.

Fabricius, Luscinus, C. (*RE* 9): Consul 282, 278. Censor 275. Often adduced as a grand old Roman, like Curius Dentatus. — *Sest.* 143.

Fadius, T. (*RE* 9): Quaestor 63. Tribune 57. Exiled, probably on a bribery charge in 52. Two letters to him (one of them notably abrasive) survive (*Fam.* 5.18 and 7.27). Formerly given the cognomen Gallus due to a manuscript error. — *Red. sen.* 21.

Fannius, C. (*RE* 9): Tribune 59. Pontifex. A consistent optimate, he was proscribed in 43 and fled to Sex. Pompeius, later to Antony. — *Har. resp.* 12. *Sest.* 113. (*Vat.* 16). Cf. *Vat.* 5.

Faustus: see Cornelius Sulla.

Fidulus, C. (*RE* Fidulius; see Shackleton Bailey, *Two Studies in Roman Nomenclature* [1976], 39) — *Dom.* 79, 80 (Fiduli), 82. *Vat.* 31.

Flamininus: see Quinctius Flamininus.

Firmidius (*RE*): satellite of Clodius. — *Sest.* 112.

Fonteian clan: — *Dom.* 116. Cf. *Dom.* 35.

Fonteius, P. (*RE* 13): Clodius' adoptive father. — *Dom.* (34–37), 77. Cf. *Har. resp.* 57.

(Fulvia) (*RE* 113): wife of Clodius, Curio, Antony. See "Pinaria."

***Fulvius** Flaccus, M. (*RE* 58): Consul 125. An ally of C. Gracchus, perished with him in 121. — *Dom.* 102, 114.

Furius Camillus, M. (*RE* 44, suppl. III): Dictator 396. Delivered Rome from the Gauls. — *Dom.* 86. *Sest.* 143.

Gabinius, A. (*RE* 11, suppl. III): Consul 58. Military lieutenant and political supporter of Pompey. As Consul backed Clodius against Cicero. Went into exile in 54 after conviction on charges of extortion. Reappears as Caesar's Legate in 48. Died in 47. — *Red. sen.* (10–13), 16, (17f., 32. *Red. quir.* 11). *Dom.* 23, 55, (60, 62), 66, 70, 102, 124–26. *Har. resp.* 2. *Sest.* (18, 20, 26, 28–30), 32 (52), 53, 55, 70, 93. *Vat.* 25. See Consuls.

Galba: see Sulpicius Galba.

Gavius Olelus (?) (not in *RE*): — *Sest.* 72.

Gellius (*RE* 1): brother of the following and supporter of Clodius. — *Har. resp.* 59. *Sest.* 110–12. *Vat.* 4. His wife: *Sest.* 110.

Gellius, L. (*RE* 17, suppl. III): Consul 72. Censor 70. On his supposed cognomen Poplicola or Publicola, see E. Badian *BICS* Suppl. 51 (1988) p. 8. — *Red. quir.* 17.

Glabrio: see Acilius Glabrio.

Glaucia: see Servilius Glaucia.

Good Goddess (Bona Dea): see Glossary of Terms. — *Dom.* 105. *Har. resp.* 8, 37. Cf. *Dom.* 110.

Gracchus: see Sempronius Gracchus.

Gracchus, the false: see Equitius.

Hannibal (*RE* 8): Carthaginian general in the Second Punic War 218–201. — *Har. resp.* 27. *Sest.* 142.

Hercules: — *Dom.* 134. *Sest.* 143.

Hermarchus (*RE* 2): of Chios. — *Har. resp.* 34.

Hiempsal (*RE* 2 and suppl. III under Iemsal): King of Numidia. — *Vat.* 12.

Horatius Pulvillus, M. (*RE* 15): Consul 509, 507. Pontifex. — *Dom.* 139.

***Hortensius** Hortalus, Q. (*RE* 13): Consul 69. Co-defender of Sestius and, before Cicero, Rome's leading forensic orator. — *Sest.* 3, 14. Cf. *Red. sen.* 23. *Red. quir.* 21.

***Hostilius** Mancinus, C. (*RE* 18): Consul 137, in which capacity he concluded a peace treaty with the Spanish town of Numantia when he and his army had been surrounded by the enemy. The Senate disowned it, and Mancinus was left at the town gate, naked with hands tied behind his back. But the Spaniards refused to accept him, and he returned to Rome, later to be reelected Praetor. His disgrace also involved his Quaestor Ti. Gracchus, who was party to the treaty. — *Har. resp.* 43.

Julian law (extortion): — (*Dom.* 23, see note). *Sest.* 135. (*Vat.* 29). Agrarian: — (*Sest.* 61).

*****Julius** Caesar, C. (*RE* 131): Consul 59 etc. Later Dictator. Pontifex Maximus 63–44. Absent from Rome in 58–49 (conquest of Gaul). — (*Red. sen.* 32). *Dom.* 22(f.), 39f., (104). *Har. resp.* (4, 45), 47f. *Sest.* (16), 39(f.), 41(f.), (52), 71, 132, 135. *Vat.* (13), 15(f.), 22, 29(f., 33), 38(f.). Julian laws: — *Har. resp.* 48.

(*****Julius** Caesar, L.) (*RE*) 143): Consul 64. — (*Vat.* 11).

*****Julius** Caesar, Sex. (*RE* 150): City Praetor 123. — *Dom.* 136(f.).

*****Julius** Caesar, Sex. (*RE* 152; cf. 153): Flamen of Quirinus. Later commanded in Syria where he was killed in a military revolt (46) — *Har. resp.* 12.

*****Julius** Caesar Strabo Vopiscus, C. (*RE* 135): Curule Aedile 90. — *Har. resp.* 43.

Junius Brutus, M. (*RE* 46a [suppl. V]: first Consul. — *Sest.* 143. See *Brutus*.

Juno: — *Dom.* (92), 144.

Jupiter (Jove): — *Dom.* 92. *Har. resp.* 20. *Vat.* 20. Jupiter Best and Greatest: — *Red. quir.* 1. *Dom.* 14 (temple of), 144. *Har. resp.* 10, 21. *Sest.* 129 (temple of). God of the Capitol (Capitolinus): — *Dom.* 144.

*****Juventius** Laterensis, M. (*RE* 16):

— Praetor 51. Committed suicide in 43 when his commander Lepidus joined forces with Antony. — *Vat.* 26.

Laenius Flaccus, M. (and his father and brother) (*RE* 2): — *Sest.* 131.

Lamia: see Aelius Lamia.

Laterensis: see Juventius Laterensis.

Lentidius (*RE* 1): henchman of Clodius. — *Dom.* 89. *Sest.* 80.

Lentulus: see Cornelius Lentulus.

Leo (*RE* 1): gladiator. — *Sest.* 135 (Lion).

Lepidus: see Aemilius Lepidus.

Liberty: — *Dom.* 108, 110f., (112), 116, 131. (*Har. resp.* 33).

*****Licinia** (*RE* 181): Vestal. — *Dom.* 136(f.).

Licinian law: — *Dom.* 51.

Licinian-Junian law: — *Sest.* 135 (see note). *Vat.* 33.

*****Licinius** Crassus, C. (*RE* 52): Tribune 145. Father of Licinia (above). — *Dom.* 136.

*****Licinius** Crassus, L. (*RE* 55): Consul 95. One of the greatest of Roman orators. — *Dom.* 50.

*****Licinius** Crassus, M. (*RE* 68): Consul 70 and 55. Pontifex (?). Joined Pompey and Caesar in 60 to form the so-called First Triumvirate. Defeated and killed at Carrhae, leading an invasion of Parthia in 53. — *Har. resp.* 12 (?), 47. *Sest.* 39, 41, 48.

*****Licinius** Crassus, M. (*RE* 56): son of the foregoing. Pontifex (?). — *Har. resp.* 12 (?).

(*****Licinius** Crassus, P.) (*RE* 61):

father of the "Triumvir." Consul 97. Censor 89. He and another son perished when Marius and Cinna returned to power in 87. — (*Sest.* 48).

*Licinius Crassus Dives, P. (*RE* 71): Praetor 57. — *Red. sen.* 23.

*Licinius Lucullus, L. (*RE* 104): Consul 74. In 73–66 waged a brilliant series of campaigns against King Mithridates of Pontus, ending ingloriously through disaffection in his army. After supersession by Pompey returned to Rome to live in ease and luxury until his death in 56. — *Har. resp.* 42. *Sest.* 58. *Vat.* 24. See Luculli.

Licinius Murena, L. (*RE* 123): Consul 62. Defended successfully by Cicero in the previous year against charges of electoral corruption. — *Dom.* 134. *Har. resp.* 42.

Ligus: see Aelius Ligus.

Lion: see Leo.

*Livius Drusus, M. (*RE* 18): Tribune 91. Pontifex. Instituted an extensive program of legislation which led to violent political conflict. Assassinated in office. — *Dom.* 41, 50, 120. *Vat.* 23.

Lollius, M. (*RE* 10): henchman of Clodius. — *Dom.* 13f., 21, 89.

*Luculli (L. Licinius Lucullus and M. Terentius Varro Lucullus): — *Red. sen.* 37. *Red. quir.* 6.

Lucullus: see Licinius Lucullus, Terentius Varro Lucullus.

*Lutatius Catulus, Q. (*RE* 7): Consul 102. His colleague was Marius, in whose victory over the Cimbri he had a share. Committed suicide in 87 under prosecution in the purge of political enemies carried out by Marius and Cinna. — *Dom.* 102, 113f., 116, 137.

*Lutatius Catulus, Q. (*RE* 8): son of the foregoing. Consul 78. Leading conservative figure until his death in 61 or 60. — *Red. sen.* 9. *Dom.* 113. *Sest.* 101, 121f.

Maelius, Sp. (*RE* 2): accused of aiming at despotic power in 440/439 and killed by P. Servilius Ahala. — *Dom.* 101.

Maenius, C. (*RE* 9): Consul 338. His column in the Forum. — *Sest.* 124.

Mancinus: see Hostilius Mancinus.

*Manlius Capitolinus, M. (*RE* 51): Consul 392. — *Dom.* 101.

Marcellus: see Claudius Marcellus.

*Marcius Philippus, L. (*RE* 75): Consul 91. Censor 86 under Cinna's regime, but joined Sulla when he returned to Italy. — *Dom.* 84. *Sest.* 110.

*Marcius Philippus, L. (*RE* 76): son of the foregoing. Consul 56. He married Caesar's niece Atia, mother of the Emperor Augustus. — *Har. resp.* (2), 11, (14f. *Sest.* 110).

*Marcius Philippus, Q. (*RE* 79): Consul 186, 169. Censor 164. — *Dom.* 130.

Marius, C. (*RE* 14, suppl. VI): Consul 107, 104–100, 86. Of Arpinum. Great general, destroyer of invading northern tribes. Driven into exile by Sulla in 88, returned to Rome by force in 87 and killed off numbers of opponents before his own death early in the following year. — *Red. sen.* 38. *Red. quir.* 7, 9–11, 19, (20f.). *Har. resp.* 51, 54. *Sest.* 37f., (48? see Cornelius Cinna), 50, 116.

(*Marius, C.) (*RE* 15): son of the foregoing. Consul 82. — (*Red. quir.* 20).

Mars: *Har. resp.* 12. *Sest.* 12. *Vat.* 25. See Mars' Field (Index II).

Mastanesosus (not in *RE*): African ruler (the name may be corrupt). — *Vat.* 12.

Maximus: see Fabius Maximus.

Memmius, C. (*RE* 8): Praetor 58. An erratic political career ended in conviction for bribery and exile in 52. Noted orator and poet, generally supposed to be the friend to whom Lucretius dedicated his poem "On the Nature of Things." — *Vat.* 33f.

Menulla (*RE*): of Anagnia, a Clodian supporter. — *Dom.* 81.

Messalla: see Valerius Messalla.

Messius, C. (*RE* 2): Tribune 57. — *Red. sen.* 21.

Metellus: see Caecilius Metellus.

Mevulanus, C. (*RE*): Catilinarian. — *Sest.* 9.

Milo: see Annius Milo.

Miltiades (*RE* 2): Athenian, won the victory of Marathon against the Persians in 490, but died the following year in jail, to which he had been consigned for his inability to pay a fine. — *Sest.* 141.

Minerva: — *Dom.* 92, 144.

Mithridates (VI, King of Pontus) (*RE* 12): arch-enemy of Rome, finally disposed of by Pompey. — *Dom.* 19, *Sest.* 58(f.).

Mother, the Great (Mater Magna, i.e., Cybele): — *Har. resp.* 24. *Sest.* 56. Mother of the Gods: — *Har. resp.* 28. Mother from Mt. Ida (Idaea Mater): — *Har. resp.* 22.

(Mucia) (*RE* 28): Pompey's third wife. — Cf. *Har. resp.* 45 and *Onomasticon.*

Mucius Cordus Scaevola, C. (*RE* 10): the story went that, foiled in his attempt to assassinate the Etruscan king Porsenna, he put his hand in the fire to show his indifference to pain. — *Sest.* 48.

*Mucius Scaevola, P. (*RE* 17): Consul 133. Pontifex Maximus. — *Dom.* 91, 136.

Murena: see Licinius Murena.

Neptune: — *Har. resp.* 20.

Ninnius Quadratus, L. (*RE* 3): Praetor in 58. On June 1 proposed a decree for Cicero's recall in the Senate. — *Red. sen.* 3. *Dom.* 125. *Sest.* 26, 68.

Numa Pompilius (*RE* 1): second king of Rome. — *Dom.* 127.

Numerius Rufus. Q. (*RE* 5): Tribune 57. — *Sest.* 82, (87), 94. See "Toothy," "Quinctius."

(Nymphs, temple of the): — (*Har. resp.* 57).

*Octavius, Cn. (*RE* 20): Consul 87. Perished in conflict with his colleague Cinna. — *Har. resp.* 54. *Sest.* 77.

Opimius, L. (*RE* 4): Consul 121. Suppressed C. Gracchus. Subsequently exiled on a corruption charge. — *Red. quir.* 11. *Sest.* 140.

Oppius Cornicinus, Cn. (*RE* 28): Senator and father-in-law of Atilius Serranus Gavianus. — *Red.*

quir. 12. (*Sest.* 74).

(**Orestes**): mythical matricide. — (*Har. resp.* 39).

Papirius, Q. (*RE* 24): Tribune before 154. — *Dom.* 127. His law: — *Dom.* 128, 130.

Papirius Mas(s)o, M. (*RE* 63) — *Dom.* 49.

Paullus: see Aemilius Paullus.

(**Peducaeus,** Sex.) (*RE* 5): Praetor 77. Cicero served under him as Quaestor in Sicily. — (*Red. sen.* 21.)

Petreius, M. (*RE* 3): Praetor 64 (?). A military man and a stout supporter of the establishment. Died fighting Caesar in Africa in 46. — *Sest.* 12.

Philippus: see Marcius Philippus.

Philoctetes: Greek hero, subject of tragedies by Sophocles and others. While journeying to the Trojan War, he contracted a festering wound from a snakebite. — *Har. resp.* 39.

(**"Pinaria"**) (*RE* 29): wife of Clodius and half-sister of the following. Probably not a Pinaria but Fulvia, later married to Curio and Mark Antony; see *Onomasticon* 76. — (*Dom.* 118, 139. *Har. resp.* 39).

(***Pinarius** Natta, L.) (*RE* 19): Pontifex. — (*Dom.* 117f., 121f., 126, 134f., 139, 141). His mother: — *Dom.* 118, 134, 139.

Piso: see Calpurnius, Pupius Piso.

Plaguleius (*RE*): henchman of Clodius. — *Dom.* 89.

Plancius, Cn. (*RE* 4): Quaestor 58, in Macedonia, where he sheltered the exiled Cicero, who later defended him against a charge of electoral malpractice. Last heard of in 45 as a Pompeian awaiting Caesar's pardon. — *Red. sen.* 35.

Plator (*RE* 2): of Orestis. — *Har. resp.* 35.

***Pompeius** Magnus, Cn. (*RE* 31 and XXI.2549): Consul 70, 55, 52. Returned at the end of 62 from years of conquest and reorganization in Asia, Pompey the Great was by common consent Rome's premier citizen, though Caesar was becoming his rival. In 58 he let Cicero fall, regardless of previous commitments, but in 57 he picked him up. Cicero did not forget. — *Red. sen.* (4), 5, 29, (31). *Red. quir.* (14), 16(f.), 18. *Dom.* 3, 13, 16, 18f., (24), 25–31 *passim*, 66f., 69, (110), 129. *Har. resp.* (38), 45–52, 58. *Sest.* 15, 39(f.), 41(f., 52), 67, 69, 74, (84), 107, (129), 133. *Vat.* 24.

Pompilius: see Numa Pompilius.

(**Pomptinus,** C.) (*RE*): Praetor 63. — (*Vat.* 30).

***Popillius** Laenas, P. (*RE* 28): Consul 132. His inquisition into the followers of Ti. Gracchus was avenged by C. Gracchus, who had him banished in 123. Recalled 121. — *Red. sen.* 37f. *Red. quir.* 6, 9(f.), 11. *Dom.* 82, 87. His sons: — *Red. sen.* 37. *Red. quir.* 6.

***Porcius** Cato, M. ("of Utica") (*RE* 16): Tribune 62. Though he never rose beyond the praetorship, Cato the Younger could be considered the soul of conservative opposition to the "First Triumvirate." Later he made common cause (if reluctantly) with Pompey against Caesar and after Pompey's death in 48 became effective leader of continuing resistance. Committed suicide at Utica in north Africa after Caesar's victory at Thapsus in 46. Revered by posterity as republican hero. — *Dom.* 20–23. *Sest.* 12, 60(f.), 62(f.).

Porsen(n)a (*RE*): King of Clusium, a town of Etruria north of Rome. — *Sest.* 48.

Postumius (*RE* 7): — *Sest.* 111.

*****Postumius** Albinus, A. (*RE* 33): Consul 99. — *Red. quir.* 11.

Postumus: see Seius Postumus.

Propertius, Sex. (*RE* 1): — *Dom.* 49.

(Ptolemy VIII Euergetes II) (*RE* Ptolemaios 27): King of Egypt, father of the following. — (*Dom.* 20).

(Ptolemy IX Lathyrus) (*RE* Ptolemaios 30): King of Egypt, father of the following. — (*Dom.* 20, *Sest.* 57).

(Ptolemy XII) (*RE* Ptolemaios 33) King of Egypt. Called Auletes, "the Piper." Driven out by his subjects in 58, restored by Gabinius in 55, died in 51. — (*Dom.* 20. *Sest.* 57).

Ptolemy (*RE* Ptolemaios 34): King of Cyprus, brother of the foregoing. Deposed in 58 by a bill of Clodius', he committed suicide. — *Dom.* 20, (52f.). *Sest.* 57, (59, 62–64).

Pulcher: i.e., P. Clodius Pulcher. — *Dom.* 22.

Pupius, M. (*RE* 8): — *Dom.* 35.

*****Pupius** Piso Frugi, M. (*RE* 10): adoptive son of the foregoing. Consul 61. — *Dom.* 35.

Pythagorean: follower of Pythagoras, sixth-century Greek philosopher and mystagogue. — *Vat.* 14.

Quinctilius Varus, Sex. (*RE* 4): Praetor 57. — *Red. sen.* 23.

"Quinctius": — *Sest.* 82. See Numerius Rufus.

*****Quinctius** (Cincinnatus?), Kaeso (*RE* 8): fifth-century patrician forced into exile by prosecution and popular hostility. — *Dom.* 86.

*****Quinctius** Flamininus, T. (*RE* 47): Consul 123. — *Dom.* 136.

Quirinus (i.e., the deified Romulus): *Har. resp.* 12.

Romulus (*RE* 1): founder of Rome. — *Vat.* 20.

Salus: see Weal.

Saturninus: see Appuleius Saturninus.

Saturnus: — *Har. resp.* 20.

Scaevola: see Mucius Scaevola.

Scato: see Vettius Scato.

Scipio: see Cornelius, Caecilius Metellus Scipio.

Scribonius Curio, C. (*RE* 10): Consul 76. Pontifex. Notable general and orator. Died 53. — *Har. resp.* 12. *Vat.* 24.

(*****Scribonius** Curio, C.) (*RE* 11): son of the foregoing. Tribune 50. Friend of Cicero's, politically volatile. As Tribune went over to Caesar, allegedly for a vast bribe. Led Caesarian expedition to Africa in 49, where he was defeated and killed. — (*Vat.* 24)

Scylla: mythical monster with savage dogs around her middle, infesting the straits of Messina, which separate the toe of Italy from Sicily. — *Har. resp.* 59. *Sest.* 18.

Seius Postumus, Q. (*RE* 12): A Roman Knight, alleged by Cicero to have been poisoned by Clodius when he refused to sell his house. — *Dom.* 115, 129. *Har. resp.* 30.

*****Sempronii** Gracchi, Ti. and C.: by their actions and legislation these two "popular" Tribunes (133 and 123–122) changed the face of Roman politics. Both were killed in office, or shortly after, by conservative opponents. — *Sest.* 105. *Vat.* 23.

*****Sempronius** Gracchus, C. (*RE* 47): Tribune 123–122. — *Dom.* 24, 82, 102. *Har. resp.* 41, 43(f.). *Sest.* 101, 103, 140. His law: — *Dom.* 24. See Sempronii Gracchi.

(*****Sempronius** Gracchus, Ti.) (*RE* 53): father of the Tribunes. Consul 177, 163. Censor 169. — (*Har. resp.* 41, 43).

*****Sempronius** Gracchus, Ti. (*RE* 54): Tribune 133. — *Dom.* 91. *Har. resp.* 41, 43(f.) *Sest.* 103. See Sempronii Gracchi.

Septimius, C. (*RE* 7): Praetor 57. — *Red. sen.* 23.

Sergius, L. (*RE* 15): follower of Clodius. — *Dom.* 13f., 21, 89.

*****Sergius** Catilina, L. (*RE* 23): Praetor 68. His plot for a coup d'état in 63 was exposed and suppressed by Cicero as Consul. Killed in battle the following year. — *Red. sen.* 10, 12, 33. *Red. quir.* 13. *Dom.* 13, 61f., 72, 75.

Har. resp. 5, 42. *Sest.* 12, 28, 42. Cf. *Vat.* 25.

Serranus: see Atilius Serranus.

*****Servilius** Ahala, C. (*RE* 32): Master of Horse 439. See Maelius. — *Dom.* 86. *Sest.* 143.

*****Servilius** Caepio, Q. (*RE* 50): Praetor (?) 91. Sworn enemy of Livius Drusus. — *Dom.* 120.

*****Servilius** Glaucia, C. (*RE* 65): Praetor 100. Ally of Saturninus, perished with him. — *Har. resp.* 51.

*****Servilius** Vatia Isauricus, P. (*RE* 93): Consul 79. Proconsul in Cilicia 78–74, he gained his triumphal cognomen by operations against the Isaurian highlanders in southeast Anatolia. Died in extreme old age in 44. — *Red. sen.* 25. *Red. quir.* 17. *Dom.* 43, 123, 132f. *Har. resp.* 2, 12. *Sest.* 130. Cf. *Red. sen.* 37. *Red. quir.* 6.

(**Sestius,** L.) (*RE* 2): father of Publius. Tribune before 91. — (*Sest.* 6f.)

Sestius, L. (*RE* 3): son of the following. Consul suffect 23. — *Sest.* (6), 10, (144, 146).

Sestius, P. (*RE* 6): Tribune 57. — *Red. sen.* (7), 20, 30. *Red. quir.* (14), 15. *Sest.* 3–15 *passim*, 31, 71, 75–85 *passim*, 87, 90, 92, (94), 96, 119, 124, 132, 144, 146. *Vat.* 2f., 11, 41. His daughter: — *Sest.* 6.

Sextus (i.e., Sex. Cloelius): — *Dom.* 47.

Sibyl, the: mythical seeress whose supposed prophecies were in the custody of a College of fifteen priests, Clodius being one. — *Har. resp.* 26 (27).

Spartacus (*RE*): leader of the

great Italian slave revolt in 73–71. — *Har. resp.* 26.

Sulla: see Cornelius Sulla.

*Sulpicius Galba, P. (*RE* 55): Praetor before 65. Pontifex. — *Har. resp.* 12.

*Sulpicius Rufus, P. (*RE* 92): Tribune 88. Embarked on a "popular" program, which was suppressed and its author killed when Sulla marched into Rome. A noted orator. — *Har. resp.* 41, 43(f.). *Vat.* 23.

Tellus: Earth Goddess. — *Har. resp.* 20. Her temple: — *Dom.* 101. *Har. resp.* 31.

(Terentia) (*RE* 95): Cicero's wife. — (*Red. quir.* 8, *Dom.* 59, 96. *Sest.* 49, 54, 145).

Terentius, Q. (cf. *RE* 44): Minor Pontiff, probably not to be indentified with Q. Terentius Culleo, Tribune 57. — *Har. resp.* 12.

*Terentius Varro Lucullus, M. (*RE* Licinius 109): Consul 73. Brother by birth of L. Lucullus and an almost equally distinguished soldier. Triumphed for victories in the Balkans. Died not long after Lucius. — *Dom.* 132f., *Har. resp.* 12. Cf. *Dom.* 110. See Luculli.

Themistocles (*RE* Themistokles 1): Athenian leader in the Persian War of 481–479. Later exiled and took refuge with the King of Persia. — *Sest.* 141.

Theodosius (*RE* 2): envoy from Chios. — *Har. resp.* 34.

Tigranes (I, King of Armenia) (*RE* 1): — *Dom.* 19, (66). *Sest.* 58(f.).

(Tigranes) (*RE* 2): son of the foregoing. — (*Dom.* 66)

Titius (*RE* 2): of Reate, henchman of Clodius. — *Dom.* 21. *Har. resp.* 59. *Sest.* 80, 112.

Titus: — *Sest.* 118.

"Toothy" (Brocchus; i.e., Q. Numerius Rufus): — *Sest.* 72, 82.

(*Tullia) (*RE* 60): Cicero's daughter. — (*Red. sen.* 1, 17, 27. *Red. quir.* 2, 5, 8. *Dom.* 59, 96. *Har. resp.* 16. *Sest.* 49, 54, 131, 144f.).

(Tullian law): — (*Sest.* 133, see note, 135. *Vat.* 29, 37).

Tullio, P. (*RE*): — *Har. resp.* 1.

Tullius, Servius (*RE* 18): King of Rome. — *Sest.* 123.

Tullius Cicero, M. (*RE* 29): the orator. — *Dom.* 44, 47, 50, 85, 102, 133. *Sest.* 11.

(*Tullius Cicero, M.) (*RE* 30): son of the foregoing. — (*Red. sen.* 1, 27. *Red. quir.* 2, 5, 8. *Dom.* 59, 96. *Har. resp.* 16. *Sest.* 49, 54, 144f.).

(Tullius Cicero, Q.) (*RE* 31): brother of the orator. — (*Red. sen.* 1, 27, 37. *Red. quir.* 3, 5, 7f. *Dom.* 59, 96. *Sest.* 49, 68, 76, 144f.)

(Tullius Cicero, Q.): (*RE* 32): son of the foregoing. — (*Red. sen.* 27. *Sest.* 144).

Vaccus: see Vitruvius Vaccus.

Valerius Messalla Niger, M. (*RE* 266): Consul 61. Pontifex. — *Har. resp.* 12.

Valerius Orca, Q. (*RE* 280): Praetor 57. — *Red. sen.* 23.

Valerius Poplicola, P. (*RE* 302): Consul 509–507, 504. — *Har. resp.* 16.

Varius Severus Hybrida, Q. (*RE*

7): Tribune 90. Accused Aemilius Scaurus of *lèse-majesté*. — *Sest.* 101.

Vatinius, P. (*RE* 3): Tribune 59, Consul 47. — (*Sest.* 113f., 132-135). *Vat. passim.*

Vesta: Roman goddess of the hearth. *Dom.* 144. *Har. resp.* 12. Vestal Virgin(s): see Glossary of Terms. — *Dom.* 136, (144). *Har. resp.* 13, 37. Cf. *Har. resp.* 4.

Vettius, L. (*RE* 6): Roman Knight from Picenum who turned informer against his Catilinarian associates in 63-62 and was prosecuted and imprisoned for making false charges against Caesar. Revealed or fabricated a plot to assassinate Pompey in 59. Died mysteriously in prison. — *Sest.* 132. *Vat.* 24-26.

Vettius Scato (*RE* 17): — *Dom.* 116.

Virtue, temple of: — *Sest.* 116, 120.

Vitruvius Vaccus, M. (*RE* 1): incited his town Privernum to rebellion against Rome (330 B.C.). — *Dom.* 101.

Weal (Salus), temple of: — *Sest.* 131.

INDEX II

PLACES

Modern names are italicized. Parentheses enclose references to passages where a place is alluded to but not named.

Achaia (sometimes refers to Greece [*q.v.*] as a whole, administered by the governor of Macedonia, but in these speeches to the Peloponnese): *Dom.* 60.
Achaeans: *Sest.* 94.
Acheron (underworld river): *Red. sen.* 25.
Aequimaelium (open area near the Capitoline, given over to a market for sacrificial lambs): *Dom.* 101.
Africa: *Red. quir.* 20. *Sest.* 50. *Vat.* 12.
Ager Gallicus: see Gallic Territory.
Alexandrians: *Har. resp.* 34. See Egypt.
Allobroges (tribe in Narbonese Gaul, the Roman province in southern France): *Dom.* 134.
Anagnia (*Anagni*, chief town of the Hernici, east of Rome): *Dom.* 81.
Apennines: *Sest.* 12.
Appian Way (principal Roman road, running south to Capua [in 312] and later extended to Brundisium): cf. *Sest.* 126.
Aquileia (*Aquileia*, town in Venetia): *Vat.* 38.
Arabia: *Dom.* 124.
Argos: *Sest.* 122.
Armenia: *Sest.* 58.
Asia (continent): *Har. resp.* 28.

Asia (western Anatolia or the Roman province): *Dom.* 52. *Sest.* 58, 68.
Athens: *Sest.* 48, 141. Athenian lectors: *Sest.* 110.
Aurelius' Platform (Tribunal Aurelii, a tribunal with steps in the Roman Forum): *Red. quir.* 13. *Dom.* 54. *Sest.* 34.

Babylon: *Dom.* 60.
Bithynia (region in northwest Anatolia): *Red. sen.* 38.
Boeotia (district of Greece, northwest of Athens): *Dom.* 60.
Brundisium (*Brindisi*, port on the east coast of the heel of Italy): *Sest.* 131.
Byzantium: *Dom.* 52. *Sest.* 56. Byzantine exiles: *Dom.* 53, 129. (*Sest.* 84). Byzantine plunder: *Har. resp.* 59.

Caeliculus (part of the Caelian hill in Rome): *Har. resp.* 32.
Campanian Consul (i.e., L. Piso Caesoninus): *Dom.* 60.
Capitol: *Red. sen.* 12, 25. *Dom.* 5–7, 15, 76, 101, 139. *Sest.* 26, 124, 131. God of the Capitol (Capitolinus, i.e., Jupiter): *Dom.* 144. Capitol Rise (Capitolinus clivus, the winding path that led from the Forum to the summit of the Capitol): *Red. sen.* 12, 32. *Sest.* 28.
Cappadocia (kingdom in central

Anatolia): *Red. sen.* 14.

Capua (chief city of Campania): *Red. sen.* 17 (29). *Sest.* 9–11, 19.

Carinae (quarter in Rome): *Har. resp.* 49.

Carthage (city in modern Tunisia): *Har. resp.* 6. *Sest.* 127. Carthaginians: *Har. resp.* 19 (Poeni). *Sest.* 142.

Chios (town and large island in the Aegean): *Har. resp.* 34.

Cilicia (Roman province in southeast Anatolia): *Dom.* 23. *Sest.* 55. Cilicians: *Har. resp.* 42.

Cimbri (German tribe, conquered in 101 by Marius at Vercellae, north of the Po river): *Dom.* 102.

Circus Flaminius: see Flaminius.

Column: see Maenius' Column.

Cyprus: *Dom.* 20, 52f., 65. *Sest.* 59, 64. Cyprian bill: *Sest.* 62.

Dardanians (Illyrian tribe on the east shore of the Adriatic): *Sest.* 93.

Dyrrachium (*Durazzo*, town on the Illyrian coast): *Sest.* 94, 140.

Egypt, King of (rex Alexandrinus): *Dom.* 20.

Etruria (district of Italy immediately north of Rome [*Tuscany*], center of power and high culture in the 7th–6th century, produced a system of divination, the "Etruscan discipline," much favored by the Romans): *Har. resp.* 20, 25. Etruscans: *Har. resp.* 18, 25. Their books: *Har. resp.* 37, 53.

Europe: *Har. resp.* 28.

Field (Campus): see Mars' Field.

Flaminius, Circus (Rome's second oldest racecourse, built in 221 opposite the Capitoline in Mars' Field): *Red. sen.* 13, 17. *Sest.* 33.

Forum (see Glossary of Terms): *Red. sen.* 6, 14f, 18f. *Dom.* 5, 49, 67, 80, 110; *Har. resp.* 6, 34, 39. *Sest.* 34f., 44, 75–79, 83, 85, 90, 95, 124, 128, 140. *Vat.* 8, 22, 34.

Gades (*Cadiz*): *Dom.* 80.

Gallic Territory (Ager Gallicus, district facing the Adriatic, north of Picenum): *Sest.* 9.

Gallogreek (i.e., Galatian, a people of north-central Anatolia): *Har. resp.* 28.

Gaul (Transalpine): *Har. resp.* 42. Gauls: *Dom.* 101. *Har. resp.* 19.

Greece: *Dom.* 60, 111. *Sest.* 142. Greeks, Grecians: *Har. resp.* 19. *Sest.* 120 (Achivi), 122 (Argivi), 141. Greek debtors: *Sest.* 94. Greek statesmen: *Sest.* 142. Greekling(s) (Graeculus, -li): *Red. sen.* 14. *Sest.* 110, 126.

Ida (mountain in the Troad in northwest Anatolia): *Har. resp.* 22.

Interamna (*Terni*, town in central Italy): *Dom.* 80.

Italy: *Red. sen.* 24–26, 28f., 38f. *Red. quir.* 1, 4, 10f., 16, 18. *Dom.* 5, 26, 30, 57, 75, 82, 87, 90, 132, 147. *Har. resp.* 5, 27f., 46. *Sest.* 12, 25f., 32, 35–38, 40f., 72, 83, 87, 107, 128f., 131, 145. *Vat.* 8.

Italians: *Har. resp.* 19. Italic War: *Har. resp.* 18.

Latiniensis ager (district near Rome): *Har. resp.* 20. Latinienses:

Har. resp. 62.
Latins: *Dom.* 78. *Har. resp.* 19. *Sest.* 30. Latin colonies: *Dom.* 78. Latin: *Har. resp.* 24.
Ligurian (native of Liguria, a region bordering the gulf of Genoa): (*Sest.* 69). Cf. *Dom.* 49. *Har. resp.* 5.

Macedonia (the Roman province in northern Greece): *Dom.* 55, 60, 70. *Har. resp.* 35. *Sest.* 13, 71, 94. *Vat.* 25.
Maenius' Column (in the Forum): *Sest.* 18 (see note), 124.
Mars' Field (Campus Martius, see Glossary of Terms): *Dom.* 75. *Sest.* 108. Field, the: *Red. sen.* 28. *Dom.* 90.
Marsi (people of central Italy): *Dom.* 116. *Vat.* 36.
Massilia (Marseilles): *Sest.* 7.
Mauretania (region of north Africa extending to the Atlantic, present day northern Algeria and Morocco): *Vat.* 12.
Minturnae (town of southern Latium): *Red. quir.* 20. Cf. *Sest.* 50.

Numantia (Spanish town), treaty of: *Har. resp.* 43.

Orestis (district of Macedonia): *Har. resp.* 35.
Ostia (city at the mouth of the Tiber River): *Sest.* 39.

Paeligni (people of central Italy): *Vat.* 36.
Palatina (one of the 35 Roman tribes): *Dom.* 49. *Sest.* 114.
Palatine (Hill): *Red. sen.* 18. *Dom.* 62, 103, 116. *Har. resp.* 16, 24, 49. *Sest.* 54.
Persians: *Dom.* 60, 124. *Har. resp.* 28.
Pessinus (town in Galatia, a district of north-central Anatolia, with sanctuary of Cybele): *Har. resp.* 28f. *Sest.* 56.
Phrygia (region of central Anatolia): *Har. resp.* 27.
Picenum (region of central Italy bordering on the Adriatic): *Har. resp.* 62.
Pisaurum (*Pesaro*, town on the Adriatic coast south of Ariminum [*Rimini*]): *Sest.* 9.
Pontus (region in northeast Anatolia): *Red. sen.* 38. *Sest.* 58.
Punic War (second, 218–201 B.C., against Carthage): *Har. resp.* 27.
Potentia (*Potenza*, coastal town in Picenum): *Har. resp.* 62.
Puteoli (*Pozzuoli*, town on the Bay of Naples, Rome's chief port before the development of Ostia in imperial times): *Vat.* 12.

Reate (*Rieti*, Sabine town northeast of Rome): *Sest.* 80.
Rock, the (Saxum): *Dom.* 136 (see note).
Rome, Roman People, etc.: *passim.*
Rostra (see Glossary of Terms): *Dom.* 123. *Har. resp.* 55, 59. *Sest.* 75f., 83f. *Vat.* 18, 21, 24, 26.

Sabine(s): *Sest.* 80. *Vat.* 36.
Samnites (gladiators): *Sest.* 134.
Sardinia: *Vat.* 12.
Scylla's strait (Scyllaeus fretus):

Sest. 18.

Senate-House (curia, in the northwest corner of the Forum): *Dom.* 13, 67, 130f. *Har. resp.* 2, 6, 47. *Sest.* 53, 75, 90, 97, 128, 144. *Vat.* 8, 10, 22.

Seplasia (street in Capua where perfume was sold): *Sest.* 19.

Sergia (one of the 35 Roman tribes): *Vat.* 36.

Spain, Spanish: *Dom.* 52. *Vat.* 12f. Spaniards: *Har. resp.* 19. Further Spain (Hispania ulterior): *Vat.* 12.

Syria, Syrian: *Dom.* 23, 52, 55, 60, 70, 124. *Har. resp.* 1. *Sest.* 55, 71, 93. Syrians: *Har. resp.* 28.

Tanagra (town in Boeotia): *Dom.* 111, 116. (*Har. resp.* 33).

Taurus (mountain range in Anatolia): *Sest.* 58.

Thessalonica (*Salonica,* city of Macedonia): *Har. resp.* 35.

Thessaly (district in eastern Greece, south of Macedonia): *Dom.* 60. *Sest.* 94.

Thracians (warlike inhabitants of a district northeast of Macedonia): *Sest.* 93.

Tiber: *Sest.* 77.

Transalpine blood: *Red. sen.* 15.

Tusculum (Latin town near modern *Frascati.* Cicero had a villa there.): *Red. sen.* 18. *Dom.* 62, 124.

Vaccus' Meadows: *Dom.* 101.

Valeria, Tabula (in Rome): *Vat.* 21 (see note).

Velia (hill in Rome): *Har. resp.* 16.

Volaterrae (*Volterra,* town in Etruria): *Dom.* 79.

Well-Curb (Puteal Libonis, in the Forum): *Sest.* 18 (see note).

GLOSSARY OF TERMS

Aedile (*aedilis*): Third in rank of the regular Roman magistracies. Four at this time were elected annually, two Curule and two Plebeian. They were responsible for city administration and for the holding of certain public games.

As: A copper coin

Assembly: There were several different sorts of popular assembly in Rome, convened by a competent magistrate for electoral or legislative purposes or to hear an address. See under Centuries, Curiate Law, and Tribes.

Augur: The priestly College of Augurs were official diviners interpreting signs, mostly from the flight and cries of wild birds or the behavior of the Sacred Chickens, before acts of public (and sometimes private) business. The College, like that of Pontiffs, was in practice almost a preserve of the nobility.

Auspices (*auspicia*): Divination from birds or other signs was officially requisite as a preliminary to major acts by magistrates, who were said to "have auspices," i.e., the power to take them.

Board of Ten (*decemviri stlitibus iudicandis*): They dealt with cases involving personal liberty.

Censor: Two magistrates usually elected every five years for a term of eighteen months. They revised the roll of citizens, with property assessments, also the rolls of Knights and Senators, removing those deemed guilty of misconduct by placing a mark (*nota*) against their names on the roll. They further supervised public contracts, including the lease of state revenues to the tax-farmers, and issued decrees as guardians of public morals. In 58 Clodius passed a bill restricting the censorial powers of expulsion, but it seems to have been rescinded soon afterwards.

Centuries, Assembly of (*comitia centuriata*): Form of assembly in which voting took place by "Centuries," i.e., groups unequally composed so as to give preponderance to birth and wealth. It elected Consuls and Praetors, and voted on legislation proposed by them. The first Century to vote (*centuria praerogativa*) was selected by lot from the wealthier voters, and its vote, considered as an omen, had a disproportionate influence on the result.

Centurion: Officer commanding a century, a company of (nominally) one hundred soldiers. There were sixty to a Roman legion.

City Praetor: See Praetor.

Clerks (*scribae*): A corporation of functionaries to assist magistrates in dealing with public accounts and records—republican Rome's nearest approach to a civil service.

Colonies: Towns, mostly in Italy, founded under government authority by settlement of Roman citizens. In the case of "Latin colonies" they gave up their Roman citizenship to become "Latins" (*q.v.*).

Commonwealth: So *res publica* may usually be translated—the Roman body politic.

Consul: Highest of the annual Roman magistrates. Two were elected, usually in July, to take office on the following January 1.

Consul suffect: Consul elected in place of one who died in office.

Consular: An Ex-Consul. The Consulars made up a corps of elder statesmen to whom the Senate would normally look for leadership.

Curiate Law (*lex curiata*): A law passed by the Curies (*curiae*), the oldest form of Roman assembly. In Cicero's time it survived only in form, each of the thirty Curies being represented by a lictor, but still had certain legislative functions, including the authorization of an adoption.

Curies: See above.

Curule magistrates: Consuls, Praetors, Curule Aediles, and certain others entitled to sit in an ivory chair, or rather stool, of state (*sella curulis*).

Decurion: Member of a governing body of a municipality corresponding to the Roman Senate.

Dictator: A supreme magistrate with quasi-regal powers appointed to deal with emergencies under the early Republic; his second-in-command, the Master of the Horse, was appointed by himself. The office was revived to legitimize the autocratic regimes of Sulla and Julius Caesar.

GLOSSARY OF TERMS

Dignity: The concept of *dignitas*, variously rendered as "dignity," "status," "standing," "prestige," "reputation," was of great importance to a Roman of the upper class, especially one who like Cicero took a prominent part in public affairs.

Edict: A public announcement or manifesto issued by a magistrate.

Epicurianism: A materialistic school of philosophy named after its founder, Epicurus, much in vogue among the Roman intelligentsia of Cicero's time.

Fasces: Bundles of rods, usually with an axe, carried by lictors in front of magistrates as a symbol of authority.

Field, the: See Mars' Field.

Flamen: Priest in charge of the cult of a particular deity. There were fifteen, three (those of Jupiter, Mars, and Quirinus) being superior to the rest.

Forum: The chief square of Rome, the center of civic life.

Freedman (*libertus*): A slave liberated by his master.

Games (*ludi*): Gladiatorial and other shows, some recurring annually and supervised by magistrates, others put on for an occasion by private individuals.

Good Goddess (*Bona Dea*): A goddess whose worship was confined to women. Her yearly festival, at which sacrifice was offered on behalf of the Roman People, was held in the house of a Consul or Praetor and supervised by his wife. See p. 1.

Gown (*toga*): Formal civilian dress of a Roman citizen. The gown of boys and curule magistrates had a purple hem (*toga praetexta*). At sixteen or seventeen, upon coming of age, a boy was given his White (or "Manly") gown (*toga pura, toga virilis*).

Greeks: In Cicero's time the word was used loosely to include the more or less Hellenized inhabitants of western Asia and Egypt as well as those of Greece proper and the old Greek settlements elsewhere.

Haruspices: See p. 103.

Honest men: So (on the basis of former English usage) I translate

Cicero's *boni* ("good men," *les gens de bien*), a semi-political term for people of substance and respectability, supporters of the established order. Their opposites he calls *improbi* ("rascals").

Imperator: Commander of a Roman army. But at this period the title was conferred upon generals by their soldiers after a victory.

Interrex: If through death or other causes the consular office stood vacant, the remaining "patrician" (i.e. curule) magistrates normally resigned and an Interrex was appointed from among the patrician members of the Senate to exercise consular functions for five days. He was then replaced by another Interrex, and so on until new Consuls were elected.

King of Rites (*rex sacrorum*): A functionary appointed for life to discharge certain religious duties formally appertaining to the Roman kings. Only patricians were eligible.

Knights (*equites*): Usually the term applies to non-senators of free birth posessing property over a certain level. They were regarded as forming a class of their own (*ordo equestris*) with special privileges and insignia.

Latins: Holders of the "Latin franchise" (*ius Latii*), an inferior form of Roman citizenship.

Legate (*legatus*): A provincial governor took several Legates, normally senators, on his staff as deputies. Caesar in Gaul made them commanders of legions. The duties, might, however, be nominal.

Mars' Field (*Campus Martius*): The plain adjoining the Tiber on which assemblies of the Centuries were held, often for elections.

Megalesia: The festival of Cybele, the Great Mother (*Magna Mater*, Greek *Megalê Mêtêr*) on 4–10 April. The Curule Aediles were in charge of it at this period.

Military Tribune: See Tribune.

Nobility: Practically, a noble (*nobilis*) at this period meant a direct descendant of a Consul in the male line. In the early Republic the Roman community was divided into patricians and plebeians, the former holding a virtual monopoly of political power. But after the consulship was thrown open to plebeians in the fourth century, many plebeian families became "noble," and the remaining patricians were distinguished mainly by disabilities, such as their ineligibility for the offices of Tribune of the Plebs and Plebeian Aedile.

Optimates: Literally "those belonging to the best" — the leading conservatives in the Senate and their supporters throughout the community. Sometimes the term is practically equivalent to the "honest men" (*boni*), though more purely political in its implications.

Patricians: See Nobility.

People's man (*popularis*): For the use as a political term, see *Sest.* 96. Cicero is fond of making play with the more general sense, "liked by people" or "devoted to the people."

Plebeians (*plebs*): See Nobility.

Pontiff (*pontifex*): These formed a priestly college in general charge of religious institutions (including the Calendar), presided over by the Chief Pontiff (*pontifex maximus*), who was Julius Caesar from 63 until his death. As with other Roman priestly colleges, the members were not set apart from the rest of the community and were often leading public figures. Cf. Augur.

Praetor: Second in rank of the annual magistrates. Eight were elected at this period. The City Praetor (*praetor urbanus*) and the Foreign Praetor (*praetor peregrinus*) handled civil suits between citizens and between citizens and non-citizens respectively; others presided over the standing criminal courts. After their year of office Consuls and Praetors normally went out to govern a province as Proconsuls or Propraetors (*pro consule, pro praetore*).

Promulgation: Advance notice of proposed legislation.

Proscription: Under a procedure first employed by Sulla in 81, lists of names were published, the persons thus "proscribed" being declared outlaws and their goods forfeit to the state. Their killers were rewarded, their protectors punished.

Quaestor: The first stage in the regular "course of offices" (*cursus honorum*), election to which carried life membership of the Senate. Since Sulla, twenty were elected annually. The two City

Quaestors (*quaestores urbani*) had charge of the Treasury, and the Quaestors assigned to provincial governors (usually by lot) were largely concerned with finance.

Rascals (*improbi*): See Honest men.

Rostra: The speaker's platform in the place of assembly (*comitium*) in the northwest corner of the Forum in front of the Senate-House, so called from the beaks (*rostra*) of captured warships which decorated it.

Salii ("Leapers"): Two colleges of priests, in Rome chiefly associated with Mars, whom they worshipped with ritual dance and song. They had to be patricians.

Senate: Governing body of the Roman Republic, numbering about six hundred and composed of magistrates and ex-magistrates.

Sesterce: A silver coin (*sestertius, nummus*) equivalent in Cicero's time to four asses, and the normal unit of reckoning.

Stoicism: Philosopohical school, named from the portico (*stoa*) in which its founder, Zeno of Citium (*c.* 300 B.C.), taught. Cato was its most prominent adherent in Cicero's time.

Tax-farmers (*publicani*): Roman taxes, as on grazing land in the provinces or excise, were for the most part farmed out by the Censors to private companies, who bid for the right of collection. The capitalists in Rome as well as the local agents were called *publicani*. In political terms, *publicani* and Knights often amount to the same thing.

Teller (*custos*): See p. 13, n. 46.

Tetrarch: Originally the ruler of a portion (one-quarter) of a larger territory; hence, "petty monarch."

Thanksgiving (*supplicatio*): A thanksgiving ceremony decreed by the Senate in honor of a military success, the number of days varying according to the importance of the victory.

Treasury (*aerarium*): The Roman state treasury was in the temple of Saturn in the Forum, managed by the City Quaestors with the assistance of the Clerks (*q.v.*).

Tribe (*tribus*): A division, mainly for voting purposes and mainly by locality, of the Roman citizen body. The number had risen in course of time from three to thirty-five. Assemblies voting by tribes (*comitia tributa*) elected magistrates below Praetor and could pass legislation proposed by Tribunes.

Tribune: (1) Of the plebs. A board of ten. The office was originally created to protect plebeians from patrician high-handedness. They had wide powers, including that of veto (by any one of them) on any item of public business, including laws and senatorial decrees. They could also initiate these. They took office on 10 December. (2) Military: officers, six to a legion. Service in this capacity was often the start of a political career.

Triumph: Victory celebrations by a general on his return to Rome. Permission had to be granted by the Senate.

Vestal Virgins: Priestesses of Vesta, the Hearth Goddess, vowed to chastity.

www.ingramcontent.com/pod-product-compliance
Ingram Content Group UK Ltd.
Pitfield, Milton Keynes, MK11 3LW, UK
UKHW041416180426
11947UKWH00007B/162